SUPER MARIO GALAXY

PRIMA Official Game Guide

Written by:
Fletcher Black

Prima Games
A Division of Random House, Inc.

3000 Lava Ridge Court, Suite 100
Roseville, CA 95661
www.primagames.com

Product Manager: Mario De Govia
Editor: Rebecca Chastain
Copyeditor: Carrie Andrews
Design and Layout: Calibre Grafix, LLC
Manufacturing: Suzanne Goodwin
Maps: Sonja Morris, Oliver Crowell, Garret Bright, Adam Crowell, Emily Crowell, and John Rice

ISBN: 978-0-7615-5713-5

Library of Congress Catalog Card Number: 2007935255

Printed in the United States of America

07 08 09 10 LL 10 9 8 7 6 5 4 3 2 1

About the Author

Fletcher Black has been playing video games since his parents first set an Atari 2600 down on the orange shag carpet of their suburban paradise. While peers declared their desire to be firefighters or astronauts, Fletcher set his sights on all things pixilated. Similarly, Fletcher earned a journalism degree from the University of Oregon, but while the other students wanted to expose political corruption or corporate scandal, Fletcher sought to reveal greater truths, such as how to beat Bowser, find all the pieces of the Tri-Force, and collect every single Pokémon. When not waist-deep in a video game, Fletcher enjoys writing, movies, travel, and shepherding his animal army. His Prima guides include *FEAR*, *Perfect Dark Zero*, *Ghost Recon Advanced Warfighter*, and *Heroes of Might and Magic V*.

We want to hear from you! E-mail comments and feedback to fblack@primagames.com.

CONTENTS

Acknowledgments

The author would like to extend special thanks to Damon Baker, Seth McMahill, Yugo Sato, Sean Egan, Erik Peterson, Tejima Atsushi, and Mr. Shigero Miyamoto at Nintendo for their tremendous support this year. Without their assistance, this book would have never achieved liftoff. Additional thanks to the team at Prima—Rebecca Chastain, Mario De Govia, and Julie Asbury—for all of their help shepherding the book. Big thanks also go to Calibre Grafix, to the talented map crew (Garret Bright, Adam Crowell, Emily Crowell, Oliver Crowell, Sonja Morris, and John Rice), and to Carrie Andrews for her ace copyediting. And finally, thanks to my grandpa, who got me hooked on looking up at the night sky when I was a little boy and who I think about every time Orion appears in the winter heavens.

SUPER

THE STAR FESTIVAL

As night settles over the Mushroom Kingdom, a lone figure runs merrily down a cobblestone path, arms outstretched in youthful abandon, like the levity of his heart could lead to takeoff at any moment. And why shouldn't he feel like flying? The night sky, streaked with stardust from the tail of a glorious comet passing close to the kingdom, provides the perfect backdrop for an audience with his princess. Tucked in his pocket is the handwritten note he has just received from her, asking him to share in the celestial sights provided by this once-in-a-century cosmic occurrence. And at the letter's end, she says she has something for him. He's been on the receiving end of her gratitude in the past, but there's something about this note. Something special.

Unfortunately, before Mario reaches the castle, the villainous Bowser interrupts the festival. No stranger to the heroic Mario, Bowser descends on the kingdom leading a fleet of airships. Bowser mounts an attack on the castle, peppering the grounds with cannonballs from his floating vessels. Mario deftly dodges the volleys, hurrying to the castle to save Princess Peach before Bowser can kidnap her again, as he's done many times before.

That lone figure en route to his princess' side is none other than Mario, brave adventurer and hero of the Mushroom Kingdom. Princess Peach has called him to the castle, eager to share something with him under the arcs of shooting stars. It's not just Mario feeling especially joyful this evening, either. The entire kingdom is alight thanks to the Star Festival dedicated to the comet's infrequent but spectacular appearance.

This year, the comet's close proximity to the kingdom has resulted in a brilliant shower of shooting stars. The Toads have collected the falling stars, bringing them to the castle. Before Princess Peach's eyes, the shooting stars became a great Power Star, shining brilliantly. Princess Peach herself even found a friendly little star, called a Luma, which she has held dear throughout the festival.

Bowser brings his airship in low to speak to the princess. He has every intention of capturing her, but something else has caught his eye—the Luma. Bowser knows

A shadow in the sky blots out the stars. A massive starship moves into view, positioning itself directly above the castle. Rather than leave his airship to pry the Luma from Princess Peach's fingers, Bowser will steal the entire castle. Three lasers erupt from the starship's bottom, searing a giant circle around the castle grounds. After carving the castle out of the earth, massive skyhooks drive into the soil. The starship slowly ascends into the heavens, wrenching the castle free of its earthly bonds.

But Bowser was not fast enough—Mario reached the castle before the starship dropped from the sky. Determined to stand between Princess Peach and Bowser, Mario holds on dearly as the castle is hoisted into outer space. However, Bowser's minion, Kamek the Magikoopa, spots the stowaway. The wizard flies down to the castle and

casts a powerful spell, shattering the stone beneath Mario's feet. Mario, knocked unconscious by the blast, floats out into space with the debris as the castle and Princess Peach vanish into the cosmos.

When Mario awakes, he finds himself on a small planetoid—but he's not alone. The Luma companion of Princess Peach escaped the castle and safely escorted Mario to the planet. The Luma promises to help Mario save his princess, but finding her in the vastness of space won't be easy. Together, the pair must travel across the universe, visiting strange worlds and bizarre galaxies in their search. Just getting off this tiny world seems daunting, but the little Luma, ever so clever, knows somebody who can help them—somebody with an intimate knowledge of the cosmos, thanks to their own search for a lost loved one.

COSMIC CAST

★★ Mario ★★

Mario is the greatest hero in the entire Mushroom Kingdom, a plumber who's traded in his wrenches for travel to the far-flung corners of the universe. In his latest adventure, Mario must chase his nemesis, Bowser, across the cosmos to rescue the fair Princess Peach. While soaring through the heavens, Mario encounters all the fantastical wonders of space, from strange comets to imaginative planets. He must also wrestle with one of the greatest forces in the universe: gravity. If Mario can use gravity to his advantage, he might stand a chance against the tricks and traps Bowser has left in his wake.

Luma

There are many Luma in the cosmos, but this particular Luma is Mario's constant companion during his space travels. This cute little star gifts Mario with some amazing skills, such as the ability to survive in deep space and unleash a special spin that helps him break free of gravity and damages various dangerous denizens. While Mario explores the galaxies, he will meet many different Luma, from helpful black Luma that manage the charts of the cosmos to green Luma that hide a special secret.

Toad

Toad is Princess Peach's trusted confidant. He and the Mushroom Kingdom are always at Peach's service, so when Bowser steals the castle and carries it into space, Toad and his friends help Mario get it and Princess Peach back. Toad and his comrades will occasionally appear to assist Mario in their mushroom-shaped starships.

Princess Peach

Princess Peach, benevolent ruler of the Mushroom Kingdom, has been friends with Mario for years. In her times of need, Peach can always rely on Mario for help. When Bowser kidnaps Princess Peach and steals her across the galaxies, she is separated from her trusted Luma. Hopefully, the Luma will help Mario rescue her from Bowser before the fiend can hatch whatever grand plot he's cooking up aboard his incredible fleet of airships.

Rosalina

Not much is known about Rosalina, the lonely princess who wanders the cosmos in the Comet Observatory, a giant starship that travels the celestial expanse. She is a great friend of the Luma, taking them in and caring for them as if they were her children.
But there is a sadness behind her eyes. What has she lost out among the stars?

Bowser

Bowser is the great fire-breathing villain of the Mushroom Kingdom, a dastardly creature bent on capturing Princess Peach and taking control of the kingdom for his own nefarious means. He commands a vast army of Goombas, Koopas, and other nasties that do his bidding without question. Mario always manages to save Princess Peach from Bowser and stop his schemes, but the brute never learns. Perhaps if Mario finally corners Bowser in the heart of the cosmos, he can pound a little sense into the scoundrel.

Bowser Jr.

Bowser Jr. has been causing trouble for Mario since they met at Isle Delfino, doing the bidding of his father, the great Koopa king Bowser. When Mario gives chase to Bowser across the universe, Bowser Jr. tries to intercept the plumber and make his father proud. But does the little Koopa underling have the guts to really stop the hero of the Mushroom Kingdom?

Psst!

Koopas, like Bowser and Bowser Jr., are based on creatures from Japanese folklore called kappa. Kappas have no standardized appearance, but many depictions present the strange monsters with turtle shells, just like the one that protects Bowser's back.

PRIMA Official Game Guide

ACROSS THE UNIVERSE

GALACTIC GUIDANCE

Before you blast off to defeat Bowser and save Princes Peach, you better know which way is up—and in deep space, that's not always easy. Mario isn't just squashing Goombas on the way to a castle; he's navigating the cosmos and encountering things he's never seen before. To help Mario win the day, you must know how to use gravity to your advantage, what kind of special suits Mario can wear to traverse the galaxies, and what it means when a strange comet flies overhead.

This guide will help you survive this incredible journey through the galaxies, which are full of jaw-dropping sights and challenging enemies. You'll be able to stay two steps ahead of Bowser, making sure that Mario and Princess Peach land back in the Mushroom Kingdom safe and sound—and with amazing stories to tell their friends.

 Game Screen

While traveling the galaxies, your view of Mario is augmented with necessary information regarding his status, such as the number of stars collected or current health.

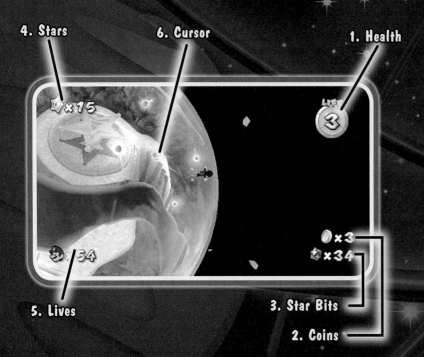

4. Stars

6. Cursor

1. Health

5. Lives

3. Star Bits

2. Coins

1. **Health:** This meter represents the number of hits Mario can sustain before falling.

2. **Coins:** Number of coins Mario has collected during the stage. The number resets to zero each time Mario falls.

3. **Star Bits:** Number of Star Bits Mario has collected during the stage.

4. **Stars:** Number of stars—Power Stars or Grand Stars—Mario has recovered in the cosmos.

5. **Lives:** Number of remaining chances Mario has to save Princess Peach.

6. **Cursor:** This marks where you're pointing the Wii Remote. This is where any Star Bits you fire will land. Use this to sweep up extra Star Bits, target enemies, or feed hungry Lumas.

Mario's health is almost always onscreen, but the other information comes and goes depending on what's happening in the game. Collecting coins and Star Bits makes the current count of these items pop onscreen. All information appears when Mario stands still for a moment, but as soon as the plumber starts running, it fades away.

Making All the Right Moves

Super Mario Galaxy uses both the Wii Remote and the Nunchuk attachment. You primarily use the Nunchuk to move Mario, while the Wii Remote handles jumping and pointing. To save Princess Peach from the clutches of the dastardly Bowser, you must be an ace with all of Mario's skills.

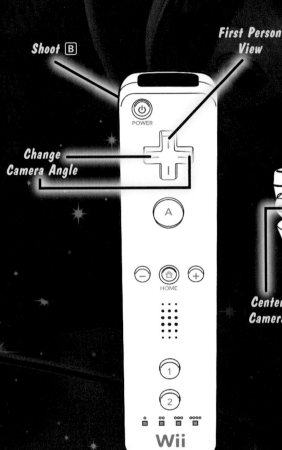

Shoot B

First Person View

Change Camera Angle

Move Mario

Center Camera

Duck

Controls

Input	Action
⊚	Move Mario
Ⓐ	Jump/Talk (when prompted)
Ⓑ	Shoot Star Bits
Ⓩ	Duck
Ⓒ	Center camera
✚	First-person view (when allowed)
✚	Change camera angle
Shake	Spin/Use Launch Star or Sling Star

PRIMA Official Game Guide

If you've played a *Mario* game before, you know all about jumping on enemies to get rid of them. Just run up to an enemy, hop into the air, and bring both feet down on the baddie. Mario can also use his jumps to activate switches.

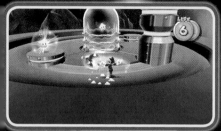

New to *Super Mario Galaxy* is Mario's spin. After meeting the Lumas, Mario is granted the ability to spin with such speed that he stuns most enemies on contact. To spin, shake the Wii Remote. Any enemy within reach is dazed. Now Mario can either touch the enemy to kick them off the planet or jump on it. How you dispose of an enemy affects your reward. If Mario stuns an enemy and boots it into space, Star Bits are released. Jumping on an enemy results in a coin.

TIP
Low on health? It might be worth getting in close and jumping on an enemy. Each coin replenishes one wedge of lost health.

Pocketful of Star Bits

The universe is full of sparkling Star Bits. Mario must collect as many of these as possible, as they are paramount to helping restore peace to the cosmos and rescuing Princess Peach. Star Bits are located everywhere—dangling in space, inside ? Blocks, and released by defeated enemies. Mario has many uses for these Star Bits. He can fire them at enemies to stun them, feed hungry Lumas, and even earn extra lives for every 50 he collects.

When you point the Wii Remote at your television, you will see a little blue star. That's your cursor. Move it around by pointing at different places on the screen. The cursor shows where you will shoot a Star Bit if you press Ⓑ. Try shooting a Star Bit at a small enemy, such as a Goomba. This rattles the Goomba. While the Goomba is stunned, Mario just needs to run at it. When Mario touches it, he kicks it off the planet, releasing more Star Bits. Use these to keep baddies at bay, making sure Mario never gets completely surrounded.

You can also use the cursor to collect Star Bits. Mario can pick them up by touching them, but it's much easier to just sweep the cursor over them— touching a Star Bit with the cursor automatically picks it up. The Star Bit crosses the cosmos, so no matter how

it's yours once your cursor touches it. So, look for anything glimmering in the skies and touch it with the cursor—you definitely want to fill Mario's pockets with Star Bits.

TIP
It never hurts to sweep the skies with the cursor in hopes of vacuuming up some Star Bits. If Mario lands on a planetoid and can see a great distance into space, run the cursor along the screen's edges to grab any Star Bits lingering there.

Multiplayer

If you have a second Wii Remote, you can play the game with a friend. The second player controls a second onscreen cursor that scoops up stray Star Bits and can fire them at baddies or thwart dangerous obstacles.

Having a friend help out with Mario's adventure is extremely useful and a lot of fun. Having another player vacuum up Star Bits while you concentrate on Mario is a great way to earn extra lives. With two cursors scouring the skies, getting 50 Star Bits is easy. Both players contribute to the same Star Bit collection, though, and they both draw from it when firing off Star Bits at enemies. So make sure you communicate and don't accidentally drain the well dry.

Two cursors are better than one when catching Star Bits as Mario rockets through the skies.

During tricky platforming puzzles, the second player can keep enemies at bay while the first player makes sure Mario maintains his balance.

The second player can also block obstacles and hazards. The second player's Star Bits can disable the ammunition fired by the cannons in the Battlerock Galaxy.

Special Moves

The heroic plumber has a menagerie of cool moves he can use from the moment he sets foot on the first planetoid in the Good Egg Galaxy, the starting planetary system. Knowing how and when to use these special moves, such as the long jump, will help Mario get ever closer to Princess Peach, so bone up on these skills before blasting off.

Long jump: This special jump is extremely useful for vaulting across large gaps between ledges. To long jump, tap Ⓩ while running to make Mario duck, then immediately hit Ⓐ to long jump. The long jump sacrifices height for distance, so don't use this jump to reach a higher ledge or platform than the one Mario is currently on.

Triple jump: Mario's triple jump is a great way to reach a really high ledge; however, you need enough distance between Mario and the ledge to utilize the jump. While running, press Ⓐ to jump. As soon as Mario lands, hit Ⓐ. Mario jumps a little higher than before, but if you press Ⓐ again as he touches down, Mario leaps into the air even higher.

Backflip: Not enough room to pull off the triple jump, but need to hop higher than usual? The backflip is a great way to get a little extra height from a standstill. First, face away from the object or ledge you want to jump to. Hold Ⓩ to make Mario duck. While ducking, press Ⓐ to jump. Like a pro acrobat, Mario backflips into the air, jumping higher than a regular jump. This jump doesn't cover much horizontal distance, so make sure Mario is right next to the ledge.

PRIMA Official Game Guide

Wall jump: Mario can spring off vertical surfaces. This is a cool way to scale great heights, but you need two flat surfaces close enough together for Mario to cover the gap between them with a single jump. To wall jump, jump against a wall and press Ⓐ just as he touches it. Mario then springs away from the wall. Keep this up to propel Mario up tall heights.

Ground pound: Mario's classic ground pound is useful for smashing heavy buttons and switches as well as stomping out an enemy. To ground pound, jump over the target. When you want Mario to slam to the ground, press Ⓩ. Make sure Mario is

precisely where you want him when you start the ground pound, because there is no pulling out of it.

Side jump: This special jump is a good way to get some immediate height as well as dodge any incoming attack. While running, quickly press the Nunchuk's control stick in the opposite direction and press Ⓐ. Mario pushes off the ground in the opposite direction he was running and does a cool flip in the air that's slightly higher than a regular jump.

Spin jump: Need just a hint of extra height while jumping? At the height of a jump, shake the Wii Remote to spin. This gives him a little upward nudge, which is often just enough to grab a ledge or pick up an object that it just out of reach with a regular jump.

⭐ **Space Travel** ⭐

🪐 **Gravity**

Since this adventure takes place in space, gravity plays an enormous part in solving the riddles of the cosmos. While using the Nunchuk's control stick to move Mario, always keep track of the plumber's direction. Gravity is always pulling down, but the essence of "down" is relative.

On spherical planetoids, Mario can run all the way around them—gravity pulls him toward the planet's center. Even though it looks like he's about to step off into space, gravity keeps him anchored to the planet. It's tricky at first, but you'll soon get the hang of thinking about the stages in true 360 degrees.

Now, not every planet's gravity is the same. Smaller planetoids have less gravity than bigger ones. While he won't break free of a larger planet's gravity, Mario can escape smaller planetoids if he jumps high enough. However, he will not always escape the gravity of smaller planets; he only does so if another gravity field is close enough to "grab" him. He will then be pulled to that new planetoid or spaceship.

TIP
Look at the "edges" of planets or floating platforms to determine whether or not Mario can walk all the way around them.

During his adventure, Mario ventures out into voids between gravity fields—and that's when he is the most vulnerable. Sometimes he will use vines or Pull Stars (more on these in the next section) or move between planets or other surfaces. If Mario loses his grip in a place with no gravity, he floats away. In flat areas, such as the huge floating platform of the Honeyhive Galaxy, if Mario drops off a sharp edge or loses his grip on a vine, he tumbles out into space. If he accidentally releases a vine or a Pull Star while between the gravity fields of two planets, he is sucked into a black hole. If light cannot escape a black hole, then surely Mario has no chance against one either.

Psst! There's a lot of cool things in Super Mario Galaxy, but the introduction of gravity is my favorite new feature. The first time I stepped off the so-called edge of a platform only to see Mario keep both feet on the ground thanks to gravity, I grinned from ear to ear. And when I started monkeying with gravitational fields to solve puzzles and travel the cosmos, I was absolutely hooked. Of course, the next time I play New Super Mario Bros. on the Nintendo DS or download a classic Mario game on the Wii's Virtual Console, I'm going to have to remind myself that Mario cannot just step off a ledge and keep on keepin' on.

Launch Stars

Some planets are too far apart for Mario to jump between their gravitational fields. In these situations, he must use Launch Stars to reach escape velocity (the speed at which an object breaks free of gravity's hold) and rocket to the next area. Launch Stars are large, orange-hued star outlines that sparkle and rotate when Mario steps near one. To blast off with a Launch Star, just stand near or inside one and shake the Wii Remote. Mario charges up enough energy to escape the planet's gravitational hold. Launch Stars have very specific paths. They always lead to the same place in each galaxy, so you never have to worry about being blasted to an unexpected location if using a previously explored Launch Star.

CAUTION Some planetoids have black holes in their centers. The pull of a black hole is greater than the pull of any nearby gravity system. Watch Mario's step on these planetoids. If he accidentally steps off a ledge, the black hole will pull him straight into it.

NOTE Sometimes Mario will encounter a Launch Star along the path of another Launch Star. If you don't shake the Wii Remote when Mario crosses the new Launch Star, he just keeps traveling to the destination of the first Launch Star. Toward the end of his adventure, Mario will encounter Launch Stars that work in tandem. To reach the final destination, he must use more than one Launch Star. If you don't shake the Wii Remote in time, Mario just falls into a fiery pool of lava.

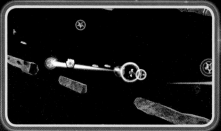

TIP

If you're quick, you can use a Pull Star to rescue Mario from floating away if you miss a jump between gravity fields. You have about two seconds before Mario drifts too far away, so if you're falling, point at any Pull Star on the screen and press Ⓐ. If you're fast (and lucky), Mario will grab it at the last second and be pulled to safety.

Pull Stars are blue stars that hang out in the space between gravity fields. Mario can use these as space hooks, grabbing each one to pull himself to the next planetoid or platform that has its own gravity. However, Mario must be close enough to use a Pull Star—he cannot latch on to one from halfway across the cosmos. When Mario is close enough to use a Pull Star, the Pull Star sparkles and is encased in a bubble.

To use a Pull Star, point the Wii Remote at it. When the cursor touches it, press Ⓐ to latch on to it. A "beam" pulls Mario to the Pull Star. If you hold Ⓐ, he will stay on the Pull Star. To move across a system of Pull Stars, simply point and click Ⓐ on each Pull Star. Mario floats between the Pull Stars until he either reaches a gravity field that pulls him in or you break his "grip" on a Pull Star, by releasing Ⓐ for a few seconds or shaking the Wii Remote. Shaking the Wii Remote just as Mario enters a gravity field brings him immediately down to the surface.

CAUTION

After releasing a Pull Star, you have only a few seconds of free-floating in space before Mario just drifts away.

There are a few instances where you want Mario to release a Pull Star in space— such as when a 1-Up Mushroom is hovering just out of reach. Without gravity, Mario can use another universal force: inertia. Inertia is the law of physics that states an object in motion will remain in motion until another mass exerts force on it. Gravity is a major force that dampens inertia, so in its absence, Mario can float freely, using the Pull Stars as makeshift slingshots.

Hungry Lumas

When exploring the galaxies, Mario encounters pink Lumas that are extremely hungry. These famished Lumas are looking for Star Bit snacks, and if Mario has enough of the sparkling goodies, the hungry Lumas will transform into new planets or even galaxies. Every Luma wants a different number of Star Bits, but the sacrifice is definitely worth it.

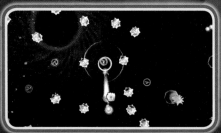

To grab these seemingly out-of-reach items, you need a straight line between Mario and the item. Somewhere between the two, you need a Pull Star. When you first latch on to a Pull Star, Mario moves the fastest. As he gets closer to a Pull Star, he slows down. You must use that initial speed burst to get the most distance. Just as Mario starts traveling toward the Pull Star, release Ⓐ and let him drift past the Pull Star and grab the item, but be ready to immediately press Ⓐ on the Pull Star. If Mario floats freely too long, he tumbles into space.

Many Galaxies have a hidden Power Star for Mario to collect, and sometimes the way to access that secret star is to feed a hungry Luma. To do this, talk to the hungry Luma by walking close to it. The Luma will say the number of Star Bits it wants to eat. Point the Wii Remote at the Luma's mouth and hold down Ⓑ to fill it with snacks. After you satisfy the Luma, it transforms. You do not need to feed the hungry Luma all the Star Bits at once. If you're a little short, look around and then come back. However, if you exit the galaxy, you must start all over when feeding the hungry Luma.

NOTE

Some of the hungry Lumas appear shortly after Mario enters the galaxy, so collect all the Star Bits you can as soon as possible.

COMET OBSERVATORY

Mario uses Rosalina's Comet Observatory as a launchpad to access all the different known galaxies in the universe. After Mario meets Rosalina at the beginning of his adventure, he arrives at her spaceship every time he exits a galaxy or whenever he returns to the game. The Comet Observatory consists of a series of platforms and Domes. Each Dome branches off to a different collection of galaxies.

The first time you start the game, only one Dome is open: Terrace. To open a new Dome and access a new group of galaxies, you must find the Grand Star in the current galaxy cluster. There are six main Domes on the Comet Observatory: Terrace, Fountain, Kitchen, Bedroom, Engine Room, and Garden. Each Dome has five galaxies except for the Garden, which only has four.

NOTE

There are additional galaxies you can find from the Comet Observatory, such as the three Trial Galaxies. We tell you how to unlock these secret galaxies and detail other cool features of the hub in the "Comet Observatory" chapter.

Gathering the Power Stars

When you enter the first Dome on the Comet Observatory, you can visit only the Good Egg Galaxy. The other galaxies in the system are obscured from view. The closed galaxies are emblazoned with a number or a question mark. The number on a galaxy represents how many Power Stars Mario must find before he can travel to that galaxy. (Power Stars are the goal of almost every mission in the game.) After you satisfy the requirement, place the cursor on the galaxy and press Ⓐ. This reveals the galaxy, and Mario can then travel there.

With enough Power Stars, Mario can explore every corner of the cosmos.

Each galaxy has a set number of Power Stars inside of it. Some galaxies have only one Power Star while others have six. (One galaxy has seven stars, but that seventh star is a secret. Don't worry—we'll tell you how to find it.) Place the cursor on a galaxy to see how many stars you have found. You find some stars by exploring an entire area of a galaxy, and others you find by winning a race or defeating a boss. When you find all the Power Stars in a galaxy, a tiny crown appears next to it on the map.

Talk to the black Luma inside each Dome to look at the map. This shows every open galaxy and whether or not you have found every Power Star inside it.

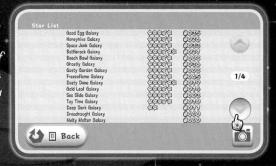

You can also check out a list of Power Stars and Grand Stars you've discovered, as well as a list of your best race times.

Daredevil Comet: The Daredevil Comet indicates that Mario must survive a mission with onlu one wedge of health. There are no coins in the mission. If Mario is hit only once, he fails and must start over, no matter how close he was to completing the mission.

When you look at a galaxy with six stars for the first time, only three blank star outlines appear. That's because the other three stars require a little extra work to find. Each of the six-star galaxies has three main missions, one hidden Power Star that requires Mario to seek out a special route in one of the main missions, and two comet-related Power Stars.

Wait—*comet-related* Power Stars?

Cosmic Comet: This comet creates a shadow Mario. Mario must race his shadow through a short course to the Power Star. If the shadow beats Mario, he loses a life and must restart the mission.

At some point while exploring a galaxy, a comet will arc overhead, which is visible from the Comet Observatory. All five comets are called "Prankster Comets"; these have a funny effect on one of the missions in that galaxy:

Speedy Comet: When this comet soars overhead, you must complete the mission within a time limit. If you don't reach the Power Star before the timer reaches zero, Mario loses a life and must start the mission over.

Fast Foe Comet: This comet speeds up the enemies in a mission. Mario has full health, but it's tough to deal with the faster enemies.

primagames.com

★★★★ 16 ★★★★

We'll let you in on a secret—there's a fifth comet. It's a purple comet that doesn't appear until Mario defeats Bowser at the center of the universe. The encounter is only available after Mario finds the fifth Grand Star and collects 60 Power Stars. After he completes a special mission inside the Gate, the purple comet starts appearing over all the six-star galaxies. The purple comet requires that Mario find 100 purple coins to earn that galaxy's final Power Star.

Continued...

There are still a great many unknowns about comets, but scientists are working hard to unlock their mysteries. Halley's 1986 appearance was investigated by the European space probe Giotto, revealing that the comet is approximately 4.5 billion years old and primarily composed of ice.

In 2005, a portion of the NASA space probe Deep Impact intentionally collided with the comet Tempel 1 to investigate the composition of a comet's nucleus. In 2006, a capsule from the probe Stardust returned to earth after a 7-billion-mile trip through deep space in which it collected particles from the comet Wild 2. The samples are still being analyzed.

Comets have always fascinated humankind. With their spectacular tails, always pointing away from the sun, comets have been viewed as harbingers of incredible things.

One of the most famous comets is Halley's Comet, a magnificent sight that only comes into earth's view approximately every 76 years. Using the calculations of Edmond Halley, the astronomer and mathematician for whom the comet is named, we can find records of the comet throughout history, dating as far back as 240 BC (and possibly even earlier). In 1910, the Earth actually passed through the tail of Halley's Comet. The most recent appearance of Halley's Comet was in 1986, and according to NASA, the next sighting of this comet will not appear until 2061.

GALACTIC GEAR

Mario may have the moves, but he needs more than his supreme jumping skills to restore order to the cosmos. He has access to special suits that grant him cool new powers and items that boost his chances for survival.

Dressed for Success

Mario always looks heroic in his trademark blue overalls, but sometimes he needs to update his look when the occasion demands it. Mario can change suits by picking up special items, such as colorful mushrooms or powerful flowers. The special suits offer Mario a host of new talents and abilities. Learning how to use these skills to defeat enemies or solve puzzles is paramount to successfully cleaning up the cosmos. So, before heading out to see the stars, check out Mario's closet and discover the latest fashion trends for today's discerning hero.

Bee Mario

What's that buzzing sound? It's Bee Mario, flitting about overhead with a cool set of teeny-tiny wings. This suit, available for the first time in *Super Mario Galaxy*, allows Mario to hover in the air for a limited amount of time and stick to special honeycomb surfaces. It's a great suit for traveling short distances through the air, such as crossing gaps in the ground or rising to collect a power-up that Mario couldn't otherwise grab in his regular overalls.

To put on the Bee Suit, Mario must find a special Bee Mushroom. It's yellow with dark brown stripes, just like the back of a bumblebee. After nabbing the special mushroom, Mario slips into the Bee Suit. There is no timer for just wearing the suit. However, bees don't like water, so if

Mario gets wet, he loses the suit. He also sheds the Bee Suit if an enemy attacks him, so bop those baddies with Star Bits to keep them from clipping Mario's wings.

Bee Mario has a limited flight time. To hover, press and hold down Ⓐ on the Wii Remote. Mario immediately starts fluttering upward, but the Bee Suit has a pretty low ceiling. From a standstill, Bee Mario can only ascend about six or seven times his height. However, if Bee Mario jumps off a ledge, his height is limited only by how much energy his wings have left.

Bee Mario must recharge after a few seconds of flying. When the Flight meter (displayed as a green circle next to Bee Mario when in flight) dips into the red, Bee Mario will drop back down to the ground. Hopefully he has some ground beneath him when the meter runs out—otherwise, Bee Mario gets a one-way trip to a black hole. The moment Bee Mario sets down on solid ground, though, the Flight meter quickly recharges and he can take off again.

Bee Mario can attack enemies while climbing on the honeycombs. If a pesky bug slips across his path, Bee Mario can jump away from the honeycomb and ground pound (use Ⓩ) to slam into the enemy.

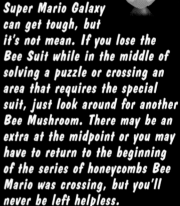

Psst!

Super Mario Galaxy can get tough, but it's not mean. If you lose the Bee Suit while in the middle of solving a puzzle or crossing an area that requires the special suit, just look around for another Bee Mushroom. There may be an extra at the midpoint or you may have to return to the beginning of the series of honeycombs Bee Mario was crossing, but you'll never be left helpless.

This is actually one of the cool things about Super Mario Galaxy. You're never punished if you slip up on a puzzle or get bonked by an enemy while in the middle of a task. Just dust yourself off and get back into it. You and Mario will get those stars and save Princess Peach.

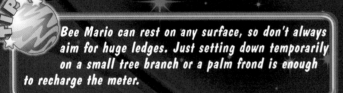

T.I.P.

Bee Mario can rest on any surface, so don't always aim for huge ledges. Just setting down temporarily on a small tree branch or a palm frond is enough to recharge the meter.

CAUTION

Bee Mario can't use all the regular moves. Special jumps, like the long jump or triple jump, are inactive while wearing the Bee Suit.

Bee Mario can also stick to special surfaces—just look for honeycombs on walls and towers. Fly Bee Mario into the honeycomb; he plants his arms and legs right into the honey and won't fall when you release Ⓐ. Bee Mario can crawl around honeycombs. If there's a gap between a couple honeycombs, just hop off, flutter up to the next sticky spot, and fly into it—Splat! Bee Mario is stuck again.

Boo Mario

The coolest power the Boo Suit grants Mario is the ability to temporarily vanish. To disappear, give the Wii Remote a little shake. Boo Mario vanishes for a few seconds. Enemies cannot harm Boo Mario while he's invisible. Even better, Boo Mario can actually pass through walls and obstacles while invisible. Are there some bars blocking Boo Mario's path? Fly over to them, give the Wii Remote a quick shake, and, while invisible, just slip right through them.

Boos have been sneaking up on Mario since *Super Mario Bros. 3*, but during this jaunt around the cosmos, Mario finally gets to turn the tables on the meddlesome ghosts. By picking up a spectral white Boo Mushroom, Mario is transformed into Boo Mario. As Boo Mario, the plumber can use several of the tricks the ghosts used to pull on him, such as temporarily disappearing.

NOTE When an action calls for you to shake the Wii Remote, there's no need to treat it like a pair of maracas. Just a little shake does the trick. And remember, always use the wrist strap when holding the Wii Remote.

If there's one thing Boos can't stand, it's the light. Boo Mario must beware of light too. Look out for spotlights and search beams sweeping around

rooms when using Boo Mario. If the light catches Boo Mario, even for a second, you lose the special suit. Hopefully, Boo Mario doesn't find himself in the spotlight while flying through space or over something dangerous.

While wearing the Boo Suit, Boo Mario can disappear and float through the air. To take flight as Boo Mario, repeatedly press Ⓐ on the Wii Remote. Each press of the button sends Boo Mario farther into the air. Several presses will have Boo Mario combing the ceiling for hidden goodies that normal Mario would never spot. This is also a good way to cross otherwise-impassable traps and hazards.

Psst! *Boo first appeared in Super Mario Bros. 3 back in 1988 (although, the game was not released in America until early 1990), and since then, the disappearing-reappearing baddie has appeared in many Mario games, including the Mario Party series, Super Paper Mario, and Mario Kart Double Dash!! Boo also starred in Luigi's big solo outing, Luigi's Mansion on the GameCube.*

Fire Mario

Fire Mario is one of Mario's most recog-nizable forms—he's been using this fireball-throwing outfit since his first adventure in the Mushroom Kingdom. To don the Fire Suit's bright red overalls, hunt down a Fire Flower. As soon as Mario picks the Fire Flower, he can start casting fireballs at enemies.

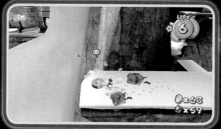
Fire Flower

Although Fire Mario is Mario's oldest superpower, debuting back in 1985's Super Mario Bros. on the Nintendo Entertainment System, this is the first time the power-up has appeared in a 3-D Mario game.

To cast a fireball as Fire Mario, point Mario at the intended target and shake the Wii Remote. Mario releases a fireball that bounces across the ground. Most baddies are thwarted with just a single fireball, but some enemies, such as a Thwomp, can shake it off with no effect. Keep shaking the Wii Remote to cast a string of fireballs and plow through a group of enemies attacking Fire Mario.

Also use Fire Mario's fireballs to light torches. It takes only one fireball to light a torch. Just point Fire Mario at the torch and let fly with the fireball. As long as there is no water between Fire Mario and the torch, the fireball will ignite it. Torches often unlock doors or reveal hidden items, so whenever there's an unlit torch nearby, look for a Fire Flower.

Ice Mario

Ice Flower

Casting a chill through his enemies is Ice Mario. Unlock this form by picking up a blue-and-white Ice Flower.

Is something frozen blocking Mario's path? Look for a Fire Flower. Fireballs melt icy things, like snowmen.

Unlike Bee or Boo Mario, Fire Mario and Ice Mario are only temporary forms. After picking up the flower that grants the special powers, use the music playing in the background to judge how much time is left for the power-up suit. When the music speeds up, the special suit is about to disappear.

Ice Mario grants Mario the ability to walk across liquid, such as water and lava. While the Ice Suit is active, step out onto the water or lava. Each step plants a frozen hexagon on the water's surface, kind of like a frozen lily pad. These pads last as long as Ice Mario stands on them. When Ice Mario steps off, the pad melts after several seconds. Use Ice Mario to cross otherwise-impassable bodies of liquid.

All water freezes under the feet of Ice Mario, including fountains. If Ice Mario jumps on the spray of a faucet or fountain, it freezes into an ice pad. Ice Mario can now use this as a temporarily platform. However, as soon as Ice Mario jumps away, the pad melts. With this talent, Ice Mario can turn a series of fountains into makeshift stairs, reaching otherwise-inaccessible ledges.

> **NOTE**
>
> *Mario can walk on the ice pads created by Ice Mario, but they are likely to disappear quickly, as they rapidly melt after Ice Mario steps away.*

To use Spring Mario's fantastic vault, press Ⓐ just as Spring Mario contracts on the ground. Release when the tightly coiled spring starts to expand. Spring Mario then rockets into the air. While in the air, use the Nunchuk's control stick to direct Spring Mario's trajectory. It's hard to direct Spring Mario with pinpoint precision, but he can at least be nudged in the right direction. Use Spring Mario to vault over especially tall walls or to reach an exceptionally high ledge.

> **NOTE**
>
> *Spring Mario shoots through the air with such force that he blasts right through bricks as if they weren't even there. However, he does land on bricks without breaking them.*

> **NOTE**
>
> *Spring Mario cannot access any of Mario's regular moves, so if enemies are en route, just rocket into the air and drop down on their heads to smash them.*

Spring Mario

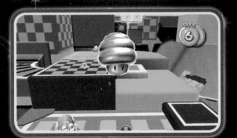

Spring Mushroom

First discovered in the Toy Time Galaxy, the Spring Mushroom grants Mario the Spring Suit. This suit grants Mario the ability to make huge superjumps, vaulting him far higher than even Mario's triple jump. The only catch, though, is that it's often difficult for Spring Mario to stay still. He wobbles and bounces, so watch out whenever he's close to an edge that drops into a black hole.

Flying Mario

Flying Star

Mario doesn't earn his Flying Suit until he reaches the Gate of the Comet Observatory. Inside this special room, a red Luma offers Mario the chance to earn the Flying Suit. If Flying Mario can collect 100 purple coins on a planetoid, the Luma will grant Mario the ability to use the Flying Suit in the Observatory. Like the Fire Mario or Ice Mario suits, the Flying Mario suit is only temporary, but it lasts significantly longer than those other suits.

Been flying around for a while and curious to know when gravity's going to reassert itself? Listen to the background music. When the music speeds up, Flying Mario is about to be grounded. However, just pick up another red star to get the suit back.

Flying Mario is decked out in black and red. Mario must be airborne to start flying. He cannot just soar into space, though. If Flying Mario tries to go too high, he's automatically pushed back down to a lower altitude.

Use the Nunchuk's control stick to control Flying Mario, who handles like an airplane—up and down are reversed. To go up, press ♥—this gives Flying Mario lift. To drop back down, press ♥, giving Flying Mario a little drag. To land, simply steer Flying Mario toward

the ground. Inches off the ground, Flying Mario drops his feet like landing gear and safely touches down. He can run around like normal, using all the regular moves. When he needs to fly again, just shake the Wii Remote and he's off!

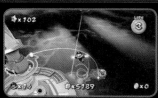

Flying Mario lets you take an airborne **Psst!** *tour of the Comet Observatory, granting you a spectacular view of Rosalina's flying home. After taking off, check out the Comet Observatory's top spire. Rosalina hid a 1-Up Mushroom there; the only way to grab it is with Flying Mario.*

Items

While touring the galaxies, Mario must pick up some souvenirs to bring back to the Mushroom Kingdom. He will collect some of his usual goodies, like coins and stars, but the cosmos is full of some pretty wondrous stuff, like Star Bits and Silver Stars. These pickups are important if Mario wants to collect the necessary Power Stars that unlock the road to rescuing Princess Peach from Bowser's clutches.

Power Star

Power Stars are the key to unlocking the cosmos and finding Princess Peach. Power Stars are the goal of every stage, save for boss encounters with Bowser and Bowser Jr. Those battles result in Grand Stars that fuel the Comet Observatory, but more on those in a moment.

Power Stars rest at the end of every stage—once Mario collects the Power Star, he is returned to the Comet Observatory. If there are additional Power Stars left in the galaxy, Mario can return and choose a new stage. Most galaxies have a handful of Power Stars, up to seven in some situations.

Power Stars are required to unlock new galaxies, so Mario must collect as many as possible. Only after collecting enough Power Stars can he blast off to save Princess Peach. So search across the heavens for those Power Stars—between Power Stars, Grand Stars, and a few special secret stars (we tell you how to get them later), there are 120 stars just waiting to be found.

Grand Stars

Grand Star

Grand Stars are required to power up the Comet Observatory. Every Grand Star Mario recovers adds energy to the great starship, opening up a new Dome. When a new Dome is open, Mario can immediately start investigating new galaxies. However, not every galaxy in the new Dome is available from the first time he steps inside. Mario must have enough Power Stars to unlock the routes to the new galaxies, and some of them require a lot of sparkle. At least one galaxy will be available when a new Dome is unlocked, though.

Coins

Coins

Mario is rarely without pocket change. The heroic plumber is always on the lookout for coins, which can be found anywhere in the galaxy. Some coins are in plain view and often serve as slight hints as to which way Mario should look, but others require a little footwork to spot. Shuffle through tall grass whenever you see it, as sometimes this shakes loose a coin. Some coins are hidden inside wooden crates or ? Blocks. Other coins are revealed if a switch is pounded

but those typically last only for a short time. Whatever coins Mario misses are lost until the next time he visits the galaxy.

Coins also replenish any lost health. One coin replaces one wedge in Mario's Health meter, located in the screen's upper-right corner. Coins will fully heal Mario, but he cannot bank coins collected while at top health for later use. If Mario picks up 50 coins in a stage during one visit, he earns a 1-Up, so keep those eyes open.

 Low on health and in dire need of a coin? Instead of stunning and kicking an enemy off a planetoid, jump on its head. This releases a coin instead of Star Bits.

Star Bits

Star Bits

Twinkling Star Bits are scattered across the universe. Mario should always scoop up Star Bits whenever possible, as he can use them for a variety of purposes, such as stunning an enemy or feeding a hungry Luma. Mario can pick up Star Bits simply by touching them, but using the Wii Remote is much easier. No matter how far Mario is from a Star Bit, pointing the Wii Remote at a glistening Star Bit picks it up. Sweep the screen with the Wii Remote when the cosmos is alive with shimmering bits to pick up dozens of Star Bits.

SUPER

Star Bits appear everywhere in the skies. In addition to the Star Bits on the ground or up in trees, look for Star Bits in the heavens as Mario zooms from one planetoid to another. Some Star Bits are tucked away in secret rooms. The coldness of space has even frozen some Star Bits in ice; Mario can free these by spinning to shatter the ice. Keep your eyes peeled for Star Bits, because Mario can use them for defense and for his health.

Collecting Star Bits grants Mario extra lives. Every 50 Star Bits he banks results in a 1-Up. However, that's 50 Star Bits in his current collection, not just 50 total Star Bits. Shooting Star Bits at enemies depletes Mario's supply. So if Mario has 45 Star Bits and fires 5 of them at a Goomba, he must collect 10 more to earn the 1-Up, not just 5 more.

Silver Star

Silver Stars are lost little stars destined to meet and create a Power Star. Like Star Chips, these little starlings come in fives. If Mario can hunt down all five of the separated Silver Stars, their destinies are fulfilled: They become the Power Star that Mario seeks to complete the stage and keep unlocking the way to new galaxies.

Star Chips

Star Chip

Star Chips are pieces of stars lost in the cosmos. They always come in fives. If Mario can find all five Star Chips in a stage, he assembles either a new Launch Star or a new Pull Star. It does not matter in what order Mario collects the Star Chips—the result is always the same. After Mario picks up the first Star Chip in a collection, the unfinished star's outline appears at the screen's top. Each Star Chip fills in one-fifth of the outline. When all five Star Chips are recovered, the new star appears. Fortunately, Mario is always shown the exact location of the fruits of his star-finding handwork.

When Mario finds the first Silver Star, it immediately starts following him around the stage. It drifts behind if Mario is vaulted somewhere across the stage or bounced really high, but it always catches up. Every Silver Star after that joins the shimmering posse, tracing Mario's every move until he finds the fifth Silver Star. As soon as all five are assembled, the Silver Stars join to become the Power Star. Mario is then given a glimpse of where the Power Star appears.

Blue Star Chips turn into a Pull Star and yellow Star Chips turn into a Launch Star.

TIP

Star Chips are rarely strewn all over a galaxy. If you spot one Star Chip, chances are good that the remaining four are on the same planetoid. Just keep looking—you'll find them!

Rainbow Star

Rainbow Star

Rainbow Stars are special power-ups that turn Mario temporarily invincible. While invincible, Mario can run through any enemy, blasting off the planetoid without worrying about losing any health. The Rainbow Star also gives Mario a serious speed boost, leaving a rainbow trail in his wake as he runs around the planets. Like all good things, invincibility soon ends. Listen to the music while tackling enemies and speeding across the landscape. When the music reaches almost terminal velocity, invincibility is about to run out. Find someplace safe!

Life Mushroom

Life Mushroom

Everybody knows Mario sustains himself on a steady diet of mushrooms. While taking a trip around the starry skies, Mario relies on this standby for extra health. Picking up a Life Mushroom fills his Health meter, and it ups the number of hits he can take from three to six. The second set of three wedges appears on top of the regular Health meter.

Mario can hold on to this extra health for the remainder of the stage as long as it never dips below four. If Mario takes three or more hits, the second set of wedges vanishes. So, keep seeking those coins—Mario needs all the health he can get while scouring the heavens for the Power Stars.

? Boxes

? Box

Coins and Star Bits are often hidden inside ? Blocks, the large yellow boxes that have served Mario well over his many adventures. To open the block and claim whatever prize is inside, stand under the ? Block and jump. Mario bops the block. If a bunch of Star Bits fall out, use the Wii Remote to scoop them up before they disappear. Unlike Star Bits, you cannot pick up coins with the Wii Remote—Mario must physically touch them.

1-Up Mushroom

1-Up Mushroom

He may be the biggest hero in the universe, but sometimes even Mario stumbles. Fortunately, he can pick up these special green-and-white mushrooms while adventuring across the galaxies. Each 1-Up Mushroom grants Mario an extra life, so check behind every rock and on every high ledge for these valuable fungi.

> **TIP**
> 1-Up Mushrooms regenerate every time Mario starts a stage, either from the very beginning or at a checkpoint if he fell into a black hole.

PRIMA Official Game Guide

COMET OBSERVATORY

A PROLOGUE

Mario's First Journey

Upon waking from the blast, Mario meets the Luma that Peach was holding on to before Bowser's attack. The Luma needs to teach Mario a few tricks about planet-hopping and star-catching, so it engages Mario in a little game of hide-and-seek before launching into a full-blown journey across a planetary system.

Bunny-Chasing

The Luma magically transforms into a cute star bunny and is joined by two friends who do likewise. They want to show Mario all about the galaxies but aren't above being a little playful about it. Before they share their secrets with Mario, he must catch all three of them on the small planetoid. As soon as Mario grabs all three, the bunnies turn back into Luma and point the way to the heavens.

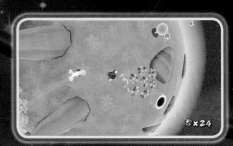

The bunnies hide in three different places on the little planet. Mario must first discover the hiding place and then chase the bunny as it flees. After he catches all three, they return to the flower path on the small mound.

x

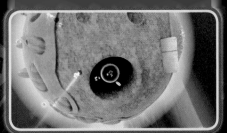

A Prologue

Comet Observatory

The third bunny is in the crater carved in the dirt patch of the small planet.

Gotcha!

There are lots of coins and Star Bits on the planetoid, so in addition to seeking bunnies, Mario should start his collection. There are Star Bits on the rooftops of the small cottages. The large hole near the flower-topped mound leads to a tunnel that travels through the planetoid's center. If Mario jumps into the tunnel's center, he shoots all the way through to the other side, picking up coins along the way.

As soon as Mario finds all three bunnies, a small castle appears on the planetoid. When Mario approaches, he spots a young woman dressed in cosmic blue, a color that exists only when the sun creeps out from behind the clouds. Her name is Rosalina, and she pledges to help Mario find Princess Peach. It seems that not only has Bowser stolen the princess, but he might be the culprit behind the thievery of special stars that help power Rosalina's Comet Observatory.

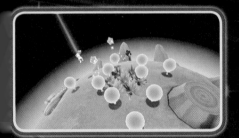

The first bunny is in the tall grasses between the rubbery bulbs.

The second bunny is in the green warp pipe. Enter either by the village or the rocks.

To help Mario track down the Power Stars and Princess Peach, he's gifted with the power of a Luma—he can use a special spin that stuns enemies and lets him break free of gravity when used next to Launch Stars. Launch Stars are the cosmic portals between planetoids.

SUPER MARIO GALAXY

Mario can use his newfound skill immediately. A Launch Star is encased in ice right behind Rosalina. Just stand next to the ice and spin to shatter the crystals and free the special star. Mario can then stand next to the star and spin again to launch to the first in a series of small planets.

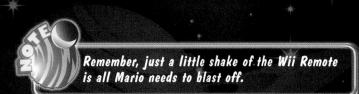

NOTE

Remember, just a little shake of the Wii Remote is all Mario needs to blast off.

Planet-Hopping

When Mario touches down on the first small planetoid, he notices that there's no Launch Star to get him to the next rock. (However, there are plenty of Goombas that he can handle with a quick spin and a kick.) Instead, Mario must seek out five Star Chips, pieces of a broken Launch Star. Star Chips look like little gold triangles, glistening on the planetoid's surface. While searching out the Star Chips, be sure to snag the 1-Up Mushroom on the rock.

This metal planet is plagued with Goombas. Instead of dealing with the Goombas individually, check out the tall spire on the planetoid's southern hemisphere. Spin next to the spire. Smacking the spire sends out a shock wave that stuns all the Goombas.

Just like the Launch Star before it, there is a Star Chip encased in ice. A quick spin breaks the ice and frees the Star Chip. After you collect all five, the Launch Star appears on the star pedestal. Mario can now launch to the next planetoid.

One of the Goombas holds a key that frees a yellow Luma opposite of the spire (you must talk to the trapped Luma for the key to appear). Picking up the key frees the Luma, which turns into a Launch Star. This Sling Star launches Mario to a larger metal planet, very similar to the last, complete with spires that upset the tiny, crawling Goombas.

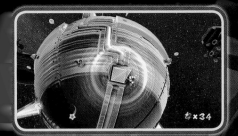

The warp pipe leads to the planetoid's interior. There's a giant star hooked up to a nefarious-looking machine, guarded by Goombas. This is surely Bowser's handiwork!

There is another key on this planetoid, but it unlocks a warp pipe. It's held by the giant Goomba on the sphere's northern half. Mario must smack the smaller spires to the south to stun the small Goombas. While traveling north, check out the rotating green ring that circles the equator. There are several coins above the ring, but watch out for the sparking ends of the green platforms. If Mario gets crackled, he loses one wedge of health.

That's a big Goomba. The titan is far too tall for Mario to jump on, so spin into it to stun it. The sound waves rattle the giant Goomba. While it's dazed, kick it off the planetoid and claim the key that opens the warp pipe.

To deactivate the machine, Mario must turn off a series of floor switches. The switches are currently yellow, but Mario must step on them to turn them blue. If he steps on a switch after turning it blue, it turns yellow again.

There are four switches along the chamber's equator, but a ring of electrified platforms runs over them. Mario must wait for the breaks in the platforms to step on the switches. Don't worry about gravity in here—no matter where he stands, gravity pushes outward from the center, keeping Mario's feet firmly on the ground.

SUPER MARIO GALAXY

After hitting the four equatorial switches, Mario must attend to the switches surrounding the imprisoned star. Goombas toddle around the switches, but a spin and kick combo makes short work of them—and releases Star Bits. After turning all the switches blue, the machine shuts down. The switches turn green and cannot be activated by stepping on them again.

This is a Grand Star. Grand Stars unleash even more energy than Power Stars. Grab hold of the Power Star and get ready for a ride.

The Power Star launches Mario across the cosmos to a darkened space station. This is the Comet Observatory, Rosalina's home among the stars. From here, Mario can access the universe, collecting Power Stars and Grand Stars, as well as hunting down Bowser.

COMET OBSERVATORY

Built from materials collected during Rosalina's great travels, the Comet Observatory is a star-bound village that houses not only Rosalina, but hundreds of Luma she adopts and cares for. From this great ship, Rosalina can peer out at all the wonderful galaxies spinning in the known universe.

Or, at least she used to. The Comet Observatory has been cast into darkness. The Power Stars and Grand Stars that used to fuel the ship have been stolen by the malevolent Bowser and put to use in his own machines. To what end, Rosalina does not know, but if she is to restore the Comet Observatory and bring peace back to the cosmos, she needs the help of a hero who is not afraid to rocket across the galaxies.

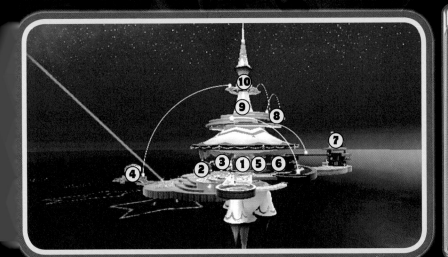

A Prologue

Comet Observatory

LEGEND

1. Star Map
2. Terrace
3. Fountain
4. Garage
5. Bedroom
6. Library
7. Kitchen
8. Gate
9. Engine Room
10. Garden

Rosalina's Paradise

When Mario first visits the Comet Observatory, the majority of the ship is dark. The reactor behind Rosalina is dim, and only a small landing is lit up. From this landing, Rosalina explains to Mario where he is and how their missions—rescuing Princes Peach and returning order to the galaxy—are intertwined. Mario will use the Comet Observatory as a hub or staging ground for his travels throughout the universe, returning here every time he retrieves a Power Star or a Grand Star. Each star will be used to augment the Observatory, either unlocking new portals or powering up the central reactor. The more energy flowing through the reactor, the more places Mario can visit in the universe.

However, until Mario starts collecting stars, the Comet Observatory remains largely empty. The Garage, which is just across from the Terrace, is inactive. The paths to the other Domes are closed. Mario cannot even reach the upper reaches of the Comet Observatory, as the lack of power mutes the once-bright warps that propel people to loftier views.

As more power flows through the Comet Observatory, special warps open up new sections of the ship.

Even though the Comet Observatory is the main hub and lacks any enemies, the starship is hardly boring. As Mario finds those much-needed stars, a variety of activities become available. There are hidden galaxies accessible only from the Comet Observatory, opened by collecting enough Star Bits to feed hungry Luma. Rosalina reads a poignant story to the Luma in the library. A special room unlocks the ability for Mario to ditch gravity and take flight, even if for a few glorious seconds.

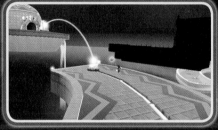

After collecting enough stars, Rosalina displays a giant board detailing the number of stars found as well as what areas are currently open for Mario to explore.

✦✦ Domes ✦✦

The Comet Observatory's main features are the Domes. There are six Domes on the Observatory, but only the Terrace Dome is open when Mario first enters the ship. Every time he boots the main boss (either Bowser or Bowser Jr.) off the galaxies linked to a specific Dome, he earns a Grand Star. This Grand Star powers the Comet Observatory's main reactor, unlocking a new Dome. The order in which the Domes are unlocked is Terrace, Fountain, Kitchen, Bedroom, Engine Room, and Garden.

Inside each Dome, a black Luma serves a guide to the galaxies. If Mario talks to the Luma, it reveals a current list of visited galaxies and how many stars have been found in that galaxy. Different galaxies have different star counts. While some galaxies have only one Power Star, others have up to seven stars or even a Grand Star. When Mario has recovered all of the stars in a particular galaxy, a tiny crown appears next to the galaxy name or on the galaxy map.

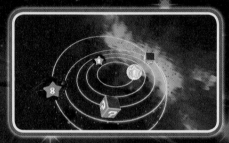

There is a blue Pull Star at the apex of each Dome. When Mario grabs the Pull Star, he can view all galaxies available from that Dome. However, on the first visit to a Dome, the full map of galaxies is obscured.

Each galaxy has a number on it. That's the required number of stars needed to unlock that galaxy. When Mario has enough stars, point to a galaxy and press Ⓐ.

Now Mario can see the galaxy and how many stars he has found. This galaxy, the Good Egg Galaxy, has six stars—but only three are available with regular visits. The other three are hidden. One of the Power Stars is accessible by finding a secret route. The other two are linked to the appearance of special comets. In the Good Egg Galaxy, one of those comets is the Cosmic Comet, which pits Mario in a race against a shadowy version of himself.

After earning enough Power Stars, Mario can unlock all the galaxies in a Dome. To check out the galaxy map from different angles, move the cursor away from a planet and hold Ⓐ. Now, move the Wii Remote to spin, twist, and skew the viewing angle. Each Galaxy icon provides a glimpse of what's in store, but Mario must travel to it to see just how crazy these planets really are.

There is always at least one Prize Block sharing orbit with the other galaxies. Most Prize Blocks link to special galaxies with only one star; one Prize Block links to two stars. However, there is no number on the Prize Block, so you won't know when it's open until a message prompts you while you're exploring the other galaxies in that particular Dome.

All those Star Bits Mario brings back to the Comet Observatory after grabbing a star go into a general bank (any Star Bits collected during a mission are abandoned if you leave the stage early). So, what do you do with them at the Comet Observatory? Feed a hungry Luma! Outside of each Dome is a Luma that could use a snack. After you earn enough stars inside the Dome, a message tells you when the hungry Luma appears.

As you open more Domes, the Luma get hungrier. By the time you're feeding the Luma outside the Engine Room, these meals prove costly. But charity never goes unrewarded—a satiated Luma opens the way to a brand-new galaxy, where you can pick up another Power Star.

🪐 Terrace

The first available Dome, the Terrace, is on the Comet Observatory's main level, to Rosalina's left. The Terrace leads to a series of fun galaxies that help Mario ease further into the fine art of planet-hopping and exploration. The Terrace also leads to the Honeyhive Galaxy, which is the first time Mario tries on his all-new Bee Suit. Bee Mario is gifted with the power of flight, allowing him to buzz across gaps and chasms.

The Loopdeloop Galaxy is also linked from the Terrace, which allows Mario to try out the fun of ray-surfing. Penguins love to watch ray-surfing, so hopefully Mario can put on a good enough show to earn the galaxy's Power Star.

Terrace Galaxies

Galaxy	Stars Required
Good Egg Galaxy	1
Honeyhive Galaxy	3
Bowser Jr.'s Robot Reactor	8
Loopdeloop Galaxy	?
Flipswitch Galaxy	?

Hungry Luma

Feed 400 Star Bits to the hungry Luma outside the Fountain Dome so Mario can rocket to the Sling Pod Galaxy. This galaxy is full of sticky pods that slingshot Mario across the night sky. Don't overshoot the Power Star at the galaxy's edge or Mario will float away.

Hungry Luma

If Mario feeds the hungry Terrace Dome Luma 400 Star Bits, it unlocks the Sweet Sweet Galaxy. The candy- and treat-themed galaxy is loaded with sugary goodness, but watch out that Mario's sweet tooth doesn't distract him from the Power Star on the cake at the galaxy's edge.

Fountain

After rescuing the Grand Star from Bowser Jr.'s Robot Reactor in the Terrace galaxies, the warp to the Fountain Dome opens. To access the Dome, Mario just needs to step in the light next to the small blue Luma. Inside, the hero can blast off for

galaxies like Battlerock, a floating fortress buffeted with cannons and Bullet Bills, or the shrinking platforms that cover the Hurry-Scurry Galaxy. After earning enough stars, Mario opens the way to wrest another Grand Star from his nemesis' clutches in Bowser's Star Reactor.

Fountain Galaxies

Galaxy	Stars Required
Space Junk Galaxy	9
Battlerock Galaxy	12
Bowser's Star Reactor	15
Rolling Green Galaxy	?
Hurry-Scurry Galaxy	?

Kitchen

The third Dome, located on the tower of plates and silverware, is the Kitchen. (Don't forget to peek under the stairs for a free 1-Up Mushroom, Mario!) Once inside the Kitchen, Mario can treat himself to a taste of the Ghostly Galaxy, a haunted realm where he earns the Boo Suit, and he meets his brother Luigi. After freeing Luigi, swimming with the penguins at Beach Bowl Galaxy, and exploring the secrets of Buoy Base Galaxy, it's time to take down those cosmic pirate ships in Bowser Jr.'s Airship Armada.

Kitchen Galaxies

Galaxy	Stars Required
Beach Bowl Galaxy	16
Ghostly Galaxy	20
Bowser Jr.'s Airship Armada	23
Bubble Breeze Galaxy	?
Buoy Base Galaxy	?

greenery for sun-scorched sands. After gathering up enough Power Stars, Mario can take the fight to Bowser again at Bowser's Dark Matter Reactor. This crazy level features some tough jumps, so get ready to shake that Wii Remote to get an extra bit of height out of each hop.

Bedroom Galaxies

Galaxy	Stars Required
Gusty Garden Galaxy	24
Freezeflame Galaxy	26
Dusty Dune Galaxy	29
Bowser's Dark Matter Reactor	33
Honeyclimb Galaxy	?

Hungry Luma

For a mere 600 Star Bits, the hungry Luma outside the Kitchen will grant Mario access to the Drip Drop Galaxy, home to a pack of penguins with serious giant eel problems. If Mario can clear out the infestation, the penguins will reward him with a Power Star. Surely that's worth a measly 600 Star Bits?

Hungry Luma

The Bigmouth Galaxy contains a lone Power Star, but if Mario wants all 120 stars, he must feed 800 Star Bits to the hungry Luma outside the Bedroom. The Bigmouth Galaxy is a lone planet, shaped like a mammoth fish. Can Mario land the catch of the galaxy?

Bedroom

The fourth Dome, the Bedroom, leads Mario deeper into the universe. The galaxies beyond the Bedroom include the Gusty Garden, a windblown collection of grassy planetoids. Here, Mario must agitate a giant worm inside an even larger apple to create a bridge to other

Engine Room

As soon as Mario grabs the Grand Star from Bowser's Dark Matter Reactor, he opens the way to the Engine Room, located on the Comet Observatory's middle tier. The Engine Room leads to a handful of tough galaxies, so get ready for some serious challenges, such as the Toy Time Galaxy's giant robot planet. The Sea Slide Galaxy is a watery ring hanging in the cosmos, populated by friendly penguins and a toothy shark named Guppy. The sea life in the Bonefin Galaxy, however, is not so friendly. Wait until Mario casts his eyes on the leviathan guarding the lone Power Star of that galaxy.

SUPER

Engine Room Galaxies

Galaxy	Stars Required
Gold Leaf Galaxy	34
Sea Slide Galaxy	36
Toy Time Galaxy	40
Bowser Jr.'s Lava Reactor	45
Bonefin Galaxy	?

Hungry Luma

Want to visit the Sand Spiral Galaxy? Then Mario must cough up 1,000 Star Bits to the gluttonous Luma outside the Engine Room, just beyond the rotating yellow platform. The Sand Spiral is a small galaxy that gives Mario the choice of the Bee Suit or the Boo Suit to help complete the challenge.

Garden

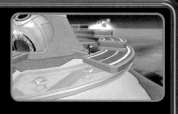

The Garden is the last of the six Domes, located at the very top of the Comet Observatory. The Garden's interior is unlike the other Domes—it looks like Mario's stepping into a massive hologram of a peaceful planet. However, the galaxies linked to the Garden are far from idyllic. The formidably named Dreadnought Galaxy is full of enemies. The Melty Molten Galaxy is full of searing fire. And the Matter Splatter Galaxy is an intense adventure through a galaxy that is constantly forming and dissolving—at the same time. The Garden does not lead to an encounter with Bowser because by the time Mario unlocks the Garden, the Comet Observatory has enough Grand Stars to travel to Princess Peach's rescue.

Garden Galaxies

Galaxy	Stars Required
Deep Dark Galaxy	46
Dreadnought Galaxy	48
Melty Molten Galaxy	52
Matter Splatter Galaxy	?

Hungry Luma

The hungry Luma outside the Garden wants to chow down on 1,600 Star Bits. It's an expensive snack for Mario, but the Luma transforms into the Snow Cap Galaxy, a two-planet system where Mario is tasked with chasing three more star bunnies.

Gate

The Gate is not a traditional Dome like the Terrace or the Engine Room, but it does lead to some space-faring thrills. When Mario unlocks the Garden, he also opens this small side chamber. From inside the chamber, Mario meets a rare red Luma that promises to let him use the special Flying Suit. This suit lets Mario take off and soar through the skies around the Comet Observatory.

Inside the Gate, Mario must collect 100 purple coins to impress the red Luma. If Mario does this, the red Luma grants Mario the Flying Suit.

After unlocking the Flying Suit, return to the red Luma on the Comet Observatory. The red star next to the Luma transforms Mario's regular overalls into the black Flying Suit.

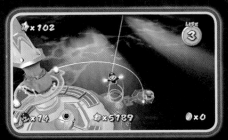

Wahoo! Flying around the Comet Observatory is a fun way to see the sights and even discover a couple secrets.

There are three hidden 1-Up Mushrooms in the Comet Observatory that Mario must use the Flying Suit to find. The first 1-Up Mushroom is atop the spire above the Loft. Fly straight up from the Comet Observatory's lower tier and set Mario's sights on the spire.

The second hidden 1-Up Mushroom is just below the Comet Observatory's lowest tier. Look beneath the Bedroom and Library. There's a green-capped mushroom! Fly around the reactor in the Comet Observatory's center and zip through the narrow opening to pick up the mushroom. The third hidden 1-Up Mushroom is tucked under the center of the island that the gate is located on.

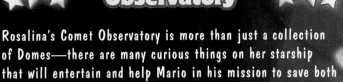

Hungry Luma

There is also a hungry Luma outside the Gate. If Mario feeds the Luma 1,200 Star Bits, it zips into the skies to become the gateway to Boo's Boneyard Galaxy. The Spooky Speedster from the Ghostly Galaxy challenges Mario to a rematch here, so don that Boo Suit and get ready to race.

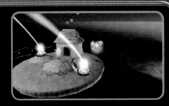

Elsewhere on the Observatory

Rosalina's Comet Observatory is more than just a collection of Domes—there are many curious things on her starship that will entertain and help Mario in his mission to save both Princess Peach and recover the stolen Power Stars. Between trips across the cosmos, Mario should explore every inch of the Observatory. He may even spot a few familiar faces while searching high and low.

PRIMA Official Game Guide

There's a Toad near Rosalina that delivers mail. Sometimes, Princess Peach sends Mario five 1-Up Mushrooms to help him in his journeys around the universe. Talk to the Toad every time a letter flashes over its head.

Every time Mario returns to the Comet Observatory, visit the Garage and open the crate to claim a helpful 1-Up Mushroom.

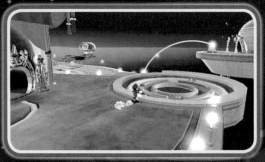

Step on the circular pads near the Bedroom and Rosalina's main platform to get an asteroid's-eye view of the entire Comet Observatory.

Luigi!

Surely Luigi isn't going to let his brother do all the hard work—or collect all the credit. After Mario rescues Luigi from the haunted mansion in the Ghostly Galaxy, Luigi appears at the Garage back on the Comet Observatory. He pledges to help Mario find the Power Stars and proves to be a plumber of his word. The only catch is that Luigi sometimes gets into trouble and needs Mario to help him out.

NOTE

If Mario falls off a platform in deep space, he tumbles into a black hole. However, should the plumber slip off the Comet Observatory, a magical bubble whisks him right back to safety.

Bro! I got a star, but now I can't get back. This picture shows where I am! HELP ME!

From Luigi

Garage

When Mario first arrives on the Comet Observatory, the Garage is completely desolate. All that sits on the landing pad is a lone crate. However, after collecting several Power Stars, Mario receives a note to visit the Garage.

The Garage is populated with Toads! The Luma are helping the Toads build a mushroom-shaped spacecraft so they can assist Mario in finding the Power Stars. Now, when Mario visits certain galaxies, he can use the Toads' ship as a platform to link planets. The Toads even find Power Stars themselves and hold them for Mario until he reaches their location in the galaxy.

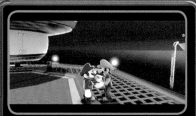

When Luigi finds a Power Star but cannot bring it back to the Comet Observatory, he sends a postcard to Mario. The Toad that delivers the mail near Rosalina signals to Mario that he has a postcard from Luigi. The postcard shows a picture of where Luigi is trapped. Mario must then go to that galaxy and find his brother. When Mario finds Luigi, he hands over the Power Star and they return to the observatory together.

While traveling through space, Rosalina has plenty of time to catch up on her reading, as well as entertain the Luma with fun storybooks. Mario can visit the Comet Observatory's Library, too, located to the Bedroom Dome's left and directly across from the Kitchen.

There is a faint outline of a large green Sling Star on the lawn below the Terrace Dome. What is this? Mario hasn't seen any green Sling Stars elsewhere in the universe—and come to think of it, are there any green Luma? The answers are out there among the planets if Mario looks in special, hidden places. There, he will find three special green Launch Stars.

When Mario brings these Launch Stars back to the Comet Observatory, they turn into green Luma. As soon as Mario collects all three, the green Luma unlock the green Sling Star. This leads to the Trial Galaxies, a trio of challenging galaxies that test Mario's dexterity. There is a normal Launch Star at the end of each Trial Galaxy, so seek out those three hidden green Launch Stars to unlock these secret galaxies.

Mario periodically gets a message that a new chapter to the storybook has been opened. The next time he visits the Library, he will see a crowd of young Luma excitedly gathering around Rosalina as she pulls what's obviously a favorite book from the shelves. Rosalina opens the book and starts reading one chapter at a time to the entranced Luma.

The story is about a young girl who… Actually, the story should be enjoyed through the eyes of the Luma, allowing you to see the colorful pictures that accompany the sweet, poignant words

TIP

Hey, since Luigi is so fond of green (check out his threads), maybe he can help Mario find one of those elusive, supersecret green Launch Stars!

NOTE

The locations of the green Launch Stars are detailed in the section for the galaxy that houses them, such as the Buoy Base Galaxy. After unlocking the Trial Galaxies, check the "Hidden Galaxies" chapter for expert tips on completing the three challenges.

TERRACE GALAXIES

GOOD EGG GALAXY
Dino Pirahna

A — Start

F — Dino Piranha

B

C

D

E

The Good Egg Galaxy is a system of small planetoids, linked together by several Launch Stars. Travelers of this galaxy must survive harrowing encounters with the stomping Dino Piranha and the lava-dwelling King Kaliente. The routes to these monsters stretch across the night sky, so buckle up and get ready to blast off for Mario's first major tour of a galaxy.

DINO PIRANHA

The first mission in the Good Egg Galaxy sends Mario on a collision course with the Dino Piranha, a vicious veggie that loves to stomp and clomp around. Before Mario reaches the Dino Piranha, though, he must do a little planet-hopping and collect five Star Chips to fashion a Launch Star on a slightly hostile planetoid.

Planet A

Mario lands on a round planet covered with grassy lawn and flowerbeds—there's even a small cottage. It looks inviting, but the welcome party is a little warmer: Electrogoombas. The shockers inch toward Mario and try to smack him with their heads. Avoid the nuisances and walk through the flowerbeds to reveal a handful of Star Bits. Scoop up the Star Bits and then focus on the Electrogoombas again. Stun each of them with a Star Bit and then either kick or spin-attack them off the planet.

This planet is not all that it seems. Walk to the planet's edge and take one giant step right off into space.

Hey, Mario's still here! The planet's gravity keeps him grounded, but the flip side is not nearly as pleasant. Where did all the sunshine go?

NOTE
Mario can also use the green warp pipe to pop out on the bottom of the planet.

CAUTION
Remember the basic rule about walking "underneath" planets. If the planet's edges are rounded, you can step to another side of the planet. If the edge is rough or sharp, you will fall off and lose a life.

The barren trees in the planet's dark half are twinkling with Star Bits. Pick them up with the Wii Remote as you explore. See that rustling in the grass? Step into the shrubbery to discover a coin. (If an Electrogoomba hits you, a coin will replenish any lost health.) Jump under the ? Block to earn additional Star Bits.

Jump onto the stairs guarded by another Electrogoomba. Jump on the enemy to pick up another coin and then step out on the balcony that extends into space. The balcony twists on its side, but gravity keeps Mario's feet firmly on the floor. There are Star Bits encased in ice out here. Spin-attack to break the ice and gather up the goodies.

Good Egg Galaxy

Honeyhive Galaxy

Flipswitch Galaxy

Loopdeloop Galaxy

Bowser Jr.'s Robot Reactor

Sweet Sweet Galaxy

SUPER MARIO

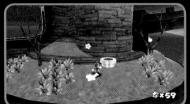

On the opposite side of the planet from the balcony, Mario can drop into an orange warp pipe. This leads into a secret room. Inside the room, head for one of the ramps with a yellow arrow against the wall. Walk up the ramp. Gravity pulls you to the floor—except now the wall is the floor. Use the ramps to reach a giant coin on the blue wall (it's surrounded by four coin pegs. Shoot each peg with a Star Bit to reveal the coin).

Grab the giant coin. A trail of musical notes starts weaving around the room, leading Mario up the ramps until he's on the ceiling. If you collect all the notes before time runs out, a 1-Up Mushroom appears on the blue wall. Hurry back across the ramps to get it—it won't last long! After bagging the

Mushroom, use either orange pipe to return to the planet's surface. The ceiling pipe deposits Mario on the cottage's roof.

Run up the curved path that leads to the tall tower. (Curved surfaces mean you can defy gravity.) There is a Luma at the tower's top. Talking to the Luma turns it into a small Launch Star. Step into the star's center and shake the Wii Remote to launch Mario back into space.

Mario lands on a tiny, bean-shaped planetoid without a Travel Star. And there's immediate danger from a snapping Piranha Plant. Maybe there's a link? Bop the Piranha Plant with a Star Bit. While it's dazed, kick it into the cosmos. After the vicious veggie vanishes, a Sproutle pops out of the surface and extends into space.

TIP

Low on Star Bits? There is a giant coin on the "bottom" of the planetoid that releases some extra Star Bits. Scoop them up with the Wii Remote. Always look for giant coins like this one; they often release special goodies.

Planets B and C

Mario lands on a small peanut-shaped planetoid. Several boulders rumble around the surface. If one of them hits Mario, just pick up a nearby coin to restore lost health. Better yet, spin into the red surface of the boulders to destroy them—they release a lot of star bits. A quick tour of the planetoid reveals that there's no way off this place. However, five small triangles glisten on the surface. Collect all five to assemble a Launch Star on the planetoid's tip. Watch out for the boulders while gathering the pieces—stepping in the boulders' ruts slows Mario to a snail's pace.

The next planetoid has a black hole in its center, so watch your step around the edges. The Travel Star is on the planet's far side, so weave around the snaking paths, avoiding the boulders and the prickly plants. There are lots of coins on the surface, so if Mario takes any damage, he can easily recover.

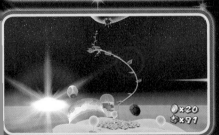

Watch out for the toothy purple Piranha Plant at the planet's top. The chompers on this thing will snap away a wedge of health, so stay back. There are two ways to defeat the plant. One, wait until it lunges forward and slam its head into the ground. While it's briefly dazed, jump on its head. Two, spin next to one of the rubbery bulbs, smacking it into the Piranha Plant. When it's gone, the Sproutle beneath it extends to the sky, offering a bridge to the next planetoid.

Psst!

There's a secret path on this planetoid. Right after Mario lands, look to the right—there's a small checkered platform leading to a warp pipe. A Piranha Plant guards it, so hit it with a Star Bit and kick it into the sky. Drop into the warp pipe.

This crazy place is a series of blue floor panels. Step on a blue panel to turn it yellow. Turning all of the blue panels yellow reveals the next route, but Mario can only step on each panel once—stepping on it again turns it back to blue. The panels lead to a 1-Up Mushroom. When Mario completes the panel puzzle, he's blasted off to Planet E.

SUPER MARIO GALAXY

Planet E

When Mario lands on the planet's sandy bottom, he notices a pair of footsteps tromping about. There's something here—but it's invisible. To flush the creature into the open, Mario must track its steps and then spin. If he tags the creature with his spin, it appears.

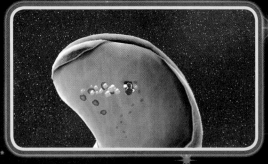

When Mario blasts off, he's surrounded by Star Bits. Sweep the cursor over them to pick them up.

Hey, check out that blue creature! Jump on it or spin-attack it to earn a bunch of Star Bits.

Planet F

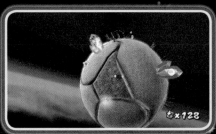

This small planetoid seems peaceful when Mario lands on it—but looks can be deceiving. After smashing the Star Bits out of the ice, walk to the planet's other side for a surprise.

Walk to the planet's topside. The makeshift stone stairs up here are crawling with Electrogoombas. Mario can stun the little guys with Star Bits and then kick them off the planet to earn extra Star Bits. If Mario is low on health, stomp on them to release coins. There is a Launch Star encased in ice at the top of the stones. If Mario can jump up and smash the ice, he can escape the planetoid via that Launch Star.

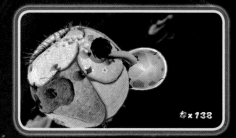

What is this, a giant walking egg? With a tail? The egg's footprints are as big as Mario, so something substantial in under that shell. To crack the shell and sneak a peek, run up to the large ball on the tail's end. Hit it with a spin. The ball shoots out into space, but the elastic tail snaps it back, shattering the egg on impact.

T-I-P

Before departing, check beneath the stones. There is a 1-Up Mushroom tucked into the shadow of the stonework.

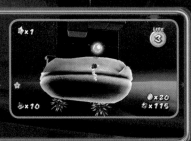

Good Egg
Galaxy

Honeyhive
Galaxy

Flipswitch
Galaxy

Loopdeeloop
Galaxy

Bowser Jr.'s
Robot Reactor

Sweet Sweet
Galaxy

Boss Battle: Dino Piranha

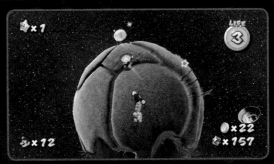

The Dino Piranha did not wake up on the right side of the nest. The beastly brute is all teeth and tail, dwarfing the plumber with its enormous size. Mario must somehow defeat the Dino Piranha in order to earn the first Power Star in the Good Egg Galaxy. Perhaps hitting the tail can crack more than just a shell?

If Mario is injured during the fight, spin-attack the coin in the ice on the planet's bottom. Mario can also hit one of the flower buds with a Star Bit to release a coin.

As soon as the battle begins, the Dino Piranha makes a beeline for Mario. The Dino Piranha is quick, so dodge the monster as soon as it roars into action. Slip alongside the Dino Piranha and

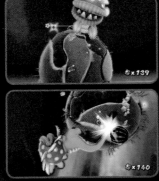

head for the ball at the end of its tail. Spin to hit the ball. The ball rockets into space before the tail whips it back, knocking the Dino Piranha right on its noggin.

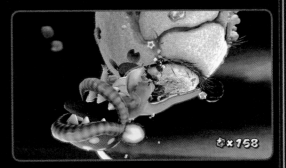

Keep slipping by the Dino piranha as it clumps around the planetoid. Watch for it to suddenly change direction, though, trying to catch Mario off guard. To ultimately defeat the Dino Piranha, hit the ball on the tail two more times, for a total of three smacks on the head.

The Dino Piranha releases several Star Bits after each smack to its head.

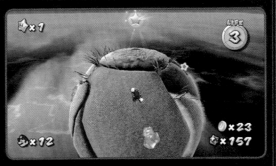

That's it—the first Power Star! Claim it to return to the Comet Observatory and show Rosalina.

45

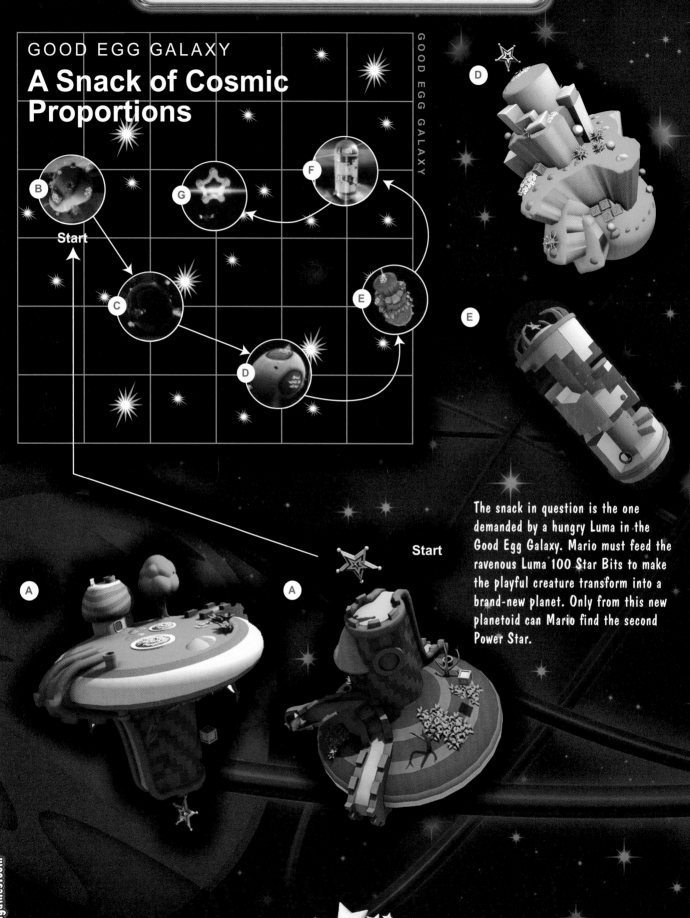

GOOD EGG GALAXY

A Snack of Cosmic Proportions

GOOD EGG GALAXY

B

Start

G

F

D

C

E

D

A

D

E

Start

A

The snack in question is the one demanded by a hungry Luma in the Good Egg Galaxy. Mario must feed the ravenous Luma 100 Star Bits to make the playful creature transform into a brand-new planet. Only from this new planetoid can Mario find the second Power Star.

Planet A

Good Egg
Galaxy

Honeyhive
Galaxy

Flipswitch
Galaxy

Loopdeloop
Galaxy

Bowser Jr.'s
Robot Reactor

Sweet Sweet
Galaxy

This mission starts off largely like the Dino Piranha mission. Mario lands on the same first planet, confronted immediately by a pair of bounding Electrogoombas. However, with the emphasis on collecting Star Bits, Mario must watch for every sparkly treat he can find. Start by seeking out the ring of stones in the cottage's lawn. Spin in the middle of the stones to release Star Bits.

On the planet's bottom, collect Star Bits from the shadow-covered trees and the Prize Block. Send Mario up the tall tower too. There is no Luma or Launch Star atop the tower this time, though. Instead, break the ice crystal to free some Star Bits and head back down to the main level. Just as Mario walks off the side of the planetoid, he spies the edge of a nearby Launch Star, but it's too far away to jump to it. Hmm.

47

There's a blue Luma at the balcony's end, just waiting for Mario. Talk to the Luma. It transforms into a series of Pull Stars. Mario can now pull himself to the Launch Star that hovers far off the planet's surface. Shake the Wii Remote to rocket to the next planet.

NOTE

As Mario blasts toward the red planet, he passes through a Launch Star. Ignore it for now; Mario must reach the red planet. The Launch Star sends Mario to an egg-shaped planetoid, and he's not ready for that place just yet.

T.I.P.

Whenever Mario blasts off from a Launch Star, watch the horizon to see the other planets in the galaxy. This is a good way to sometimes spot hidden routes. If you see a planet you didn't visit during the three regular missions, chances are that's the location of the hidden star in each galaxy.

Mario touches down on a small red planetoid that rumbles as boulders criss-cross the surface. There are several Star Bits on this planetoid, so get the tiny Sling Star on one of the stone pedestals. Shake the Wii Remote to launch up through the Star Bits and grab a spare coin. There is a ? Block on the planet's opposite side, next to an iced Launch Star. After popping the ? Block and collecting the Star bits, shatter the ice and use the Launch Star.

Planets B and C

The Launch Star that allows Mario to escape this planet is stuck in the ice. Spin to shatter the ice and free the star. However, before blasting off the planet, check out the rubbery bulbs next to the prickly plants. Stand on the bulb's opposite side, facing a prickly plant. Spin to hit the bulb. It stretches away from its springy base, smashing the plant. Now Mario can pick up a few Star Bits—just make sure he gets out of the way before the bulb bounces back in his direction.

After collecting the Star Bits from the prickly plants, hit the ice to unveil the Launch Star.

★★ Planet D ★★

Ready to feed the Luma? Stand in front of it, point the Wii Remote at it, and hold Ⓑ to shoot Star Bits into its mouth.

The satisfied Luma licks its chops and transforms, as promised. It screams into space and becomes a brand-new planet. The Luma leaves behind a pink Launch Star, which Mario can use to visit the new planet.

This planet is shaped like a big Yoshi Egg! There are Star Bits encased in ice, so grab those before visiting the hungry Luma on the planet's top. The cute little Luma tells Mario it will transform into something special if he feeds it 100 Star Bits. Mario has 100 Star Bits, right?

★★ Planet E ★★

If Mario doesn't have 100 Star Bits, use the planet's Launch Star to return to the red planetoid and try to pick up more Star Bits.

NOTE

You must feed the hungry Luma to finish this mission. If Mario uses the Launch Stars, he just completes laps around the galaxy.

Mario lands on the new planet's grassy bottom, next to some rubbery bulbs and a little wandering Goomba. The Launch Star to escape the planet's gravity is at the top, so the hero must scale the nearby cliffs. Before taking off, though, rustle through the tall grass to get a coin.

Good Egg Galaxy

Honeyhive Galaxy

Flipswitch Galaxy

Loopdeloop Galaxy

Bowser Jr.'s Robot Reactor

Sweet Sweet Galaxy

SUPER MARIO GALAXY

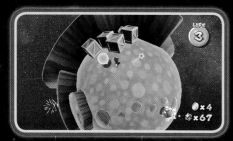

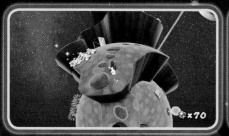

A Goomba is hiding behind these wooden crates. The crates have coins in them, so break them open with a spin. However, this also frees the trapped Goomba. Mario can stun and kick the Goomba for some Star Bits, or smack the Goomba with the bulb to earn a coin.

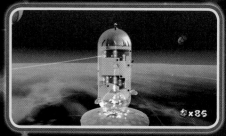

The Launch Star at the planet's top blasts Mario to the giant capsule-shaped planet orbiting in the background.

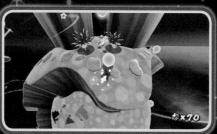

Use backflips to scale the tall cliffs or jump up the smaller ones to reach the planet's next level. There are more crates up here, as well as more Goombas. A little farther up, Mario spots a 1-Up Mushroom in a small alcove. There are three prickly plants between him and the Mushroom, though. Use the bulb to pop the three plants, then wall-jump up to the next level, grabbing the 1-Up Mushroom on the way.

Planets F and G

Front

Back

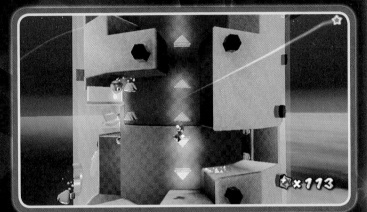

Whoa. Now Mario can walk all the way around the capsule, on the ceiling, until he reaches the starting point. This is a good way to feel out the gravity changes and grab some Star Bits.

The planet's exterior has been affected by the cold of deep space—there are Star Bits frozen in the ice. Walk around the planet's circumference to scout the capsule's interior. There are a lot of Star Bits and Goombas inside—as well as a 1-Up Mushroom. After kicking around some of the topside Goombas, look for what appears to be an empty ice crystal. Spin next to it to reveal the entrance to the capsule's interior. Jump inside to start exploring the topsy-turvy gravity and discover the hidden Launch Star that sends Mario right to the Power Star.

To reach the capsule's top, Mario must jump under the orange wall that is farther up the planet's side. At the height of his jump, spin to get an extra boost. This propels Mario high enough to be pulled into the opposite gravity field and yank him up (or is it down?) to the ceiling.

Now Mario can walk to the right and get the 1-Up Mushroom that was visible through the capsule's clear shell. After picking up the extra life (which is stationed in front of a blue wall that pulls Mario back down to the "floor"), jump up to the next bit of orange so Mario is flipped back to the ceiling. The Launch Star is in a clear dome at the capsule's top, but three Goombas patrol it. Make short work of them by jumping on their little heads and then approach the Launch Star. Shake the Wii Remote to gain energy and then blast off, breaking through the capsule's shell.

The arrows on the walls inside the capsule indicate the direction of gravity. When Mario walks in front of a blue wall, gravity pulls him down. However, when he steps in front of an orange wall, gravity lifts him up, pulling his feet to the ceiling, which is actually the ground in that particular gravity field. Give it a try when Mario enters the capsule—walk to the right and head for the orange surface.

Good Egg Galaxy

Honeyhive Galaxy

Flipswitch Galaxy

Loopdeloop Galaxy

Bowser Jr.'s Robot Reactor

Sweet Sweet Galaxy

LEGEND

⚑ Star Chip

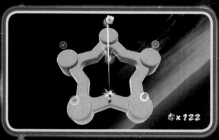

After Mario collects all five Star Chips, five Pull Stars appear at the extremes of the planet. Now Mario can get the Power Star. Just walk to the middle of the bend between the Pull Stars. Point at the Pull Star on the planet's opposite side. Mario is hoisted into the air and pulled right into the Power Star.

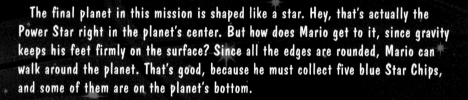

Great success!

The final planet in this mission is shaped like a star. Hey, that's actually the Power Star right in the planet's center. But how does Mario get to it, since gravity keeps his feet firmly on the surface? Since all the edges are rounded, Mario can walk around the planet. That's good, because he must collect five blue Star Chips, and some of them are on the planet's bottom.

KING KALIENTE'S BATTLE FLEET

GOOD EGG GALAXY
King Kaliente's Battle Fleet

The Good Egg Galaxy's third Power Star is guarded by King Kaliente, a squidlike entity that bathes in a lava lake on the outskirts of the planetary system. Kaliente protects his lair with a small fleet of Bowser's airships, so before challenging the tentacle-waving boss, Mario must set sail across the stars.

Planets A, B, and C

The quest for King Kaliente's Power Star starts in the same place as Mario's previous missions in the Good Egg Galaxy. However, this time the Launch Star leading off the beginning planet is located on the roof of the small cottage just behind the pair of meddlesome Electrogoombas.

A triple-jump will put Mario right on the rooftop, but it's better to use the orange warp pipe on the planet's bottom. That way, Mario can pick up an extra 1-Up Mushroom before blasting into the heavens to find King Kaliente. The orange pipe on the secret room's ceiling places Mario on the cottage's roof, ready to use the Launch Star to vault to Planet A.

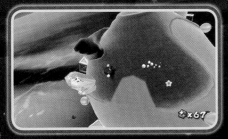

Oh no, a Toad is frozen in ice! Quick, Mario, break the ice with a spin and free the Toad.

The Toad tells Mario how to use the coconuts on the ground to his advantage: Mario must shuffle into them to roll them across the ground. Spinning next to them kicks the coconut at a nearby target.

 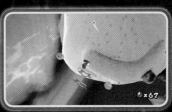

To get off this small planet, Mario must find the hidden Launch Star. Look for the prickly plant in the shade of the tall palm tree. The Launch Star is under the prickly plant's dangerous fronds, but there are no rubbery bulbs nearby. Instead, roll a coconut next to the prickly plant and spin. Knock the coconut into the plant to eliminate it, revealing the Launch Star.

Break open every wooden crate with a spin attack. There's often a coin inside.

There's a Pokey lording over the next planetoid. Mario cannot touch Pokeys because they hurt, just like a...prickly plant? This calls for a coconut! Roll one of the planetoid's many coconuts close to the Pokey. Stand on the coconut's opposite side, facing the Pokey, and give a little spin. The coconut flies into the Pokey, removing its segments.

Good Egg Galaxy

Honeyhive Galaxy

Flipswitch Galaxy

Loopdeeloop Galaxy

Bowser Jr.'s Robot Reactor

Sweet Sweet Galaxy

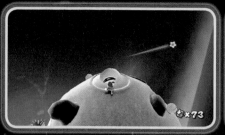

TIP

Mario can use the Rainbow Star's power to pop the Chomps on the asteroid's surface. Before time runs out, go topside and smash the Chomps to free even more Star Bits.

Just its head remains, upside down with its eyes in the sand like a scared ostrich. Spin to knock the Pokey head off the planet and locate the next Launch Star. Use the Launch Star to rocket to a very small asteroid, currently crowded by two Chomps.

After using up the Rainbow Star's powers, check for a Launch Star on the asteroid. This launches Mario to the next planet, a floating disc that sports some impressive firepower. Surely, Bowser has been here.

Drop into the green warp pipe on the tiny asteroid to check out a secret chamber that plays tricks on Mario's eyes.

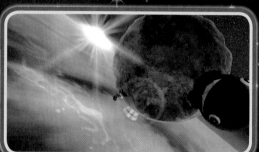

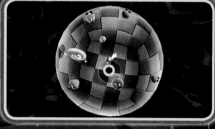

The secret room's interior is spherical with enough gravity to keep Mario's feet on the floor no matter where he stands. There are several Goombas inside. You can make short work of them with stomps, but that giant coin looks intriguing—pick it up to reveal a Rainbow Star. When Mario grabs the Rainbow Star, he temporarily turns invincible. He runs faster, plowing into any enemy with absolute impunity. Awesome! Now, take out those Goombas while scooping up the resulting Star Bits with the cursor.

⭐ Planet D ⭐

Top

Bottom

Mario lands on the bottom of Planet D, which is bathed in darkness. There are several enemies patrolling the disc's lower half, including some aggressive Chomps that come over the planet's edge. Hey, if those Chomps can cross to the planet's bottom, then there's enough gravity for Mario to walk to the top half. However, getting off this disc's bottom half isn't a cakewalk. There are multiple electrical fields on the disc's base. They slowly circle the disc, but Mario can easily jump over them.

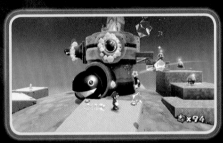

However, the electrical fields that rotate around the disc's equator are tougher. These beams are augmented by Bullet Bill cannons. If Mario lingers near the equator, the Bullet Bills spot him and lock on to his position. Mario must then run toward a rock, hoping to trick the Bullet Bill into hitting it instead.

This disc's top half is littered with half-buried blocks. Many of them are adorned with coins, but those are traps. There is a giant pillar in the disc's center that releases Chomps and expels Bullet Bills. The Bullet Bills are high enough that Mario, close to the disc's edge, does not arouse suspicion. However, if Mario steps on a block to get a coin, he enters the Bullet Bills' line of sight. Now they give chase.

To get off this disc, Mario must climb the stone steps that lead to a Launch Star atop the Bullet Bill cannons. The Launch Star is encased in ice and patrolled by a trio of Electrogoombas—two things that slow Mario down. And this is no place to be slow, because those Bullet Bills will hone in on Mario the second they spot him. Stun those Electrogoomas with Star Bits, wait for the Bullet Bills to launch, and then make a run for the Launch Star. Pass under the Bullet Bills' radar and kick the Electrgoombas off the disc. While sweeping the sky for Star Bits, spin to break open the Launch Star. Now, let's get off this crazy disc.

★★★ Planet E ★★★

The next stop is a series of airships in orbit around King Kaliente's lair. Mario flies to the closest ship, touching down on the deck. As soon as he lands, the welcome party springs into action—a pair of squidlike monsters that spit fireballs at Mario from the second airship.

★★★ 55 ★★★

Mario cannot reach the second airship without dropping the gangplank between the two squid. He must somehow stop those monsters, as the coconuts they spit between each fireball volley are his ticket to the next ship. When one of the monsters spits a coconut across the gap between the ships, Mario must hit the projectile with a quick spin. This bounces the coconut back across space, surprising the brute. Just one coconut to the head of each gatekeeper squid is enough to lower the gangplank.

TIP

These airships look like pirate ships, and everybody knows what's on a pirate ship: ill-gotten booty. Check the transom on the ship's stern for some coins.

With the Life Mushroom in hand, jump to the aft of the second airship. Several Electrogoombas patrol the aft, but a few well-aimed Star Bits puts them on their heels long enough for Mario to kick them overboard. The Launch Star is on the aft cabin roof. Spin to shatter the ice around it and then launch to the last planet in this mission, King Kaliente's lava lair.

After crossing the gangplank, crack open the lone wooden crate on the second airship's portside. There's a Life Mushroom in there, and Mario could use the extra health before challenging King Kaliente for that Power Star.

⭐ **Planet F** ⭐

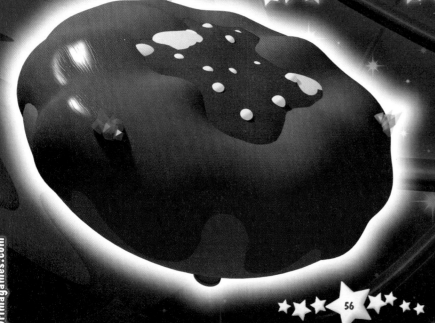

The airship Launch Star vaults Mario to the bottom of King Kaliente's home. The underside of the lair is quiet, save for a little yellow Luma that wants to chat. The Luma points out the two small lamps on the ground. If Mario fires a Star Bit at the lamp, it turns into a coin. This is a good way to replenish any health lost in the upcoming brawl with King Kaliente.

When Mario crosses to the planetoid's top half, King Kaliente erupts out of the lava lake that dominates the center of his lair. King Kaliente is a giant, sporting two large tentacles that do not attack Mario but defend against any attacks he might try. To defeat this boss, Mario must recall a tactic used earlier in this galaxy to deal with distant enemies.

King Kaliente sinks into the lava and unleashes a handful of Lava Bubbles. Mario can either fall back and run away from the nuisances or use Star Bits to neutralize them.

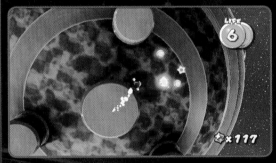

King Kaliente starts the battle by breathing a trio of fireballs across the lava. Run from the attack, heading for the Star Bits decorating the lair's edges. Break open these Star Bits with a spin. To earn extra lives, scoop up these Star Bits and any released by King Kaliente after a successful attack.

To win the Power Star, Mario must strike King Kaliente with two more coconuts. The next time Mario knocks a coconut back at the king, he puts up his tentacles to deflect the coconut back at Mario. Mario cannot dodge this attack. He must zoom over to the coconut and spin again to send it right back. King Kaliente, not ready for the second attack, doesn't put up his tentacles—bam! Now Mario just needs to hit the king one more time (the next attack requires a return volley too) to end his reign over the Good Egg Galaxy.

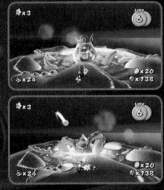

After breathing fireballs, King Kaliente spits a coconut at Mario. Rush toward the coconut and spin just as it closes in on Mario, who knocks the coconut back at King Kaliente. The boss doesn't expect this and puts up no defense. The coconut bonks him right on the crown. Wise to Mario's game, the king won't take the next attack so easily.

After defeating King Kaliente, Mario can lay claim to the Power Star and return to the Comet Observatory. Mario now has three Power Stars and one Grand Star.

Good Egg Galaxy

Honeyhive Galaxy

Flipswitch Galaxy

Loopdeeloop Galaxy

Bowser Jr.'s Robot Reactor

Sweet Sweet Galaxy

SUPER

DINO PIRANHA SPEED RUN

GOOD EGG GALAXY
Dino Pirahna

A — Start

B

C

D

E

F — Dino Piranha

GOOD EGG GALAXY

When Mario returns to the Good Egg Galaxy, it's bathed in the red-orange glow of the Speedy Comet. This comet hides a Power Star in the Dino Piranha mission of the Good Egg Galaxy. Mario must reach and finish off the boss monster within four minutes. Is Mario up to the challenge?

A

A

D

Mad Scramble

Four minutes may seem like enough time to reach the Dino Piranha, but when enemies get in Mario's way and you want to scoop up every Star Bit on the screen, the clock will run down faster than expected. So, to finish this mission, Mario must streamline his plan of attack. The goal is to cover distance with as little sightseeing as possible.

Waste no time messing around with monsters on the first planet. Mario must get off this rock quickly, so skip the Star Bits and Electrogoombas and immediately head for the planet's bottom half. Use either the green warp pipe or just step off the edge to flip to the planet's bottom. Run up the tower to the waiting Luma. Talk to it to unlock the Launch Star and blast off to the next planetoid.

Mario must still collect five Star Chips to create the Launch Star on the small, peanut-shaped planet. There's a new hitch to this planet now—the boulders have been replaced with fast-moving Chomps. Mario must duck in and out of their way to get the Star Chips and complete the Launch Star.

CAUTION

Watch for the muddy grooves on the tiny planet. The speedy Chomps can catch Mario as he trudges through the muck, knocking him down.

As soon as Mario touches down on the bean-shaped planetoid, go for the Piranha Plant blocking the Sproutle. Don't worry about the giant coin and any Star Bits unless there is still close to three minutes on the clock.

When Mario hits the carved planet, head for the secret warp pipe just beyond the shrinking platform. Hop to the warp pipe, dislodge the Piranha Plant with a spin and a kick, and drop inside to cross the system of ? Switches. Grab the 1-Up Mushroom on the switches, then use the Launch Star to rocket to the next planetoid.

NOTE

Don't take the switch-filled area detour unless you have over two minutes on the clock. If Mario is already running out of time, just run for the purple Piranha Plant.

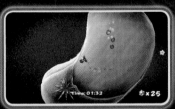 

No time to fuss with the invisible creature on the next planet's sandy underbelly, no matter how much those Star Bits call to you. Mario must scurry to the planet's top and jump up the stones. Avoid the Electrogoombas and break the ice to unlock the Launch Star. Blast off for the Dino Piranha's lair. Hopefully, Mario still has at least one minute on the clock, although the more, the better.

Good Egg Galaxy

Honeyhive Galaxy

Flipswitch Galaxy

Loopdeloop Galaxy

Bowser Jr.'s Robot Reactor

Sweet Sweet Galaxy

59

The Dino Piranha isn't happy to see Mario again. The boss monster roars into action after Mario breaks open his shell. Since time is of the essence, Mario must cut close to the Dino Piranha as he screams toward its tail. Smack the ball at the tail's end three times to knock the Dino Piranha silly.

The clock doesn't stop just because Mario defeated the Dino Piranha. Until that Power Star is in the plumber's hands, the seconds continue to fade like the stars in the morning sky. So act fast, take hold of that Power Star, and return it to the Comet Observatory before time runs out.

LUIGI ON THE ROOF

After you rescued Luigi from the haunted mansion in the Ghostly Galaxy, he decided to pitch in with his own star-recovery services. Unfortunately, Luigi tends to get stuck in places and requires a little assistance from Mario to get home. In the Good Egg Galaxy, on his first Power Star, Luigi discovers he's afraid of heights.

Finding Luigi

Luigi actually isn't very far from the starting point in the Good Egg Galaxy—he's stuck on the little cottage's roof. Those Electrogoombas must have Luigi spooked, because he refuses to budge. Mario must scramble to the roof to rescue poor Luigi and recover the Power Star.

The Mario Bros. are back in action!

Good Egg Galaxy

Honeyhive Galaxy

Flipswitch Galaxy

Loopdeloop Galaxy

Bowser Jr.'s Robot Reactor

Sweet Sweet Galaxy

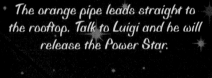

Drop to the first planet's underside and seek out the orange warp pipe. Mario slips back into the secret room with the giant coin. Pick up the coin and follow the trail of musical notes to retrieve a 1-Up Mushroom. After grabbing the tasty treasure, use the orange pipe on the ceiling to reach the cottage roof.

HONEYHIVE GALAXY

The Honeyhive Galaxy is the first place Mario encounters his newest threads, the Bee Suit. With the Bee Suit, he can float around the multitiered Honeyhive Kingdom, a large system of planets under the benevolent rule of the Queen Bee. If Mario can help the bees with their multitude of problems that have cropped up since Bowser's arrival, they will bestow on him a collection of Power Stars.

Bee Mario Takes Flight

When Mario first arrives in the kingdom, the bees are a bit skeptical of his presence. However, as soon as he discovers the Bee Suit and learns how to buzz around like a pro, the bees open up. They tell him about the trouble their queen is in and point the way to her throne. Can Mario help the queen and earn the Power Star?

The orange pipe leads straight to the rooftop. Talk to Luigi and he will release the Power Star.

Main Kingdom

LEGEND

🍄	1-Up Mushroom
🐝	Bee Mushroom

The Power Star appears next to Luigi on the roof. Luigi sure looks relieved to see his brother again.

PRIMA Official Game Guide

SUPER MARIO GALAXY

The main planet in the Honeyhive Galaxy is giant compared to the Good Egg Galaxy's planetoids. There will be a lot less planet-hopping in the Honeyhive Galaxy adventures, although this first mission—"Bee Mario Takes Flight"—offers a considerable tour of the

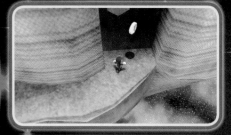

kingdom. As soon as Mario lands, he can chat up a soldier bee that introduces him to the kingdom of the honeybees.

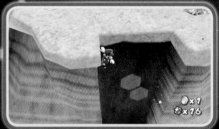

Right away, there are some extra goodies for Mario to pick up. Before walking into the kingdom, turn the camera to look away from the trees and bees. There is a giant "M" constructed of Star Bits hanging in space. Pick them up with the cursor. Also, peek over the railing behind the small sign. There's a 1-Up Mushroom back there.

There is a ledge to the trapeze's right. Jump up to it and peek over the other side. A small pond is back there, so it's safe to hop down. Walk to the right to discover a shallow alcove in the cliffs that lead straight down to the black hole. Mario can wall-jump up the alcove, grabbing some coins. Hop out at the alcove's top to reach a high ledge that was previously only visible at the height of a trapeze swing.

CAUTION

The Honeyhive Kingdom does not operate under the same kind of gravity as the Good Egg Galaxy. Mario cannot walk off the planet's edge and just keep going. Stepping off the edges of this galaxy leads right to a nasty black hole gurgling just below the planets, so watch where Mario walks.

There are Piranha Plants up here! The hungry plants seethe and snap at Mario, but a quick spin knocks these veggies off the planet. One of the Piranha Plants guards a warp pipe. After disposing of it, drop into the pipe to discover an optional secret room.

A dirt road winds through the kingdom. Follow it until Mario reaches another bee soldier. There is a flowery trapeze above the bee soldier. Jump up and do a little spin to grab onto it. Swing back and forth, gaining a little height with each arc. Mario is soon high enough to grab the coin floating above the trapeze. Release to drop back to the ground and continue adventuring.

Drop off the ledge with the Piranha Plants (watching out for a boulder that rolls out of the cave just below) and look for a nearby fountain. There is a giant coin in the waters. When Mario picks up the coin, the Bee Mushroom appears on the lowest tier of the kingdom. This special Mushroom gives Mario his Bee Suit, so get down there and check it out as soon as possible.

When Mario drops down the green warp pipe, he enters a chamber full of rolling boulders. There are ramps on the walls that let him defy gravity, such as walking on the ceiling. There is a giant coin on the room's floor. Use the ramps to reach it. Picking it up reveals a Rainbow Star that makes Mario temporarily invincible.

TIP

Spin in the center of the stone circles to release a bunch of bonus Star Bits.

Now Mario can run back up the ramps and plow into the boulders. Each boulder releases a host of Star Bits, but like the Rainbow Star's effects, they are temporary. While Mario shatters the boulder, use the cursor to sweep up the Star Bits left in his wake.

As soon as he becomes Bee Mario, the plumber has the ability to fly. Check the meter next to him to see just how much hover power he has left for each flight.

As Bee Mario, investigate the ledge just across from the Piranha Plants. There are some pesky bugs over here, but the three ice crystals full of Star Bits are worth the risk.

Use the Bee Suit's flight powers to buzz up to the ledge with the large waterfall. Watch out for the water—bees hate water, so if Bee Mario gets even a drop on him, he loses the special suit. Hover over the water to grab the coins and pop the coin flower with a Star Bit to claim the twinkling treasure. As soon as Mario pockets the coins, buzz up to the ledge behind the waterfall. There's a dark tunnel with some bugs, but it's the only way to reach the Queen Bee.

Good Egg Galaxy

Honeyhive Galaxy

Flipswitch Galaxy

Loopdeloop Galaxy

Bowser Jr.'s Robot Reactor

Sweet Sweet Galaxy

PRIMA Official Game Guide

Aim at each bug with the cursor and shoot a Star Bit at it. The Star Bit stuns the bug, forcing it on its back. Bee Mario can still kick and spin, so when the bugs are vulnerable, rush in and bop those pests right out of the kingdom. When the tunnel is clear, buzz up to the ceiling to pick up a trio of coins.

TIP *Use shadows to spot secret items. While on the tunnel's floor, you cannot see the coins, but you can see their three small shadows. So remember, if you see a shadow on the ground, look up. Stargazing never hurts in this adventure.*

There is a Bee Mushroom at the slide's bottom in case Mario lost his Bee Suit in the tunnel. Fly up the ledge to the Bee Mushroom's left to spot a pair of coin-covered blossoms. Buzz up to the flowers to pollinate Mario's pocketbook with these coins before heading to the honey-drenched ledges along the back of the kingdom.

Mario must drop down the hollowed-out tree trunk to see the back side of the kingdom. However, before heading down, walk around the trunk to pick up a 1-Up Mushroom.

Whee! A slide covered with Star Bits waits for Bee Mario just below the trunk.

Buzz over the gaps between the ledges. Watch out for the honey rivers Mario's feet can get stuck. It's not such a big deal right now, but in return visits, this poses a problem for times when the Bee Suit is unavailable. Use the Launch Star over the honey pool at the ledge's end to leave the main kingdom and investigate a patch of beautiful (and gigantic) blooms.

⭐ Tall Flowers ⭐

LEGEND

🍄 Bee Mushroom
🍄 1-Up Mushroom

Jump across the petals to reach the Launch Star on the tallest bloom. Watch out for water spouts.

Bee Mario arrives in a gorgeous flower garden, but the blossoms are a little too high to reach by basic buzzing techniques. Mario must find another way to launch himself up to the blooms and keep moving to the Queen Bee, whom he can see in the distance. This garden area is tough for a bee, as the ground is primarily covered in water. Several enemies rummage around the water, and Piranha Plants snap from their places on the few patches of solid land. Bee Mario must zip from lily pad to land, avoiding the water.

There's a 1-Up Mushroom on the flower ranging over space. If Mario misses his landing and runs out of flight time, he falls into the black hole.

Hop on the highest flower and shake the Wii Remote to rocket to the Queen Bee via the Launch Star.

To reach the giant flowers, Mario must seek out pink flowers that start at only half the height of the larger blooms. There is one next to the spare Bee Mushroom in the garden's corner. Walk up to the flower and shake the Wii Remote—Mario swings up the stem just like a Sproutle. However, his weight causes the stem to bend back. When Mario reaches the blossom, the flower whips forward, sending Bee Mario high into the air. While in midair, hit Ⓐ to buzz over to one of the large petals.

★☆★ **Queen Bee** ★☆★

LEGEND

🐝 Bee Mushroom

Good Egg Galaxy

Welcome to the Galaxy

Honeyhive Galaxy

Flipswitch Galaxy

Loopdeloop Galaxy

Bowser Jr.'s Robot Reactor

Sweet Sweet Galaxy

SUPER MARIO GALAXY

★★★ 65 ★★★

Mario lands on the base of a large wall covered with honeycombs. As Bee Mario, he can stick to these honeycombs and climb the wall. Without the Bee Suit, however, he's stuck on the ledge. If Mario lacks his Bee Suit, spin-attack the seed on the ground to grow a Sproutle around the base of the Queen Bee's planetoid.

The Queen Bee tells Mario her troubles—she has a terrible itch. If he could please take care of it, he will be handsomely rewarded.

The Sproutle leads to a Bee Mushroom, and there are several Star Bits along the vine path. After picking up the Bee Mushroom, keep flying around the base. There are six coins floating above the wide gap between the two ledges at the planet's base.

The queen's throne area is covered with water and flowers. Mario needs a Bee Suit to help the queen, so if he falls in the drink, seek out a replacement Bee Mushroom on the garden's outskirts. Watch out for Piranha Plants and bugs in the garden. Snugly fit into his Bee Suit, send Mario over to the queen's body to see about scratching that itch.

Buzz up to the first honeycomb hexagon and fly into it—Bee Mario immediately sticks. Now, just keep climbing up the honeycombs, collecting coins along the way. If there is a break in the honeycombs, jump away from the wall and buzz over to the next line of hexagons. Steer into the wall and Bee Mario will stick to it again. Use Mario's shadow to make sure he's over the honeycomb—if the shadow is touching a hexagon, the hero can safely land.

Check out the giant coin to the right of the honeycombs, near the wall's top. Grab the coin to free a bunch of extra Star Bits.

Keep buzzing up the honeycombs until Mario reaches another ledge. Spin next to the seed to release a Sproutle that leads right to the Queen Bee's throne.

Star Chips—that's what's been annoying the poor queen. Bee Mario sticks to the queen's body when he touches it, so crawl around Her Majesty to pick up five Star Chips. After grabbing the fifth Star Chip, a Launch Star appears directly behind the Queen Bee. The queen is so grateful for your help.

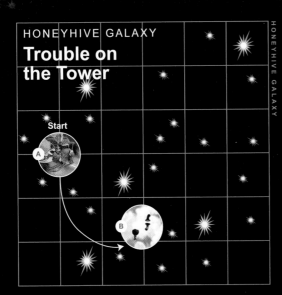

Use the Launch Star behind the queen to return to the kingdom's main planet.

Mario meets a bunch of Toads on the treetops of the Honeyhive Kingdom. The Toads have found a Power Star during their travels, but they're unsure of how to get down from the tree. With Mario here, they can finally escape. To thank Mario, they hand over the Power Star they found in the kingdom. Now Mario—and the Toads—can return to the Comet Observatory to start a new search for another Power Star.

TROUBLE ON THE TOWER

HONEYHIVE GALAXY
Trouble on the Tower

Start
A
B

Welcome back to the Honeyhive Kingdom. Since Mario's last visit, the bees have come under siege by a new threat: Mandibugs. The creepy-crawlies are all over the kingdom, including the tower that hovers over the giant trees on the main planet. If Mario can beat back the bugs, surely the bees can spare another Power Star?

Main Kingdom

LEGEND

🍄	1-Up Mushroom
🍄	Life Mushroom

Good Egg Galaxy

Honeyhive Galaxy

Flipswitch Galaxy

Loopdeeloop Galaxy

Bowser Jr.'s Robot Reactor

Sweet Sweet Galaxy

67

Mario's second trip to the Honeyhive Kingdom starts much like the first—a quick glance to the heavens to collect the M-shaped constellation of Star Bits and a fence-hop for a 1-Up Mushroom. However, from here on, things have changed in the kingdom. There are no Bee Mushrooms—they've vanished. Instead, the countryside is littered with breakable stone wheels. Mario can shatter the wheels with a ground pound.

Run up the dirt road to spot the stone wheel near the trapeze. When Mario smashes this wheel, it frees a Sproutle. The Sproutle extends across the large gap between the kingdom's left and right sides. Since there are no Bee Mushrooms, this is the only way to safely cross over the black hole directly below the gap.

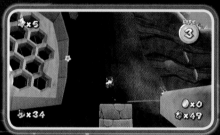

Before crossing the Sproutle, smash the rest of the stone wheels on the kingdom's right side. Tall stacks crumble under the weight of a single ground pound, releasing hoards of Star Bits. This is a great way to earn a 1-Up.

Mario easily swings across the first Sproutle. Stop shaking the Wii Remote when he reaches the Sproutle's end so he drops right on to another vine. (If you don't stop shaking the Wii Remote, you risk accidentally making Mario spin in midair, missing the second vine and falling into the cosmic void.) When Mario grabs the second Sproutle, shake again so he winds around the vine and drops down near another stone wheel.

This stone wheel covers a spring. The ? Block over the spring is too high to reach with a regular jump, so ground pound the wheel to open up the spring. Now Mario can smash the spring and bounce right into the ? Block, earning a handful of Star Bits. There is another spring to the right of the giant tree on this land, but before vaulting off to the next area, check around the kingdom for some extra treasures.

The stone wheel behind the tree hides some extra Star Bits.

There are three coin flowers on the outcropping overlooking the black hole. Shoot the flowers with Star Bits to nab them.

After grabbing the goodies, walk to the spring behind the small Sling Star. Bounce on the spring and shake the Wii Remote to activate the Sling Star. This lifts Mario to a ring-shaped platform with a big red button. A Wiggler circles the button, though, so be careful. Mario can defeat the Wiggler with a spin and a jump. The resulting shock wave tips the Wiggler over, but don't gloat—when that thing turns back over, it's furious. It runs at double-speed and will knock Mario to the ground if he doesn't avoid it.

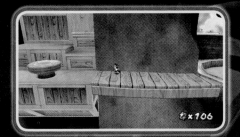

Striking the button extends a bridge to the planet's rear. There is a large wooden button on the ground on the bridge's other side. Ground pound it to lower the platform, revealing a system of ledges Mario can wall-jump across. Wall-jump up the planet's rear to the kingdom's topmost platform.

NOTE

Anything with that jagged-blast symbol on it, such as the two buttons, can be ground pounded.

The Launch Star that connects the kingdom to the tower is between two wooden walls. Wall-jump to reach it.

Mario lands on a strangely shaped planetoid high above the kingdom. Gravity keeps him anchored to the tiny planetoid while he dispatches some Piranha Plants. There is a similarly shaped planetoid just below the first one. The two planetoids share gravity, so when Mario jumps from the bottom of the upper planetoid, he twists in the air and lands on the bottom surface.

The Launch Star rockets Mario out into space, passing the tower at great speed. Hey, where is he going?

Good Egg Galaxy

Honeyhive Galaxy

Flipswitch Galaxy

Loopdeeloop Galaxy

Bowser Jr.'s Robot Reactor

Sweet Sweet Galaxy

PRIMA Official Game Guide

There is a Life Mushroom on the checkered floor below the tower. Drop down to grab the Life Mushroom and earn some extra health. Watch out for the Mandibug guarding the Life Mushroom. After dispatching the pest, use the spring to the right to vault back to the walkway.

A small Sling Star sends Mario to another little planetoid. The gravity pulls him to the wall where he can easily grab a giant coin, which releases a Rainbow Star. With the Rainbow Star's power, Mario runs right through a Wiggler patrolling a hollow tree trunk on the small planetoid. After defeating the Wiggler, jump into the trunk to fall back down to the tower.

While dropping through space, pick up the line of Star Bits that stretch between the tree trunk and the tower.

⭐⭐ Tower ⭐⭐

The tower is a set of wooden platforms that create a good lookout for the bees. However, the Mandibugs have swarmed the tower and are keeping the bees out. To help the bees, Mario must scale the tower and dispatch a pair of nasty Mandibugs at the top. His first move is to cross a gap in the walkway via a nearby trapeze.

Use the trapeze to jump to the wooden platform above the walkway. There is another Mandibug up here. It guards three coins and a large red button. This button controls the windmill on the tower's front—this is Mario's way up. So, defeat the Mandibug and smack the button with a ground pound to start the windmill and ascend the remainder of the tower.

There are Mandibugs on the walkway. These purple-backed bugs use their pincers to attack when they charge forward. Mandibugs move only in a straight line, though, offering Mario a way to get the drop on the enemies. If he stands in front of a Mandibug, taunting it, it rushes forward. Just jump in the air and ground pound its back (notice the same symbol from the buttons?) to send it packing.

Ride the windmill to the tower's top to spot the two Mandibugs causing the most trouble for the bees.

Defeating the two Mandibugs frees the tower from infestation and releases a Power Star.

These two Mandibugs are playing totem pole—the smaller one sits on the larger one's back. Mario must ground pound the smaller bug first. To do this, trick it into making a beeline for Mario. Sidestep the forward charge and then leap over the Mandibugs. Ground pound to smash the smaller one.

This makes the larger Mandibug angry—it turns red with fury and starts moving erratically. Use the same technique to take out the larger bug. Tease it, then get behind it and smash its back with a ground pound. If either of the Mandibugs hits Mario, he can fish coins out of the tiny lamps on the floor with Star Bits.

BIG BAD BUGABOOM

The poor bees of the Honeyhive Kingdom are under attack again—the Mandibugs have returned, but this time, they are marching lockstep with their leader, the giant Bugaboom. Mario must don the Bee Suit and zoom to the galaxy once more to free the bees from the predatory pests, returning peace to the Queen Bee's flowery realm.

Main Kingdom

As soon as Mario lands on the main planet in the bee's kingdom, he spots the scourge of the Mandibugs. The little monsters skitter across the ground, lunging at anything that comes near them. Easily defeat the Mandibugs by taunting them to rush forward. While the Mandibug is blindly charging, step behind it and jump into the air. As the Mandibug backs up to its original position, ground pound its back, squashing it.

Many of the same goodies are available in this mission, such as the Star Bits in the sky behind the starting point and the secret room below the green warp pipe. After gathering up these treasures, turn to the fountain next to the boulder cave. Mandibugs are patrolling the grounds up there. Dispatch the bugs with ground pounds to help the bees.

The Queen Bee waits for Mario at the tunnel's end, behind the waterfall. Bop the three Mandibugs in the tunnel to reach the queen and use her Launch Star.

There's a bubble cannon in the fountain. Jump on the block in front of the cannon and hitch a ride to the kingdom's other side.

The Launch Star rockets Mario to the Bugaboom's orbiting lair.

The bubble rockets Mario over the treacherous black hole. There are necessary power-ups on the kingdom's other side, such as a Life Mushroom that grants extra health in preparation for the boss battle with the Mandibug leader, Bugaboom. The Life Mushroom is guarded by a Mandibug, so squish the insect to get the power-up. The Bee Mushroom is on a small lily pad in the stream that circles a massive tree. Snag that Bee Mushroom—Mario has a better chance against Bugaboom if he's sporting the Bee Suit.

After donning the Bee Suit, drop down the green warp pipe overlooking the black hole. This whisks Mario to the kingdom's lower level. There are coins on the waterfall ledge, but before Mario can claim those prizes, he must flutter over three bubble cannons. If a bubble catches him, Mario flies all the way across the kingdom. If he's not careful, he'll smash into a bug or fall off the planet's edge.

Buggy Lair

Mario touches down on a small island. There is a Bee Mushroom next to a flower, just in case Mario needs to pick up the Bee Suit again. Vault to the next island with the flower to pick up three coins and replenish any lost health. When you're ready, use the flower on the island to hop to Bugaboom's lair.

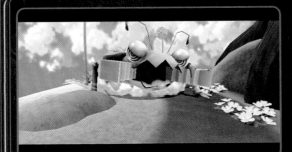

LEGEND

🍄	1-Up Mushroom
🍄	Bee Mushroom

Boss Battle: Bugaboom

Bugaboom isn't pleased by the disturbance, but it relishes the chance to exact revenge on the plumber who destroyed his army of Mandibugs. The massive Bugaboom shrieks with a fierce battle cry, extending its vicious pincers in a show of force. Don't back down now; the bees need Mario more than ever, so get ready to take flight and play the role of royal exterminator.

Like its Mandibug minions, the Bugaboom's weak spot is its back. The green giant's shell in emblazoned with the ground pound symbol. Fly on top of the Bugaboom and perform a crushing ground pound. It drops to the dirt, shaking Mario off its back.

(continued on next page)

Good Egg Galaxy

Honeyhive Galaxy

Flipswitch Galaxy

Loopdeloop Galaxy

Bowser Jr.'s Robot Reactor

Sweet Sweet Galaxy

SUPER MARIO GALAXY

PRIMA Official Game Guide

Uh-oh. The Bugaboom looks angry, and Mario won't like it when it's angry.

The third time better be a charm, because the Bugaboom looks madder than a hornet.

The Bugaboom takes flight, circling the tree. Since the bug boss is several feet off the ground, Mario must think vertically if he wants to get the drop on the beast. With half the planet doused in water, losing the Bee Suit is easy. Fortunately, there is always a Bee Mushroom handy for taking flight.

The Bugaboom flies around the tree again, but this time, it doesn't remain level for very long. The creature frequently turns on its side, preventing Mario from landing on its vulnerable back. In addition, the Bugaboom drops a torrent of exploding shells from the spout on its belly, so stay off the ground—especially the ground right below the flying boss.

Mario doesn't have enough flight time to buzz higher than the Bugaboom, so he must seek out a staging ground above the bug. With the Bee Suit, Mario can buzz up to the honeycombs on the tree and wait for the Bugaboom to pass by, or he can swing around a flower stem to launch himself over the bug.

Whether Mario uses the honeycomb or the flower to ambush the Bugaboom, he must hover over the boss's back. The Bugaboom remains level while flying, so if Bee Mario is running out of buzz, he can just land on the creature's back to recharge his wings. Perform another ground pound to smash the Bugaboom back to the ground.

To finish off the Bugaboom, Mario must time his ground pound. Wait for the Bugaboom to come around the tree and then shimmy up a flower stem. As the Bugaboom closes in, fling Bee Mario into the air. At the height of the vault, start hovering toward the boss. It soon drops into a horizontal position, but only briefly. Ground pound the Bugaboom one last time to free the bees from its tyranny.

The Bugaboom leaves behind a Power Star. Grab it to return to the Comet Observatory and see about unlocking some new galaxies.

TIP

There is a 1-Up Mushroom on the tree root that extends beyond the rim of the Bugaboom's planetoid.

HONEYHIVE COSMIC MARIO RACE

When the Cosmic Comet arcs over the Honeyhive Galaxy, it casts a mischievous spell on the kingdom. When Mario drops down to the system's main planet, a familiar-looking fellow greets him—Cosmic Mario. This strange celestial spirit beckons Mario to a race—who is Mario to turn down such a playful challenge?

Cosmic Race

When Mario touches down on the planet, there's still time for gathering Star Bits or checking for hidden 1-Up Mushrooms. However, when Mario steps forward, a twinkling sprite greets him. This cosmic spirit eggs him into accepting a race challenge across the Honeyhive Kingdom. The winner lays claim to a Power Star. Mario eagerly accepts the challenge.

The two contestants line up on the starting point, eyeing each other before the starting signal.

The race is short, but Cosmic Mario already knows the course's general layout. Mario, on the other hand, must constantly check the arrows that point the way. If Mario veers off-course, Cosmic Mario will pull ahead. And once this happens, it's tough to catch up. To get past Cosmic Mario, cut him off at the first corner, cutting in front of him at the small edge in the road.

Hop on the small blocks below the waterfall. Either backflip into the air or spin at the crest of a normal jump to grab the ledge and pull Mario up. Watch out for Cosmic Mario, as he may try to get in Mario's way.

> **NOTE**
>
> Cosmic Mario will try to thwart Mario's efforts at every turn. Mario bounces off Cosmic Mario if they collide. If Cosmic Mario cuts Mario off at a turn, he can bop Mario back a few paces, preventing him from winning the race.

Backflip from the boxes straight to the tunnel behind the waterfall.

Drop down the hollow tree trunk. There is no 1-Up Mushroom behind the trunk in this mission, so don't waste precious seconds looking for it.

SUPER MARIO GALAXY

PRIMA Official Game Guide

Whoosh down the ramp below the tree trunk. Steer away from the outer wall. If Mario bumps it, he slows down.

making big jumps. If he tries to jump from the honey, he just slips off the edge and plummets into the black hole. This is where Cosmic Mario really tries to catch up, so don't slow down.

Backflip from the giant block at the ramp's bottom to the system of honey-drenched ledges behind the kingdom.

The Power Star hovers over the honey pool. If Mario tries to walk through the honey, Cosmic Mario will close the gap. If Cosmic Mario is breathing down Mario's neck, jump out and spin to the Power Star, claiming it right before Cosmic Mario's starry-eyed, er, star eyes.

The Power Star is to the left of the ledges, but the honey can really bog Mario down. Stay out of the gooey sweetness—it slows him down and prevents him from

LUIGI IN THE HONEYHIVE KINGDOM

Rescuing Luigi

Bro! I got a star, but now I can't get back. This picture shows where I am! HELP ME!

From Luigi

Luigi's search for the Power Stars leads him to the Honeyhive Galaxy. However, something scary has chased the poor guy up a tree. When Mario, at the Comet Observatory, receives the postcard from Luigi, he must return to the galaxy and select the "Bee Mario Takes Flight" mission. This sends him soaring to Luigi's rescue.

Buzz up to the narrow ledge that extends the waterfall's width. Walk left to cross to the kingdom's other half.

In order to help Luigi, Mario must find a Bee Suit. Run up the dirt road to the fountain next to the boulder cave. Dodge any rolling rocks and grab the giant coin at the fountain. The Bee Mushroom now appears on the ledge below the fountain. Drop down and don the Bee Suit to earn the power of flight and start the search for Luigi.

Drop from the ledge to the ground below. There is a pool of water and a bug, so if Mario touches either one, he loses the Bee Suit. Stun the bug with a Star Bit, then kick it off the landing. When the coast is clear, jump up and tap Luigi to shake him off the tree.

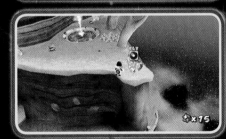

Luigi thanks Mario for helping him out of that tree—and reveals the Power Star he recovered from the Honeyhive Galaxy.

Luigi is on the kingdom's left side, so Mario must somehow cross the gap between the planet's two halves. Buzz Bee Mario up to the branch that holds the flower trapeze. Take a short breather on the branch to recharge flight time and then take off for the Piranha Plant—covered ledge just above. After taking care of the Piranha Plants (and checking out the secret room below the warp pipe), buzz over to the ledge with three ice crystals and a few pesky bugs. Shatter the ice to grab the Star Bits.

Good Egg Galaxy

Honeyhive Galaxy

Flipswitch Galaxy

Loopdeloop Galaxy

Bowser Jr.'s Robot Reactor

Sweet Sweet Galaxy

PRIMA Official Game Guide

As Mario soars toward the Flipswitch Galaxy, he spots a sea of bright blue floor switches. These are the same switches that kept the first Grand Star hooked up to one of Bowser's evil machines, so if Mario can solve this puzzle world, maybe he can discover another secret star.

★ Painting the Planet Yellow ★

HONEYHIVE GALAXY
Painting the Planet Yellow

Start

A

HONEYHIVE GALAXY

The mission begins on the top side of the Flipswitch Galaxy. There are three sides to this puzzle surface, connected by a series of rounded railings. Mario can only cross to the puzzle's other side via these rounded silver railings. If he steps off the edge of a floor switch anywhere else, he drops right into the black hole at the heart of the puzzle.

To solve the puzzle, Mario must turn all the switches from blue to yellow by stepping on them only once. If he leaves a switch and steps on it again later, it returns to blue. He can, however, jump all he wants while still on the same switch—it does not change color unless he completely steps off the switch.

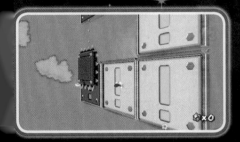

To start solving the puzzle, step over the railing to the puzzle surface on the left. This is the best place to begin turning the switches yellow. Walk down the side of the puzzle surface, opposite the sliding platform. Walk over to the red sliding platform, but don't get too close—there are spikes on the edges that knock Mario back and steal one health wedge. Jump from the bottom switch to the platform and ride it across the gap to the topmost switch on that side. Now, finish flipping the switches and return to the top surface.

Walk across the switches on the puzzle surface's top, jumping over the red shock waves unleashed by the purple robot in the far corner. Close in on the robot and then jump on its head, temporarily

The robot's head pops up to reveal a springy neck.

Walk to the puzzle galaxy's right side. There is another sliding red platform that boxes the area. Watch out for the platform as it slides across the surface. There is a coin over the surface, but wait until Mario solves the puzzle to grab it. He cannot risk getting bumped off the puzzle by landing right in front of the platform's spikes.

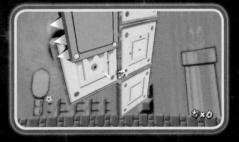

When Mario flips all the switches yellow, they turn green. He can now walk across the three surfaces of the galaxy without worry. Plus, the red platforms stop moving. Now's a good time to collect those coins safely.

Boing! Use the purple robot's springy head to bounce up to the Power Star and save the galaxy.

SUPER MARIO

Psst!

Hey, that backdrop looks familiar. Instead of a star field, the Flipswitch Galaxy's heavens are painted with a classic scene from the original *Super Mario Bros.*, released on the Nintendo Entertainment System in 1985. Check it out—8-bit warp pipe navigated with a simple D-pad and two-button controller. Now you're holding a controller that measures velocity, angle, and distance.

Times, they are a changin'.

LOOPDELOOP GALAXY

Talking penguins surfing on the backs of manta rays just for entertainment? Which crazy corner of the universe is this? It's the Loopdeloop Galaxy, a water-logged race track where penguins compete for record times on a twisting course through the wild blue yonder. Can Mario master the manta well enough to cruise across the finish line?

When Mario drops down to the Loopdeloop Galaxy, the penguins are more than happy to see a new racer. Chat up the little penguins near the starting line to learn all about the fine art of ray-surfing before approaching the emperor penguin holding court near the water. The big penguin is happy to give Mario a few lessons regarding ray-surfing on a short course before sending him on to the real deal.

⭐ Surfing 101 ⭐

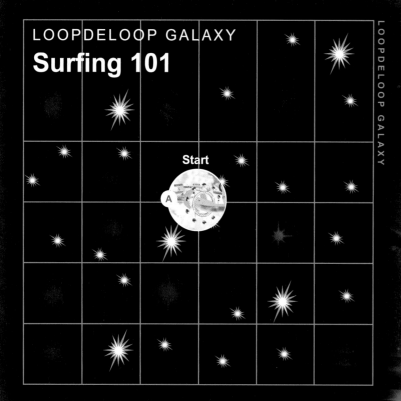

LOOPDELOOP GALAXY
Surfing 101

Start

A

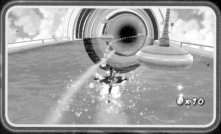

0 x 10

The short course is lined with coins. The penguin explains how to turn the manta ray and follow the line of coins. Point the Wii Remote at the screen. Twist the remote from side to side to tilt the ray. Gentle motions result in sweeping turns. A quick twist translates into a sharp turn. To speed up, hold down Ⓐ.

TIP

Use speed on straight stretches. The record for this race is 1:30, but if Mario zooms along the straightaways with a speed boost, he'll put that record to shame.

and sacrifice time or safety for a little pocket change. What matters is finishing the race under 1:30, not crawling across it with heavy pockets. The 1-Up Mushroom is always a pleasing prize, especially since it keeps Mario in the game in case he accidentally steers the ray off the side of the track.

After completing the introductory lesson, it's time for the big race. The penguins show Mario to the starting line.

Remember, speed down those straight stretches by holding 3. Watch for billboards with arrows—these indicate sharp turns that Mario must slow down to negotiate.

Use easy twists to gently glide along the shallow turns in the first part of the course.

There are a couple of jumps on the track. Race the ray up the ramps with speed boosts, then sail back down. Direct the ray in the air with the Wii Remote to make sure Mario doesn't drop right off the track.

There are two sharp turns before the finish line, which is shaped like a giant sun. Slow down so Mario doesn't slide right off the watery track. If he does, try to steer the ray onto the stretch of track below and then surfing back up to the finish line for a second try. Slow down for these last two turns and ease across the finish line. If Mario skates through under 1:30, he's golden.

There are coins and 1-Up Mushrooms on the track. Steer toward the coins to collect them, but don't go out of the way

Hooray! The penguins are impressed with Mario's ray-surfing skills. The emperor penguin owes Mario a gold medal, which turns out to be a Power Star. Hop up on the first-place pedestal to claim the Power Star and show the universe that Mario is the champ at ray-surfing.

Good Egg Galaxy

Honeyhive Galaxy

Flipswitch Galaxy

Loopdeloop Galaxy

Bowser Jr.'s Robot Reactor

Sweet Sweet Galaxy

⭐⭐⭐ 81 ⭐⭐⭐

BOWSER JR.'S ROBOT REACTOR
Megaleg's Moon

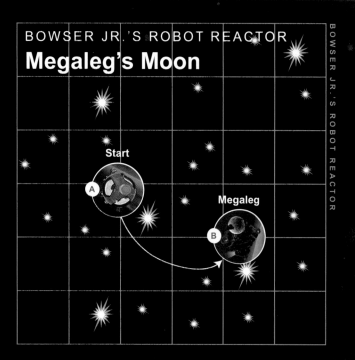

Start

A

Megaleg

B

Mario crashes to a small metal planetoid with a black-hole core. The planetoid's surface is covered with cages containing a variety of items, like coins and 1-Up Mushrooms. But the most important is the caged Launch Star, which Mario must break free in order to vault off this planetoid and launch a full-scale attack on Bowser Jr.'s metal monster, Megaleg.

Bowser Jr. patrols the edge of the Terrace galaxies, keeping watch for the meddlesome Mario while his dad continues working on his nefarious schemes. After Mario unlocks Bowser Jr.'s Robot Reactor, the hero must zip across the cosmos to battle Bowser's underling for control of another rare Grand Star. Only a Grand Star can further power up Rosalina's Comet Observatory.

Megaleg's Moon

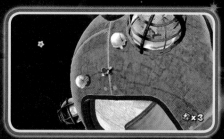

To break open the cages, Mario must discover the Bullet Bill cannon on the planetoid's other side. When a Bullet Bill blasts out of the cannon, Mario must walk in front of it to get its undivided attention. The Bullet Bill's eyes turn red, indicating it has a lock on Mario. Mario can now lead the Bullet Bill to a cage, but he must be fast. The Bullet Bills move pretty quickly, so Mario must stay several steps ahead.

Lead the Bullet Bills into the cages to earn the 1-Up Mushroom and a small collection of coins. After blasting open the treasures, lead a Bullet Bill to the cage with the Launch Star. Free the caged Launch Star and use it to rocket to Bowser Jr.

> **NOTE**
> Watch out for the robot Goombas on the planetoid's surface. Mario can spin to knock these little menaces into the black hole or tip them over with a stomp on the unguarded underbelly to earn a coin.

Look at the size of that thing! That's not a moon—that's a space station.

🪐 Planet B

As Mario touches down on the small moon dominated by the massive Megaleg, Bowser Jr. swoops low on his airship.

He doubts Mario can withstand the crushing might of Megaleg's titanic limbs, so he's confident about scooting off to the next galaxy and leaving Mario to his demise. It's time to prove that little creep wrong.

Boss Battle: Megaleg

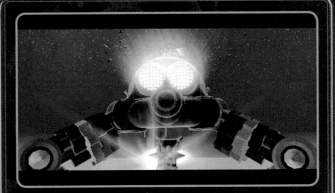

Megaleg is a walking cannon battery. The three giant legs that support Megaleg's cockpit are so large they have their own gravity system. If Mario can climb up those legs and reach the core, perhaps he can trick one of the dozens of Bullet Bills streaming from Megaleg's cannons into giving the brute a self-inflicted wound.

At the battle's start, Megaleg slowly stomps around the minor moon. Quickly dip to the moon's southern hemisphere and check out a series of cages, which contain Star Bits and coins. If Mario gets into trouble, he can lead a Bullet Bill down here and pop one of the coin cages to replenish his health.

When the titan drops one of its huge feet to the moon's surface, Mario must head for the green arrows. Jump onto the leg and let Megaleg's gravity capture Mario. Mario sticks to the leg, turning the green arrows red. This means the Bullet Bills farther up the leg are aware of Mario's presence and are getting ready to fire.

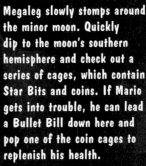

(continued on next page)

★★★ 83 ★★★

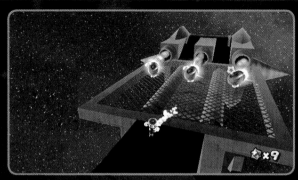

Weave between the trio of Bullet Bills that scream down Megaleg's limb. A quick zigzag confuses the red-eyed Bullet Bills into crashing into each other.

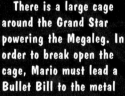

Jump across the grinding gears that connect the legs to Megaleg's body.

There is a large cage around the Grand Star powering the Megaleg. In order to break open the cage, Mario must lead a Bullet Bill to the metal mesh. Run around the multiple cannons until a Bullet Bill spots Mario, then lead it up to the cage. It takes only one Bullet Bill to break open the cage and reach the Grand Star.

Oh no, there's a backup security system in place. As soon as the domed cage vanishes, a wall pops up, protecting the Grand Star from Bullet Bills. Crisscross the Megaleg core to ensnare more Bullet Bills. When those eyes go red, the Bullet Bill is locked. Now, run toward the cage. At the last second, jump out of the way and let the Bullet Bill crash.

The Bullet Bill shatters only one piece of the cage, which regenerates after just a few seconds. Mario must lead another Bullet Bill through the hole in the cage wall to break the glass surrounding the Grand Star.

Feeling nimble? Try leading a Bullet Bill over the wall by flipping in front of the cage. The Bullet Bill arcs upward and then comes smashing down on the glass dome over the Grand Star.

Breaking the glass dome powers down the Megaleg. Every joint explodes, sending pieces of the mechanical monstrosity across the cosmos. The Grand Star drops to the moon's peaceful surface. Mario just needs to touch the Grand Star to claim it and return to the Comet Observatory.

This Grand Star fuses with the Comet Observatory's beacon, powering up the starship. Energy flows to the Fountain Dome, allowing Mario to access a whole new system of galaxies.

SWEET SWEET GALAXY
Rocky Road

Start

A

Terrace

Good Egg Galaxy

Welcome to the Galaxy!

Honeyhive Galaxy

Flipswitch Galaxy

Loopdeloop Galaxy

Bowser Jr.'s Robot Reactor

Sweet Sweet Galaxy

The hungry Luma outside the Terrace wants 400 Star Bits to snack on. After Mario feeds the little Luma, the happy starling zooms across the cosmos and becomes an entirely new galaxy to explore: Sweet Sweet. What delicious treats await Mario in this candy-coated galaxy?

Rocky Road

The road before Mario isn't just rocky, it's holey. Various shapes and cutouts have been pressed out of the candy highway that stretches between the starting point and a safe platform made entirely of cookies. There are several coins on the candy conveyor and Star Bits on the walls, so sweep the cursor across the wall while taking an afternoon jaunt. Jump over the holes in the candy, taking care not to slip through the cutouts.

The gravity in Sweet Sweet is as light as a soufflé. Mario bounds higher than normal, allowing him to easily cross the holes. However, make sure he doesn't accidentally jump right on the electric barrier that spans the width of the candy highway.

The candy avenue to the right is also moving, but instead of flowing at Mario, it's moving from left to right. The bridge is perforated with holes of all shapes and sizes that Mario must avoid slipping through while jumping toward the next cookie safe zone.

85

Two Toads point Mario around the next corner, toward a candy wheel. The wheel spins between the walls of cake that flank the narrowing passage. Mario must jump over the holes in the wheel. There is a 1-Up Mushroom on the wheel, right at the bend in the passage.

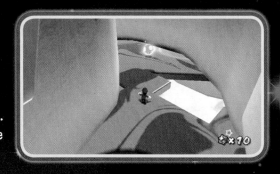

After grabbing the Mushroom, head left and jump to the chocolate-covered platform that looks out over a big cake. That cake is topped with a Power Star, so Mario better get moving.

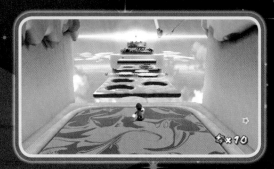

The Power Star is atop the cake. The Toads on the cake celebrate their delicious discovery, but Mario has more important things to do than satisfy his sweet tooth. He must collect the Star Bits on the cake's second tier and grab the Power Star.

Jump across the candy cutouts that float through the air. Watch out for the electrical fields. If Mario's zapped, he may fall through a hole or off one of the small circular ledges.

FOUNTAIN GALAXIES

SPACE JUNK GALAXY

The Space Junk Galaxy is composed of discarded debris pulled together by gravity and floating lazily out in the cosmos. Old rockets, space station building blocks, and a field of clutter may not look like prime places to hide Power Stars, but Mario soon discovers that Space Junk Galaxy affirms the old adage of "one plumber's junk is another plumber's treasure."

SPACE JUNK GALAXY
Pull Star Path

PULL STAR PATH

⭐ Pull Star Path ⭐

The Pull Star Path is aptly named—Mario must use the blue Pull Stars to cross the empty spaces between the orbiting junk places. His first tour of the galaxy is largely trouble-free, but before he claims the Power Star by navigating the last debris field, a host of spiders drops in to spoil the space stroll.

Space Junk Galaxy

Battlerock Galaxy

Rolling Green Galaxy

Hurry-Scurry Galaxy

Sling Pod Galaxy

⭐ Planets A, B, and C ⭐

Mario lands on a small floating platform with a shallow gravity field. It's enough to keep his feet on the metal as he walks on the platform's underside, collecting some errant Star Bits. However, the gravity is no match for the force of the Pull Stars between the platform and the drifting crystal.

When Mario is pulled from the platform toward the crystal, a quick shake of the Wii Remote breaks the Pull Star's hold. Since the crystal is larger than the starting platform, Mario is pulled into its gravity field. There are Star Bits encased in ice on the crystal; free them with a quick spin attack.

⭐⭐⭐ 87 ⭐⭐⭐

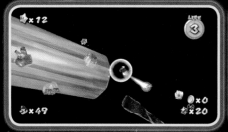

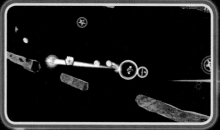

Leave the crystal via the Pull Stars on the opposite end of the planetoid from the starting platform. These Pull Stars tug Mario into the cold reaches of space, leaving him vulnerable to drifting away. To keep him moving along safely, constantly reach for the next Pull Star by pointing at it with the Wii Remote and pressing Ⓐ.

There are several coins between the Pull Stars that lead toward a trio of floating spheres, locked together by their own gravity system.

Mario drops down to an old rocket ship, drifting idly in the glow of a distant star system. Star Bits rain from the heavens, crashing on the rocket's hull. Pick up the Star Bits while breaking the ice crystal that contains coins.

At the last Pull Star, next to the L-shaped asteroid, shake the Wii Remote to drop Mario on the closest sphere in the trio. The sphere's gravity ensnares him. Mario can now run all the way around it. However, if he jumps next to one of the other two spheres, that sphere's gravity pulls him into it. Bound between the three planetoids to collect five Star Chips.

The Star Chips form a Launch Star that blasts Mario across the Space Junk Galaxy. He bursts through an ice crystal full of Star Bits, so use the cursor to scoop those up as Mario screams toward the next planet.

After grabbing the coins, run to the rocket's tip. There are two Pull Stars above the rocket, enclosed in small spheres. Mario can grab the Pull Stars with the cursor, so lift him up to the closest sphere. Jump toward the next sphere. At the height of the jump, snag the Pull Star in the sphere's center. Mario is caught by that sphere's gravity field.

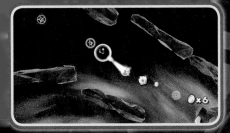

Use the nearby Pull Stars to yank Mario off the sphere and drag him into an asteroid field.

Drag Mario through the lines of coins between the Pull Stars.

Planet F

There is a T-shaped platform floating beyond the last Pull Star in the chain. When Mario reaches the Pull Star closest to the platform, shake the Wii Remote to break the Pull Star's hold and drop down to the platform. Fuzzy spiders are waiting for him there; use Star Bits to stun the spiders and then kick them out into space for extra Star Bits.

The platform's edges are round, which means Mario can walk around the whole thing without falling into space. Check out the platform's "bottom." The camera twists to reveal another cadre of spiders; these arachnids protect three coins and

a ? Block full of Star Bits. After defeating the spider and claiming the goodies, walk up the arrow to kick the last spider off the platform and check out the T's top.

Oh no, the poor Toads are frozen in ice! Mario must free them with spin attacks.

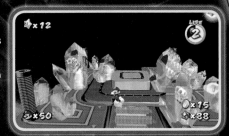

CAUTION

There's a frozen Goomba on this platform, so don't free it by mistake.

After Mario frees all the Toads, their spaceship zooms through the cosmos and goes into low orbit near the platform.

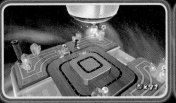 

The Toads' spaceship has its own gravity field. Jump toward the spaceship to be captured by its gravity field. Walk to the top of the Toads' ship to use the Sling Star. This Sling Star launches Mario to the debris field that hides the Power Star.

Space Junk Galaxy

Battlerock Galaxy

Rolling Green Galaxy

Hurry-Scurry Galaxy

Sling Pod Galaxy

SUPER MARIO GALAXY

LEGEND

⭐ Silver Star

Carefully walk across the bricks, giving them time to click together and form a path through space. Mario must collect the five Silver Stars, so head toward the first Silver Star on the left. There are six coins next to it, but when Mario closes in on them, no block slides under his feet. He must make a leap of faith. A block appears under the coins, catching Mario as he lands.

The debris field is an oddity—there are several circles of coins floating out in the ether, but there is no way for Mario to walk or pull himself toward them. Plus, where's the Power Star? Perhaps those little Silver Stars at the edges of the debris field can help?

Keep following the path through the debris field, catching up with the other Silver Stars. When Mario meets a Silver Star, it follows him for the remainder of the mission. Pretty soon, Mario has a gaggle of Silver Stars in his wake.

Walk to the platform's edge, facing into the debris field. As Mario nears the edge, blocks snap together, pulled into place by the debris field's strange gravity. As Mario walks forward, more blocks snap into place. However, after several steps, the first set of blocks blasts apart.

The coins in the debris field's upper-right corner look unreachable. However, when Mario jumps toward them (on another leap of faith), a group of red triangles snap together to create a safe landing pad. Similar triangles click together under the Silver Star.

NOTE

Use the map to see how all the bricks and blocks would look if somebody glued them together as they snapped into place.

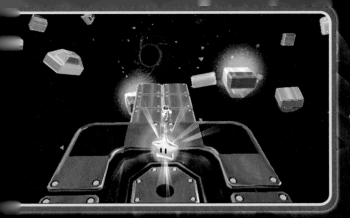

The five Silver Stars join together to create a Power Star. The Power Star soars over to the platform on the debris field's edge.

KAMELLA'S AIRSHIP ATTACK

SPACE JUNK GALAXY
Kamella's Airship Attack

Start

A

B

C

Space Junk Galaxy

Battlerock Galaxy

Rolling Green Galaxy

Hurry-Scurry Galaxy

Sling Pod Galaxy

Kamella, queen of the Magikoopa, travels the cosmos with her fleet of airships in search of Mario. Bowser is too busy with his plotting to stop Mario's meddling, so he charges minions like Kamella to do his dirty work.

Planets A and B

Mario soars across the cosmos, zeroing in on the first airship in Kamella's fleet.

drops into the Space Junk Galaxy, landing on one of oads' orbital mushrooms. It's just a quick hop to the next ship—the gravity between the two crafts is weak. Mario blast off via the Launch Star atop the red ship. This sends ocketing toward Kamella's airship armada, a fleet of deep-

SUPER

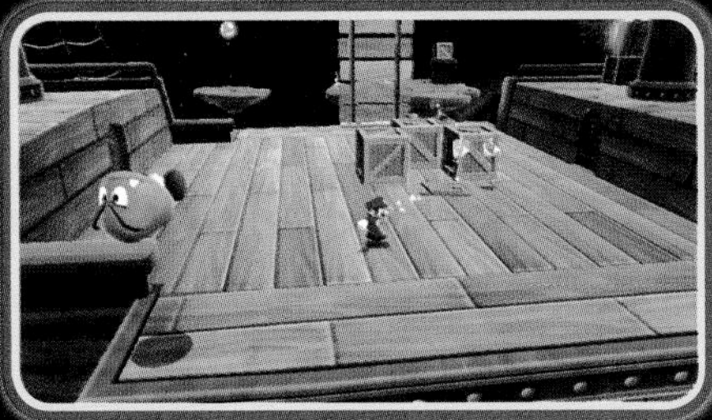

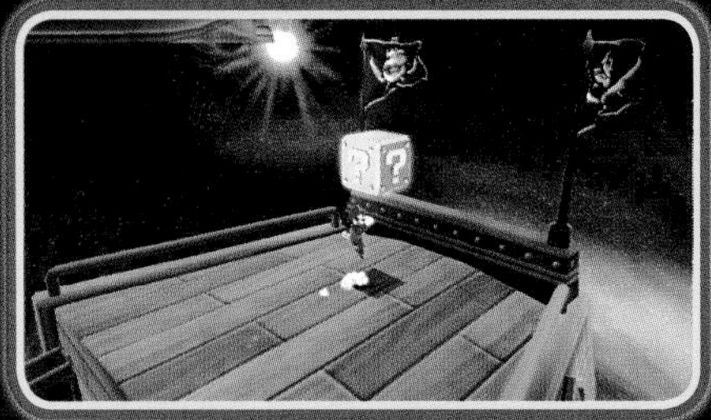

A pair of Goombas patrols the first airship's deck. One of them is hiding in the middle of the four wooden crates in the deck's center. Break the crates to earn some extras Star Bits and release the Goomba. Stun it with a Star Bit, then kick it off the ship to claim even more Star Bits. After eliminating the Goombas, empty the ? Block on the ship's aft—it's full of Star Bits.

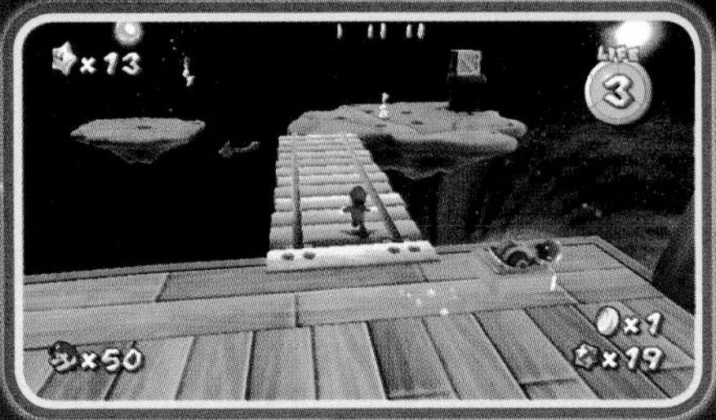

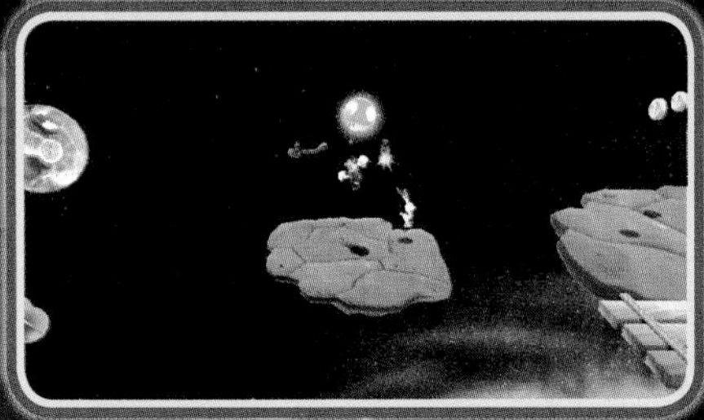

Spin next to the lever on the deck to drop the gangplank. This plank connects the airship to a pair of floating rocks. The rocks are populated by two space bunnies jumping and spinning through the air. Follow the blue bunny across the gap between the rocks to claim a 1-Up Mushroom (Mario must spin while jumping to reach it).

The Sling Star to the next airship is in the wooden crate next to the bunnies. Break the crate and spin into the Sling Star to blast off.

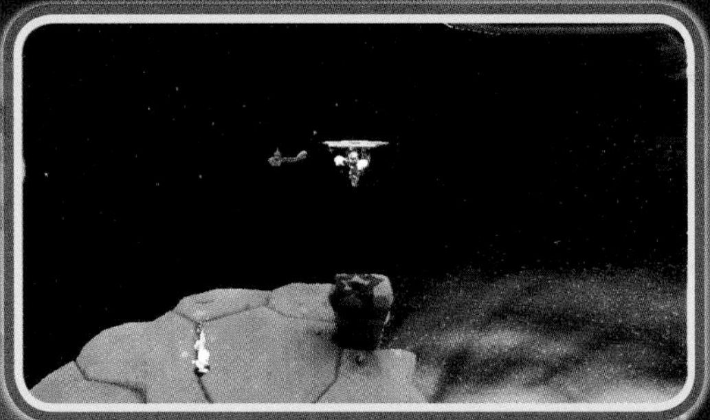

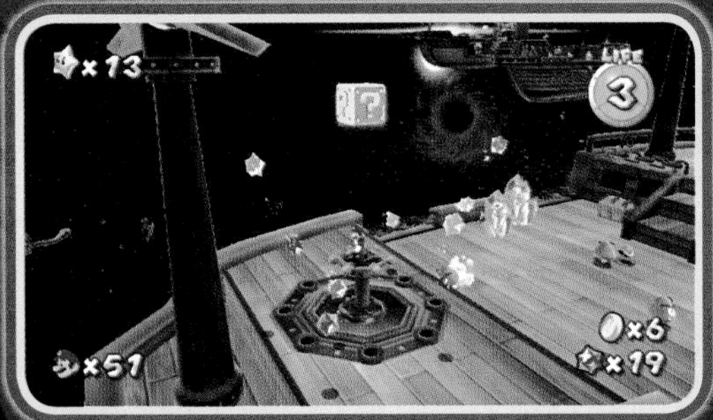

When Mario lands on the next ship's deck, a handful of Goombas spring into action. Jump away from the enemies and step on the green spigot handle on the ship's bow. Spin while standing on the handle. It rises into the air, releasing a stream of Star Bits. Plus, Mario can now jump straight up and spin to bop the ? Block full of Star Bits.

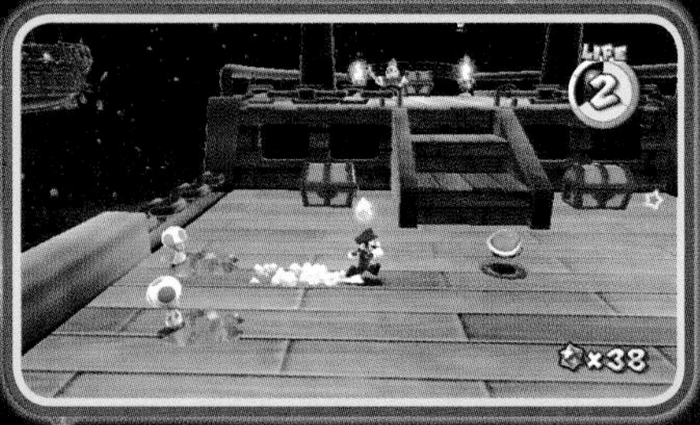

There are two Toads on the deck, frozen in ice. Free them to learn a new trick—Mario can pick up and throw Koopa shells to attack enemies and open locked treasure chests. To pick up a shell, walk over it. Mario hoists it to his shoulder. To throw it, shake the Wii Remote. Mario hurls the shell in the straight line.

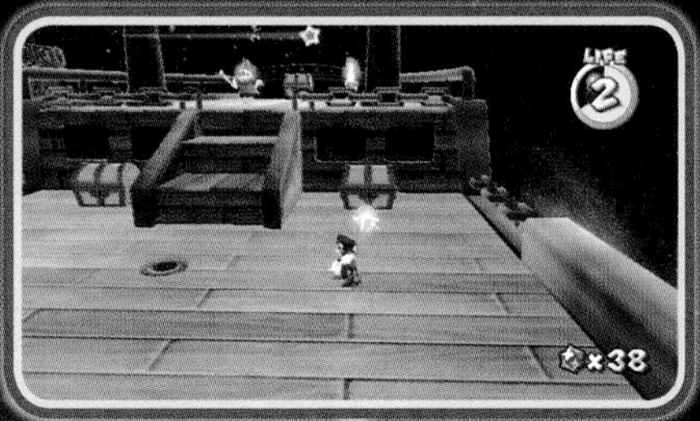

Open the treasure chests flanking the stairs to discover coins and Star Bits.

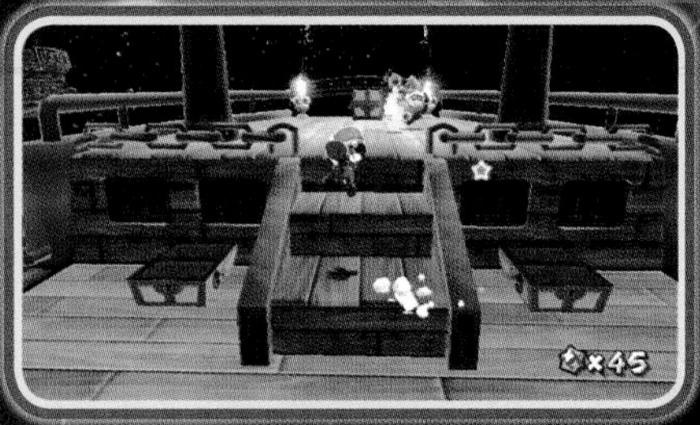

Lug a shell up the step and throw it at the Magikoopa when it's between magic spells. Watch out for those fireballs—they make Mario run in a circle until his biscuits stop burning.

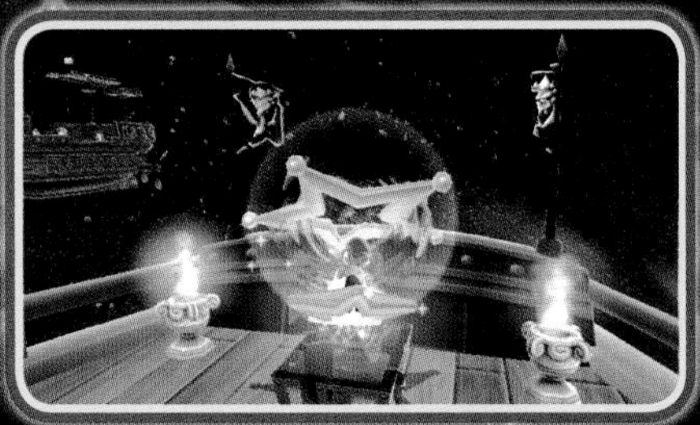

The treasure chest on the ship's aft, guarded by the Magikoopa, contains a large Launch Star. Use this to zoom to the next pair of airships and continue the fight.

Mario lands on a wooden platform teetering at the top of a ship's mast. There's a lone Goomba up here; Mario can either push it off with a few Star Bits or try to stomp it. Be careful next to the platform's edges, though. If Mario falls down to the deck, he cannot get back up here—which would be too bad, because the smokestack leads to a neat secret.

Two squid guard the gangplank that normally connects the two airships. They spit only fireballs across the gap. To knock out the beasts and lower the gangplank, Mario must throw shells across the gap. Koopas trundle along the deck, providing a steady supply of shells. After hitting a Koopa, pick up the empty shell and aim for each squid.

The treasure chest on the deck's right side contains a Life Mushroom.

Psst!

Want a bunch of Star Bits? When the coast is clear, run toward the tall smokestack opposite the wooden platform. Even if Mario spins at the height of his jump, he still cannot reach the smokestack's lip. So, before jumping, point at the Pull Star next to the stack. When Mario leaps toward the smokestack, the Pull Star goes active. Grab it with Ⓐ before Mario crashes to the deck. Release the Pull Star when over the stack. Mario falls into a secret room full of Star Bits. There is a small Sling Star on the room's other side that vaults Mario back to the deck.

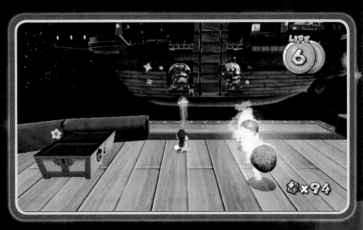

The treasure chest on the left contains a red shell. These home in on targets, so even if Mario's aim is slightly off, the red shell arcs toward the squid.

After bopping each squid with a shell, the gangplank drops. Run across the bridge and use the Sling Star to reach the carpeted deck. Who deserves the red carpet all the way out here?

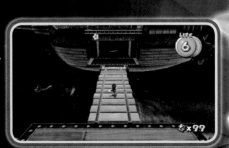

Space Junk Galaxy

Battlerock Galaxy

Rolling Green Galaxy

Hurry-Scurry Galaxy

Sling Pod Galaxy

TIP
There are two coins on the ship's bow, but Mario must carefully sidle across a narrow plank to reach them.

Wicked Kamella rules over all Magikoopa. She uses her size and magical powers to intimidate foes, casting dangerous spells that sear her rivals. Mario spots the source of Kamella's power right away—a Power Star in the tip of her magic wand. To retrieve that Power Star, Mario must defeat Kamella.

After Mario hits Kamella with two shells, she calls in reinforcements. Two Magikoopa appear on the ship's deck and start filling the air with streaking fireballs. (The Magikoopas never cast shells—only Kamella can use that spell.) Mario must now avoid up to three fireballs at a time while trying to survive long enough to grab a shell.

Kamella swoops around the ship, waving her magic wand and casting fireballs at Mario. The only way to do any damage is to throw a shell at Kamella, but there aren't any on the deck at the battle's start. So, avoid the fireballs and look for coins; shoot the lamp on the mast with Star Bits to earn one. If Mario has full health, leave them be for now. Should Kamella's aim prove true, Mario will need them to survive the battle.

If the deck gets too hot, consider making those Magikoopas walk the plank. You can throw a shell at them and jump on their heads just before they cast a spell. If Mario waits until after they cast their fireballs, the Magikoopa disappear just before his feet touch their heads. After dispatching the Magikoopa, Mario has an easier time managing Kamella's fireballs. After the third shell to the face, Kamella vanishes for good.

The key to besting Kamella is watching her wand. When she raises it and red sparks surround the tip, she's about to cast a fireball. However, if a green mist appears, she's about to cast a shell. Mario must grab these shells and throw them back at her. After picking up a shell, jump so the shell misses the railing and hits Kamella right in the kisser when you throw it. She reels back, releasing Star Bits.

Feeling nimble? Spin just as the shell is about to hit Mario—he grabs it right out of the air.

Kamella drops her magic wand, freeing the Power Star. Pick it up off the deck to end the mission.

SPACE JUNK GALAXY
Tarantox's Tangled Web

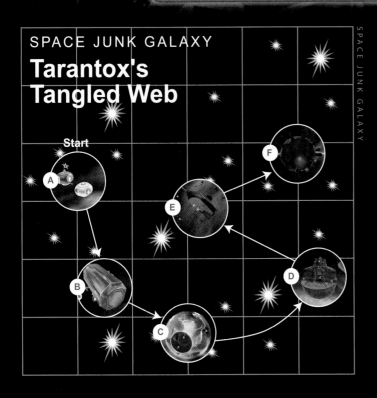

Start

A
B
C
D
E
F

SPACE JUNK GALAXY

Somewhere in the coldest reaches of space, a creature spins a silvery web strong enough to ensnare stars. Mario must go on a space safari to find this monster and retrieve the Power Star tangled in its sticky handiwork.

Space Junk Galaxy

Battlerock Galaxy

Rolling Green Galaxy

Hurry-Scurry Galaxy

Sling Pod Galaxy

★ Planets A and B ★

spiders now. Use Star Bits to stun the spiders and kick them off the crystal. After claiming the frozen Star Bits from the ice, walk to the crystal's opposite end.

Via the Pull Stars, drag Mario across space. Pull him through the coins while traveling between the asteroids. At the L-shaped asteroid, use the lower set of Pull Stars to enter the glass-covered planetoid's gravity field. To reach the planetoid's surface, let Mario drift beyond the final Pull Star. Shake the Wii Remote to break free of the Pull Star and get captured by the planetoid's gravity.

e Toads let Mario use their space-ips as a staging ground for this ssion. When the plumber arrives in e galaxy, he drops down to the yellow ip. The Toads beckon him to the red ip, where he can reach to a Pull Star d start dragging himself to the crystal anetoid. This planetoid is infested with

Back

Front

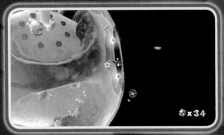

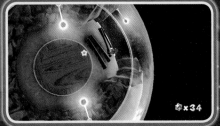

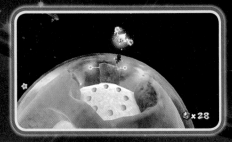

There's land just below the glass ball that encapsulates the planetoid. Near the last Pull Star is a hole in the glass that leads to the lower surface. Several Goomba roam the planetoid's interior, guarding Star Bits. Why are there so many Star Bits on this planetoid?

There's a hungry Luma on this planetoid! The goal right now is to reach Tarantox, but be sure to return to this mission later to check out that Luma.

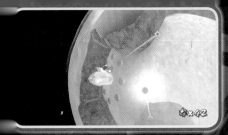

Mario lands on the small planetoid, which has a spider problem. The fuzzy enemies wobble down a small road. Aim at the spiders and stun them with Star Bits, then kick them into the great void. They release even more Star Bits—scoop them up as Mario walks to the little Toad stuck to a Sling Pod, a gooey bulb that Mario can use to fling himself through space. Free the little guy by using the Sling Pod in the same way as when Mario is stuck in it. The Toad may not have wanted to be stuck to the gooey Sling Pod, but using the Sling Pod is Mario's ticket to the Power Star.

Space Junk Galaxy

Battlerock Galaxy

Rolling Green Galaxy

Hurry-Scurry Galaxy

Sling Pod Galaxy

xplore the planetoid's interior, ollecting coins and Star Bits. The one circles hide Star Bits, so spin the center of the rings and pick up e goodies. After harvesting the Star its, follow the wooden path through the anetoid to find the Sling Star. Spin der the Sling Star to escape velocity d blast off this planetoid.

Jump on the Sling Pod. Mario automatically sticks to it. Place the hand cursor on the Sling Pod and hold Ⓐ. Drag the pod away from its base, creating tension. Aim for the Sling Pod on the cube dead ahead. Line up the two Sling Pods and release Ⓐ.

NOTE

Mario crashes through a giant Star Bit as he soars to the next planetoid. Quickly run the cursor over the Star Bits before Mario reaches the next planetoid's surface or they vanish.

The Sling Pods snap back into place, throwing Mario free. Mario zooms through space and lands right on the sticky surface of the next Sling Pod.

Use this Sling Pod to fling Mario to the old rocket ship. The rocket has no Sling Pod to land on, but the crumbling ship has enough gravity to pull Mario in for a soft landing.

PRIMA Official Game Guide

Check the rocket's bottom. There's a Life Mushroom encased in ice. Grab it—Mario needs full health before challenging this galaxy's boss for the Power Star.

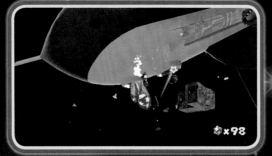

Several coins are caught in the web. Run the cursor over the coins to free them—they drop to the ring that surrounds the spiderweb. However, save as many of the coins as possible for the fight ahead, as Mario may need some health pick-ups during the battle.

There is a Sling Pod at the rocket ship's base. Stick to it and use the line of coins stretching across open space as a guide for lining Mario up with a small rock covered with spiders. This is the only stop between the rocket ship and a large, mysterious pod floating in deep space.

When Mario is at full health, jump to one of the small white balls of webbing. He sticks to it like he does on Sling Pods. Pull back the same way, lining Mario up with a huge ball of tightly wound webbing. Break open the webbing and see just what's hiding under there.

Use the Sling Pod on top of the debris to throw Mario across space and to the giant purple pod. It looks dangerous, but Mario senses the Power Star is nearby. Line him up with the purple pod and pull back the Sling Pod. Release to send Mario flying through space. He crashes through the pod's tightly woven shell, revealing a huge spiderweb and large ball of sticky threading.

Boss Battle: Tarantox

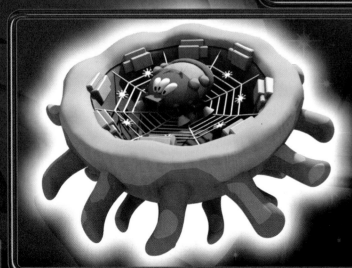

Lumbering at the giant web's center is Tarantox, a three-eyed space spider. Those three eyes allow Tarantox to cast glances all over the cosmos, searching for prey. The ample arachnid's web is full of coins, but Tarantox would surely clear a little space for a prize like Mario.

Boss Battle: Tarantox (cont.)

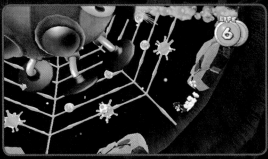

Tarantox's lair is large enough to support its own gravity, keeping Mario's feet on the ring that encircles the web. That's good, because Mario better start running the moment the battle begins. While rotating, Tarantox drools acid from its snout.

The monster stores this acid in pockets, which Mario can pop to stop the attack. Use the white web balls to launch Mario across the ring, breaking the acid pockets so Tarantox stops spitting—at least, temporarily.

Run around the ring to spot Tarantox's weak spot— its rump. Blast Mario into the weak spot to flip Tarantox on its back.

Tarantox has three red bulbs on its underbelly. Hitting all three of these wounds the giant spider, so use the web balls to attack. Send Mario flying into each bulb before Tarantox flips back over and recovers. If Mario successfully attacks all three bulbs before Tarantox flips, the monster is significantly weakened. And angered.

As soon as Tarantox flips back over, it douses the ring in acid. Run between the acid streams, waiting for Tarantox to take a breather.

TIP

Need extra health, but already used the coins? Ground pound the stone platforms around the ring. He shatters the stone, releasing a hidden coin.

Blast Tarantox's rear pouch again to flip the spider over.

Mario has less time to pop all three red bulbs on Tarantox's under-carriage now, so be quick about it.

When Tarantox falls, it leaves behind the Power Star, stuck in the web's center. Fling Mario into the ring's middle to grab the Power Star and return to the Comet Observatory.

SPACE JUNK GALAXY
Pull Star Path

Start

A

G

B

F

D

C

E

Time: 03:40

Zip across the Pull Stars in the asteroid belt.

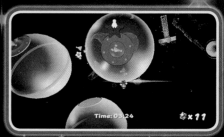

Time: 03:24   ✦×11

Quickly gather up the five Star Chips of the three spheres to create a Launch Star.

Time: 03:13

The Launch Star blasts Mario around the glass sphere, breaking an ice crystal containing several Star Bits. Collect the Star Bits before he lands on the rocket ship.

The Speedy Comet casts its spell over the Space Junk Galaxy, beckoning Mario to return for a recently discovered Power Star. If Mario can zip across the debris-filled galaxy and gather the five Silver Stars in under four minutes, the Speedy Comet vanishes, leaving the Power Star in its wake.

Cruising the Pull Stars

×14   Life 3

×53   Time: 03:59   ●×0   ♦×0

There are many extra coins and Star Bits littered around the galaxy to distract Mario from the task at hand—but avoid going out of your way to pick up anything sparkling. Use the Pull Star to drag Mario to the first crystal planetoid and scoop up the line of coins leading to the next Pull Star. If Mario misses one, just keep moving forward.

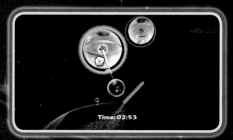

Time: 02:53

Iced coins on the rocket ship beckon, but Mario must resist the urge unless he has at least three minutes left on the clock. Run to the rocket ship's top and use the Pull Stars in the spheres to keep moving across the galaxy.

Time: 02:25 ●x18

Pull Mario quickly through the next asteroid belt. There are coins in this field, but for the sake of speed, don't line Mario up with them. Just hop from one Pull Star to the next, shuffling between the asteroids until he reaches the T-shaped platform with the spiders.

The Debris Field

Time: 01:58 ●x25 ●x29

No time to lose—run down the platform, hitting the spiders with Star Bits to keep them at bay. The Prize Block on the platform's bottom is a temptation Mario can ill-afford right now.

Time: 01:31 ●x63

Time: 01:22 ●x63

Run to the platform's top and free the frozen Toads. Watch for the Goomba on ice while shattering the crystals. When all the Toads are free, their captain drops his spaceship into low orbit. Jump into the ship's shallow gravity field and hoof it to the Sling Star on the roof.

Speed across the debris field. The bricks and blocks work overtime, snapping into place under Mario's feet. The goal is to gather the five Silver Stars, which

Time: 00:27 ●x63

are in the same places as the normal Pull Star Path mission. Jump across the rapidly constructing-deconstructing platforms to bring together the Silver Stars and find the Power Star.

The Power Star appears on the first platform in the debris field. Hurry back to claim the prize!

YOSHI'S UNEXPECTED APPEARANCE

Yoshi's Unexpected Appearance

Start

A
B
C
D

Remember that hungry Luma in the "Tarantox's Tangled Web" mission? It's time to return to the Luma with the rumbling tummy and indulge its taste buds with some Star Bits.

Space Junk Galaxy

Battlerock Galaxy

Rolling Green Galaxy

Hurry-Scurry Galaxy

Sling Pod Galaxy

Planets A and B

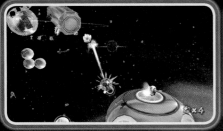

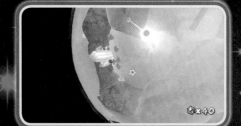

The hungry Luma needs 50 Star Bits, so Mario must collect as many of the Star Bits he encounters on his travels as possible. The first planetoid beyond the Toads' spaceships, the crystal, has several Star Bits frozen in ice. There are two spiders scrambling around the crystal too. Spin to stun the spiders, then kick them into space to earn even more Star Bits.

Watch out for Goombas bumbling about on the interior surface. The Goombas are worth a few Star Bits, so spin next to the creatures to stun them, then boot them away to pick up extra Star Bits. Keep exploring the interior to find 50 Star Bits and then return to the hole in the glassy outer sphere. Use the Pull Star to shuttle Mario up to the hungry Luma.

As Mario is pulled through the asteroid belt, he collects several coins. However, Star Bits are out here too. While pulling Mario close to a Pull Star, move the cursor over the small L-shaped rock to pick up seven Star Bits. The hungry Luma will sure appreciate it!

Feed that Luma those 50 Star Bits. The Luma rewards Mario by transforming into a new planetoid.

As Mario uses the Pull Stars to head for the glassy sphere, he spots the hungry Luma. There is also an ice crystal with several Star Bits on the sphere's surface, so capture those goodies before dropping to the planetoid's interior.

That's a nice-looking planetoid. Who's your decorator?

Planet C

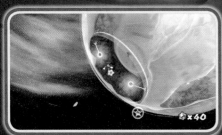

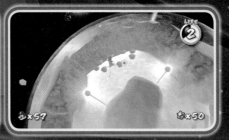

Mario should have around 40 Star Bits by the time he reaches the planetoid. He needs 50, so it's time to enter the sphere and collect the remaining Star Bits from the surface. There are stone rings that reveal Star Bits if Mario gives a little spin in the circle's center.

Use the Launch Star on the glass's surface to blast off to the wooden Yoshi head. There's a whole swarm of Goombas crawling all over Yoshi's mug. In order to release the hidden Power Star, Mario must eliminate all the Goombas.

> **CAUTION**
>
> Watch out for two little steam geysers on Yoshi's nose; they're right on the nostrils.

Scramble all over the planetoid, spinning and kicking away the Goombas. Bouncing on the Goombas consecutively without hitting the ground will give you an extra life for each one after the seventh. When all the Goombas are gone, the Power Star appears on Yoshi's snout.

BATTLEROCK GALAXY

At the heart of Battlerock Galaxy is a fortified attack platform, built into a massive asteroid. From this position, the denizens of the system closely monitor any incoming encroachers and launch countermeasures. Mario must outsmart these measures, which are led by Topman, if he wants to recover this galaxy's Power Stars.

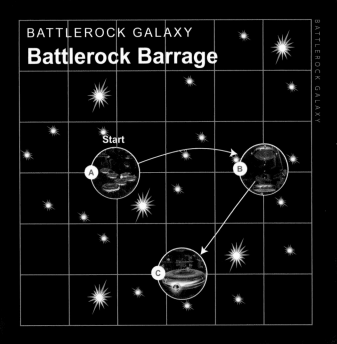

BATTLEROCK GALAXY
Battlerock Barrage

Battlerock Barrage demonstrates the defensive measures Topman and his tribe have installed on their asteroid. After assembling a Launch Star to approach the base, Mario must survive a gauntlet of cosmic cannons that pepper the horizon with exploding shells. It's a tough ordeal, but Mario must persevere to get the first Power Star of the galaxy.

Space Junk Galaxy

Battlerock Galaxy

Rolling Green Galaxy

Hurry-Scurry Galaxy

Sling Pod Galaxy

PRIMA Official Game Guide

Watch out for the metallic Goombas on the twin discs. They'll try to needle Mario as he explores the area.

Mario drops into Battlerock, landing on a collection of floating discs. Each disc has enough gravity to hold Mario if he walks over the edge to check for goodies—such as coins—on the underside, but not enough to hold him permanently. Leaping across the discs is easy, and necessary, as he must assemble five blue Star Chips to create a series of Pull Stars.

Robotic Goombas wander the discs, complicating Mario's mission. Mario cannot kick these little enemies off the discs like a regular Goomba. He must stun them with a spin and then stomp the weak, exposed belly to finish it off.

After collecting all five blue Star Chips (check under the discs), a series of Pull Stars appear, extending to the Sling Star that is normally out of reach. Work the Pull Stars to reach the Sling Star and blast off to the next section of the Battlerock Galaxy, a twin set of discs.

Mario must reach the upper disc; however, it doesn't have strong enough gravity to pull him in if he jumps toward it. There is purple robot in the middle of the bottom disc. Bounce on its head—it has a springy neck! Jump on the robot again to vault to the upper disc. Walk to the upper disc and stand on the blue screw. Spin to drive the screw into the disc and make it move.

LEGEND

🍄	1-Up Mushroom
⭐	Power Star

The disc starts floating toward the base, activating the asteroid's defenses. The dozens of cannons on the asteroid empty volley after volley into space, using their sheer numbers to keep intruders out. Mario must avoid the cannon blasts and remain on the disc until it passes through the gauntlet of cannons.

Mario can just hop over the short fences.

Space Junk Galaxy

Battlerock Galaxy

Rolling Green Galaxy

Hurry-Scurry Galaxy

Sling Pod Galaxy

> [!NOTE]
> Mario's disc has enough gravity to hold his feet down when he walks to the lower half, but those spinning balls that travel the disc's circumference will give him quite a shock. Watch out for them when ducking down to the disc's bottom to avoid cannon fire.

The disc eventually docks next to two immobile discs at the end of the cannon-covered wall. The Power Star is right in front of Mario, but it's sealed in a cage. Mario must somehow break the cage open—and fortunately for him, two Bullet Bill cannons are built into the asteroid's wall. If Mario can taunt one of the Bullet Bills, it will follow him across the two discs and blast free the Power Star.

There's more than just cannons to deal with here—electric fences block the disc's approach. Mario must run between the two sides of the disc to avoid the fences. A line of coins mark the first time Mario must duck to avoid shock treatment, but future fences can only be dodged with a diligent eye.

The disc closest to the Bullet Bill cannons has four cages on its upper surface. The cages are loaded with coins, Star Bits, and a spring. Mario must break open some of these cages to clear a route for a Bullet Bill to reach the Power Star's cage. Stand on the disc's edge to get a Bullet Bill's attention, then jump behind the cages to trick the projectile into crashing.

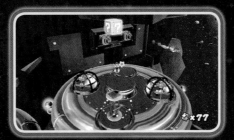

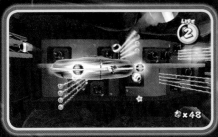

Sometimes, Mario must stand on the disc's edge to avoid two fences at the same time. Cool moves, Mario, but watch out for those balls.

The spring bounces Mario up to a ? Block full of Star Bits.

The giant coin on the disc's path extends lines of Star Bits from two cannons. Pick them up with the cursor while avoiding the cannonballs.

There's a 1-Up Mushroom on the underside of the disc next to the Bullet Bill cannons. Mario must stand on the disc's edge and jump outward to get the farthest Bullet Bill's attention, then lead it to the cage.

SUPER MARIO GALAXY

After clearing a path for the Bullet Bill, tease one of the Bullet Bills into following Mario and then carefully guide it back to the first disc. Lead it straight to the cage and then jump over it just as it crashes. The cage breaks apart, freeing the Power Star. Grab that star to return to the Comet Observatory.

BREAKING INTO BATTLEROCK

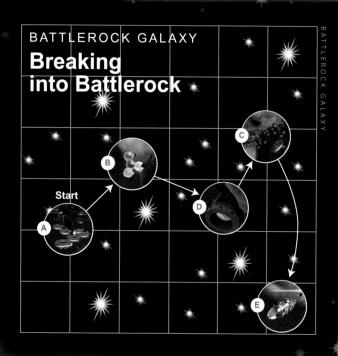

BATTLEROCK GALAXY

Breaking into Battlerock

BATTLEROCK GALAXY

Throw a Bob-omb next to the Launch Star cage and stand back.

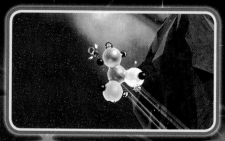

Mario blasts off from the Launch Star, zooming around the asteroid on a collision course with a molecule-shaped planetoid. Wait—are those Chomps?

Now that Mario has managed to outsmart the galaxy's defenses, it's time for the hero to infiltrate the base. The Power Star is actually on the asteroid's other side, forcing Mario to go the long route around the rock.

Planets A and B

Mario starts on the Battlerock Galaxy's outer edge, standing on a series of discs in orbit around the asteroid. The Launch Star that rockets Mario to the base is trapped inside a cage, but there are no Bullet Bill cannons in sight. How will he reach that Launch Star? Bob-ombs. The moment Mario picks up a Bob-omb, its fuse ignites, giving him only a few seconds to get rid of it before it explodes. Mario can use the Bob-ombs to blast open the cages full of Star Bits (and in a later mission, he absolutely must do this), clearing a path to the Launch Star cage.

When Mario lands on the planet, he drops next to a Bob-omb dispenser. He must use the Bob-ombs to reach a cage with a Rainbow Star on the planetoid's other side. It's not that far of a walk,

but those Chomps make the journey difficult. Grab a Bob-omb and make a mad dash for the cage. Throw the Bob-omb down next to the cage and dodge the Chomps until it explodes.

The Rainbow Star turns the tables on the Chomps—now Mario can blast right through them, clearing the planetoid's surface. The shattered Chomps release Star Bits. These are extremely useful for feeding the hungry Luma on the planetoid's surface, which opens the path to the hidden star in this galaxy. After you free the planet of Chomps, use a Bob-omb to release a caged Luma on the planetoid. The Luma turns into a Sling Star, rocketing Mario to an asteroid field.

Space Junk Galaxy

Battlerock Galaxy

Rolling Green Galaxy

Hurry-Scurry Galaxy

Sling Pod Galaxy

Planet C

LEGEND

🍄 1-Up Mushroom

🍄 Life Mushroom

Carefully pull Mario through the field, dragging him to the power-ups floating among the mines. The 1-Up Mushroom is tough to get—Mario must use inertia to float beyond the Pull Star and grab it. Before he floats too far away, grab another Pull Star and drag him back into the minefield. The goal is the Launch Star on the minefield's far side.

Mario lands on a lone disc just outside a minefield. The crate on the disc's bottom contains a 1-Up Mushroom. After grabbing the power-up, walk to the disc's edge and grab the closest Pull Star. Mario must pull himself through the field, careful not to touch any of the mines. If he does, the mine explodes, breaking Mario's grip on the Pull Stars. He has only a second to grab another Pull Star before drifting too far away to recover.

The Launch Star blasts Mario down to the surface of the Battlerock station.

Planet D

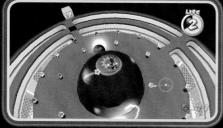

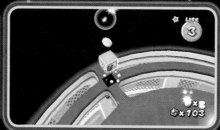

When Mario drops to the surface, he lands beside a dome with a large red button. Triple jump or backflip up to the button, then ground pound it to release a flurry of Star Bits. Pick them up with the cursor before dropping down to the floor of the area. There are two spinning spheres that will shock Mario, so keep back. After grabbing the Star Bits, jump over the spheres and empty the Prize Blocks to earn coins.

Mario blasts through the crystal, freeing the Launch Star. Now he must use a Bob-omb to break the cage on the ceiling and jump into another cannon.

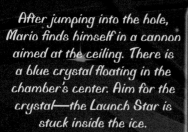

Use the warp pipe on the ground to slip inside the large structure. Mario pops out next to a large cage. There's a hole in the floor inside the cage. With nowhere else to go, Mario must grab a nearby Bob-omb and shatter the cage to investigate the hole.

Fire Mario at the Launch Star. Just as he touches it, shake the Wii Remote to blast him out of the chamber.

After jumping into the hole, Mario finds himself in a cannon aimed at the ceiling. There is a blue crystal floating in the chamber's center. Aim for the crystal—the Launch Star is stuck inside the ice.

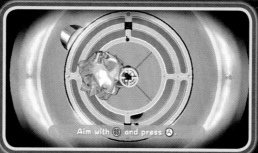

Aim with ✛ and press Ⓐ.

Mario bursts through the chamber's wall, zooming through space en route to a colorful rocket ship.

Planet E

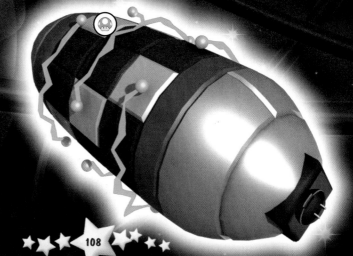

⊙×103

⊙×103

The hole at the rocket's top leads to another cannon. Jump into the cannon and aim for the Power Star, which is in the center of a cluster of spinning platforms. Mario must fire himself straight at the star. If he hits one of the platforms, he falls back to the rocket.

Mario lands near the rocket's base. There is a Bob-omb dispenser where the exhaust should be. Grab a Bob-omb and hotfoot it across the rocket's side, jumping over the rotating electrical fields. Use the Bob-omb to break the cage on the rocket's top. However, there is a 1-Up Mushroom between here and there, which is well worth the stop. Bomb the cage, grab the Mushroom, then return to the rocket's base to get another Bob-omb.

TOPMANIAC AND THE TOPMAN TRIBE

TIP

Throw the Bob-omb right between the 1-Up Mushroom and the cage at the rocket's top. The blast is big enough to shatter both cages, eliminating the need for a second dangerous trip back down the rocket.

⊙×103

BATTLEROCK GALAXY

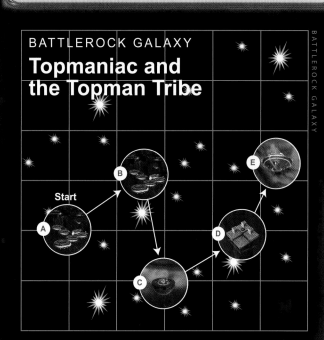

Topmaniac and the Topman Tribe

Start

A B C D E

The king of Battlerock Galaxy, Topmaniac, lords over his galaxy from a disc situated high above the asteroid. Reaching Topmaniac is no easy task—Mario must venture right through the heart of the asteroid, avoiding troublesome traps, to earn the Power Star in a man-versus-machine battle royale.

SUPER MARIO GALAXY

★★★★ 109 ★★★★

Mario begins his journey on the outer rim of Battlerock Galaxy, standing on a trio of discs. The second and third discs in the collection are dominated by two pesky Montys, molelike creatures that pop above and belowground to hassle the hero. To defeat a Monty, ground pound right next to its hole just as the baddie shows its head. The Monty is flipped upside down, its little feet wiggling in the air. Spin next to the Monty to knock it out of its hole and earn some Star Bits.

Planet C

TIP

There's a giant coin under the third disc. Pick it up to make a bunch of Star Bits appear.

Mario lands softly on the edge of the bowl-shaped planetoid. A Luma is stuck in a case at the arena's center. Mario could easily pop that cage, but it's surrounded by electrical barriers. To shut off the juice, he must spin next to the red Topman twirling about the planetoid. Knock it into the barriers to deactivate them.

Use the Pull Stars beyond the third disc to reach the next set of hovering platforms.

Backflip onto the tall cylinder to reach a Life Mushroom hidden just out of view. Remember, look for shadows to sniff out hidden items.

There is a small Sling Star on the first disc, but a giant robot is guarding it. If Mario gets too close, the robot fires a laser at him. Jump on top of the robot to stun it. While it's dazed, jump to the Sling Star and shake the Wii Remote to reach the middle disc. When Mario touches down, the disc starts moving through a short minefield. Dodge the mines while collecting coins. When the moving disc closes in on the third platform, jump to it and head for the Launch Star to blast off.

After the Topman short-circuits the cage, the grateful Luma turns into a Launch Star.

⭐⭐ Planet D ⭐⭐

The Launch Star sends Mario to a ledge on the Battlerock asteroid's side. A Monty guards some wooden crates—there must be something valuable in them. Ground pound to shake the Monty off the platform and then break open the crates. The one in the back obscures a green warp pipe. That's the entrance into the base interior. Let's get going!

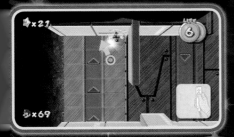

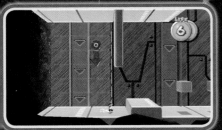

Mario drops into a side-scrolling area, but his feet are firmly stuck to the ceiling. The gravity in this hall is artificial, connected to a series of arrow-shaped switches. The arrows point in the direction gravity pulls Mario. Spin to knock the arrow around so it points down, slamming Mario to the floor.

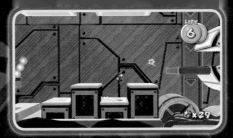

Run inside the next spindle, but wait for it to turn vertical. Now, wall-jump up the passage to grab a 1-Up Mushroom.

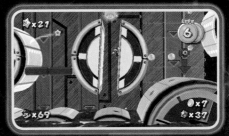

Run to the right, jumping across the platforms to reach a pair of spindles over a sea of bubbling lava.

Grab the giant coin in the first spindle's center, then pick up the resulting Star Bits.

At the hall's end, spin-attack the arrow to redirect gravity toward the ceiling. Mario "drops" to the roof.

CAUTION

As long as Mario stays against the blue wall, he sticks to the ceiling. If he touches any area of the orange wall, he's pulled back down to the floor, and possibly right into the lava.

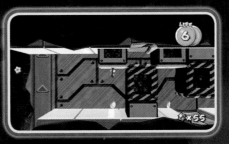

Keep following the blue walls to fall "upward" into another hallway. Jump between the crushing pillars.

Space Junk Galaxy

Battlerock Galaxy

Rolling Green Galaxy

Hurry-Scurry Galaxy

Sling Pod Galaxy

SUPER MARIO

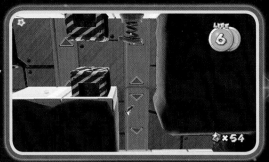

Bounce on the springy purple robot to vault to the orange wall and drop back down to the floor.

Topman into the beams. The first Topman disables the red beams. The second Topman turns off the green beams. The door then opens, reorienting gravity. Mario is pulled into the corridor. Fortunately, there's a Launch Star at the bottom that rockets him to the last planetoid, Topmaniac's throne.

A green warp pipe at the hall's end sends Mario to a round chamber. There's another purple robot in the center, emitting shock waves that Mario must jump over. Empty the Prize Block to get extra Star Bits, then jump on the robot to make it stop attacking. Now, use the robot's springy neck to bounce to a Sling Star high above the chamber's center.

Mario blasts off from the Battlerock asteroid to catch up with Topmaniac and his Topman henchmen.

Mario pops to another round room, but this one is occupied by two Topmen. The room's exit is protected by a set of electrical beams. Mario must knock each

Planet E

Bottom

Top

112

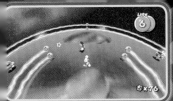

Mario lands on the bottom of Topmaniac's throne. The metallic planetoid has enough gravity to hold Mario to the underside of the floating disc. He must run to the disc's upper side, but a cabal of Topmen try to block his way. Jump over the electrical beams and avoid the Topmen.

A blue Luma is on the upper deck, selling power-ups. For 30 Star Bits, Mario can have either a Life Mushroom or a 1-Up Mushroom. The Life Mushroom grants Mario an extra three wedges of health, so buy that before jumping to the planetoid's top to challenge Topmaniac.

Boss Battle: Topmaniac

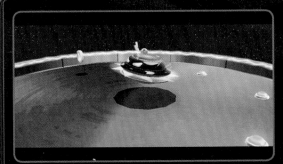

Topmaniac, ruler of the Topman tribe, spins wildly about his throne platform, cutting and ripping with his razor-sharp spikes. The boss's only weak spot is the top of his head (helpfully painted red), and jumping on it causes the spikes to temporarily retract. To bring the boss down, Mario must disable Topmaniac's spikes and knock it into the electrical field surrounding the arena three times.

Topmaniac immediately goes on the offensive when Mario reaches his arena. His spikes pop out and he starts darting around the circle. Mario must jump on Topmaniac's red head plate to disable the spikes, so jump up and use a spin to get a bit of extra height. Drop down on Topmaniac—no ground pound is necessary—to temporarily daze him. While Topmaniac is stunned, he spins in place, giving Mario a clean shot at spinning him into the electrical barrier.

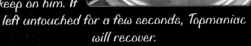

It may take a couple spins to knock Topmaniac into the barrier, but keep on him. If left untouched for a few seconds, Topmaniac will recover.

The Topmaniac arena has several lamps you can shoot with Star Bits to earn coins.

After knocking Topmaniac into the electrical barriers twice, he calls in reinforcements. Two Topmen drop into the arena and try to bounce Mario either into Topmaniac's spikes or into the electrical barrier. The two henchmen have spikes on their heads, so Mario cannot jump on them. He can only spin and deflect them into the barrier to get rid of them and clear the way for a third strike on Topmaniac.

After blasting Topmaniac into the barrier for the third time, the Topmen king falls and reveals the Power Star.

BATTLEROCK'S GARBAGE DUMP

The hidden star in the Battlerock Galaxy can be found from the "Breaking into the Battlerock" mission. Mario must track down the hungry Luma again, bringing a bounty of Star Bits to satisfy its voracious appetite. The satisfied Luma shows Mario the way to the secret Power Star.

To the Hungry Luma

Mario's quest starts the same as before—he must use Bob-ombs to blow apart cages that contain Star Bits and a Launch Star. Capturing every Star Bit on these first five discs is important, so check the underside of each disc and sweep up any stragglers with the cursor.

When Mario has over 30 Star Bits, talk to the hungry Luma. Feed the Luma and it becomes both a Launch Star and a new planetoid.

The Launch Star blasts Mario back to the molecule-shaped planetoid, still crawling with aggressive Chomps. Grab a Bob-omb from the dispenser and use it to free the Rainbow Star trapped in the nearby cage. Now invincible, Mario can bulldoze through the Chomps. This releases scores of Star Bits, so be ready to scoop them all up with the cursor while plowing through the Chomps.

Garbage Duty

Mario arrives at the new planetoid to discover it's covered with junk and scrap. The maid robot tottering around the planet isn't pleased about it either. The robot promises Mario a special treat if he helps get rid of all this garbage in under just 30 seconds. When Mario agrees, the robot activates four Bob-omb dispensers. Mario must use these bombs to clear the surface before time runs out.

Thirty seconds goes by fast, especially since the fuses on these Bob-ombs haven't been accelerated. Mario can have only four Bob-ombs in play at the same time too. Once the Bob-omb from a specific dispenser explodes, a new one appears—and not a moment sooner.

TOPMANIAC'S DAREDEVIL RUN

When the Daredevil Comet rises over the Battlerock Galaxy, Mario must return to Topmaniac's throne and teach the thug a second lesson in good manners. Mario has only one wedge of health to finish the job, though, and the Topmaniac's spikes aren't any less sharp.

Dishing It Out

To clear the garbage in time, use the lamps on the ground as a guide. Throw the Bob-ombs as close to the lamps as possible. From these spots, the blast radius will clear out multiple scrap piles. Pick up a Bob-omb and run toward the lamp so Mario can make the throw. His aim doesn't have to be absolutely precise, but the room for error isn't terribly wide either.

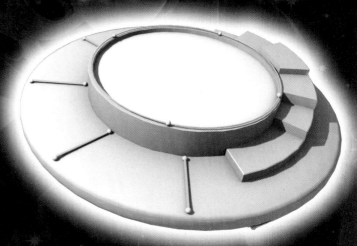

Top

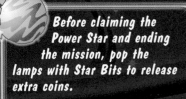

When Mario cleans up all the trash, the maid robot delivers on its promise—it hands over a Power Star.

TIP

Before claiming the Power Star and ending the mission, pop the lamps with Star Bits to release extra coins.

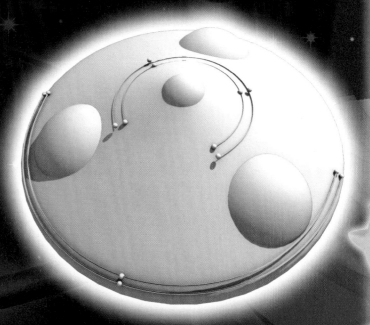

Bottom

Space Junk Galaxy

Battlerock Galaxy

Rolling Green Galaxy

Hurry-Scurry Galaxy

Sling Pod Galaxy

SUPER MARIO GALAXY

When Mario returns to the scene, he's dumped directly on the bottom of Topmaniac's planetoid—no need to push through the asteroid's center. The first challenge is to safely reach the planetoid's top, a task complicated by spinning Topmen and electrical barriers. Jump over the barriers and climb the stairs on the platform's upper half to call down Topmaniac and start the fight.

Luigi's found another Power Star in the Battlerock Galaxy—but he's been trapped in a cage and cannot return to the Comet Observatory. He sends a postcard to Mario, showing his exact location. It's time to return to the Battlerock, start the "Battlerock Barrage" mission, and rescue Luigi one last time.

When the battle begins, Topmaniac buzzes around the arena. Mario must stay in the air as much as possible to avoid the boss's spikes. Jump on the red plate to stop the spikes and stun Topmaniac. When the metal menace is dazed, push it into the electrical barriers. After two shocks, Topmaniac asks for help from his closest aides—spiky-headed Topmen.

Getting to Battlerock

Steer clear of the smaller Topman and concentrate on Topmaniac. Be careful when jumping—the spiky-headed Topmen might slide right underneath Mario's feet as he comes down.

Mario starts his rescue mission on the Battlerock Galaxy's edge, just as before. He must collect the five blue Star Chips from the discs to forge Pull Stars that yank him closer to the asteroid and its row of cannons. Pick up the giant coin to reveal a slew of Star Bits. Remember, pocketing 50 Star Bits earns Mario an extra life.

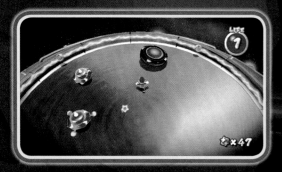

Push the Topmaniac into the barrier a third time to finish the fight and earn the Power Star.

Luigi is stuck under the first of the two discs. Not only is he in a cage, but the four pillars around him act to deflect any stray Bullet Bill attacks.

When Mario reaches the twin discs, he must use the purple robot to vault to the upper platform. The blue screw is still atop the upper disc. Spin the screw to start an attack pattern on the Battlerock. Now it's just up to Mario to dodge the cannons long enough to reach poor Luigi.

Mario must use the Bullet Bills to break the cages and free the extra coins and Star Bits. Don't forget the 1-Up Mushroom on the second disc's bottom.

⭐ Saving Luigi ⭐

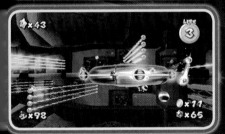

Crossing the cannon gauntlet remains a treacherous task. The cannons keep blasting away, filling the sky with explosive shells. Mario must dodge the shells, surviving the journey to the final two discs on the asteroid's exterior. Here, Mario will find Luigi—stuck in a cage like the Power Star was in the first run through this mission.

After retrieving the 1-Up Mushroom, walk back to the disc's edge and jump out to catch the ire of a Bullet Bill. Its eyes turn red with rage, and it changes course to follow Mario. Run ahead and jump across the gap between the two discs. If Mario stays too close, the Bullet Bill may dip low when following Mario's jump and crash early. Lead the Bullet Bill right to Luigi's cage and then jump over it just as the projectiles crash down.

Luigi rewards Mario with a Power Star—but not just any Power Star. This is a green Power Star. It matches the color of the transparent Launch Star on the Comet Observatory. Return to the Comet Observatory and check out the site.

Space Junk Galaxy

Battlerock Galaxy

Rolling Green Galaxy

Hurry-Scurry Galaxy

Sling Pod Galaxy

SUPER MARIO GALAXY

ROLLING GREEN GALAXY

The Rolling Green Galaxy is like a golf course hanging in the middle of the cosmos, eternally blessed with sunny weather and light winds. The planetary system is a collection of grassy platforms, shaped and smoothed with different contours. Rolling the Power Star, encased in a plastic sphere, through the course proves a fun challenge for Mario.

★ Roll through the Clouds ★

Roll the sphere around the hole at the platform's end to pick up several coins. When Mario drops through the hole, the sphere rolls down a long, winding track.

At the galaxy's start, Mario must jump on a sphere that holds the Power Star. He has no means of freeing the sphere, so he must roll it across the course until reaching the mechanism that can crack this shell. To start the course, roll forward to the small plateau and jump on it. Roll the ball to the ring.

> **NOTE**
> To control the sphere, hold the Wii Remote perpendicular to the floor. Tilting the Wii Remote from this position rolls the sphere. The farther you push the Wii Remote in any given direction, the faster the sphere rolls. To slow down, pull the remote back in the opposite direction. To jump, press Ⓐ.

Mario drops to a long fairway scattered with Goombas, coins, and Star Bits. The course is fairly flat at first, but as he rolls forward and starts weaving around the holes in the platform, the ground begins to dip and tilt. Picking up the giant coins on the course creates strings of Star Bits. Follow the trails to pick up enough Star Bits to earn an extra life.

The sphere is vaulted to a stretch of grass patrolled by several Goombas. The Goombas are no match for the sphere's weight. Mario just needs to roll over the Goombas to flatten them and earn a coin. The only catch is that rolling over a Goomba causes the ball to do a little hop, which is dangerous near the platform's edge. If Mario's going too fast, squishing a Goomba can launch him over the edge.

Carefully roll along the course's edge to pick up coins. It takes 50 coins to earn an extra life, but if Mario keeps rolling off the edge while trying for the coins, he'll leave the mission with fewer chances than when he started.

Use the Star Bits trail as a guide for rolling across the course.

CAUTION

Collecting the coins on the hills requires Mario to build up some speed, but if he doesn't slow down at the hill's top, he risks rolling right down the other side—and straight off the course.

Hop across the gap in the course to get a 1-Up Mushroom. Slow down as the sphere reaches the small platform, then gingerly squash the Goombas. When the coast is clear, jump to the stone pedestal to grab the power-up.

Pick up the giant coin on the left path to find even more Star Bits. Just watch where Mario rolls!

The sphere is finally launched to the last platform. Roll it into the blue-ringed hole right in front of the flag. The sphere gets stuck in the hole, but the mechanism cracks it open and releases the Power Star within. Mario must climb the flagpole to reach the star. At the pole's top, hit Ⓐ to jump straight up and snag the Power Star.

A curving stone bridge leads to the course's back half. There are even more Goombas back here, and the coins are now on small hills. Two paths lead to a hole at the course's rear (the hole is a launcher that pops the sphere up to the final platform). The left path is incredibly curvy and requires a delicate touch. The right path just has a little gap in it. It's less dangerous but also offers less reward, as the left path has a giant coin that offers extra Star Bits.

HURRY-SCURRY GALAXY

The Hurry-Scurry Galaxy is no place to dillydally. The galaxy earns its name from the collapsing platforms that comprise its planetoids. The instant pressure is applied to the platform, it begins to shrink until nothing is left but thin air—and a direct line between the unlucky traveler and a ravenous black hole.

Space Junk Galaxy

Battlerock Galaxy

Rolling Green Galaxy

Hurry-Scurry Galaxy

Sling Pod Galaxy

PRIMA Official Game Guide

Shrinking Satellite

Shrinking Satellite brings Mario to the Hurry-Scurry Galaxy for a Power Star hidden at the center of a cluster of shrinking platforms. Mario must retrieve a host of musical notes to close the black hole, revealing the Power Star's location before gravity pulls him to an unfortunate end.

To reach the Power Star, Mario must negotiate an avenue of shrinking platforms. As soon as he touches a platform, it starts to collapse on itself until nothing is left. Keep moving across the path of platforms to reach a Launch Star that bounces Mario to the orbiting cluster of shrinking platforms.

Watch your step, Mario—keep moving before the entire platform vanishes under your feet.

There's no time to mess with the Goomba. Let it charge Mario, then jump over it. The Goomba plummets off the path while Mario survives.

Path to the Power Star

LEGEND

🍄 1-Up Mushroom

There's a 1-Up Mushroom on the path, but it rests on a shrinking platform. To get the Mushroom, jump over a couple platforms so they do not collapse. When Mario lands on the Mushroom, the floor beneath it starts to vanish, but Mario can walk back across the still-stable platforms to reach a solid ledge containing some Toads.

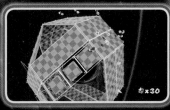

Space Junk
Galaxy

Battlerock
Galaxy

Rolling Green
Galaxy

Hurry-Scurry
Galaxy

Sling Pod
Galaxy

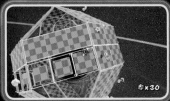

The second Mario touches down, he must start moving. The floor beneath him is disappearing, and he must collect every musical note before all the platforms vanish. Follow the trail of musical notes around the planetoid, taking care not to step on any platforms that don't support a musical note. Leave as many steps in place as possible, just in case Mario needs a safe place to jump to.

The Launch Star is to the Toads' left, directly under a shrinking platform. Jump up to punch the Prize Block as many times as possible to earn coins before the floor completely vanishes. When Mario drops into the Launch Star, shake the Wii Remote so he rockets off to the second planetoid.

The musical notes are not in a straight line. Mario must run around the entire planetoid, changing directions and jumping over gaps left in the surface from previous musical notes. Always keep moving—standing still is the worst possible thing to do in this mission.

After collecting the last musical note, the black hole at the planetoid's heart transforms into a Power Star. Stand in the center, or "side," of the planetoid and let gravity do the rest. Mario falls through the planetoid's disappearing surface, but he drops straight to the Power Star.

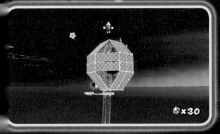

As Mario soars, he can see the musical notes appearing on the planetoid made entirely of shrinking steps.

BOWSER'S STAR REACTOR

At the edge of the Fountain Galaxies, Mario finally catches up to Bowser. The Koopa King is perturbed that the hero survived battles against fierce foes such as Kamella and Tarantox but understands that if you want something done right, you have to do it yourself. The tyrant takes a moment away from his plotting—why does Bowser need a Star Reactor, anyway?—to stop Mario's meddling before he can recover any more Power Stars.

The Fiery Stronghold

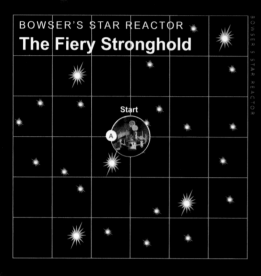

The Fiery Stronghold is a strange castle in the cosmos that leads across deep space to the king's secret Star Reactor. Mario must survive the palace's tricks and traps to finally reach Bowser and challenge him to a duel on the spherical Star Reactor, a powerful machine fueled by a Grand Star's energy. If Mario can push Bowser out of the galaxy, he can take the Grand Star back to the Comet Observatory.

Mario touches down at the beginning of a colorful road that loops through the heavens. The road has enough gravity to hold him while he walks upside down, collecting coins from the winding highway while avoiding fire traps. Mario can just jump over the fire traps—he doesn't risk escaping gravity and floating away.

Outer Defenses

When Mario reaches the castle's exterior, a Thwomp tries to smash him. Wait for the stream of flames from the nearby cannon to cease before ducking under the Thwomp.

platform back toward the magenta wall and jump up to be yanked to the ceiling—er, floor. Avoid the fire trap and Thwomp, then jump on the yellow platform to move away from this crazy wall.

Palace Problems

Space Junk
Galaxy

Battlerock
Galaxy

Rolling Green
Galaxy

Hurry-Scurry
Galaxy

Sling Pod
Galaxy

The palace's exterior walls are bathed in blue and magenta. This isn't just a paint job; it's a clue about the direction of gravity. Blue pulls Mario straight down while magenta pushes him up. With a black hole sucking in all free matter just below the wall, Mario must use the gravity fields to keep both feet on firm ground. Walk to the right until he reaches three coins. Jump straight up to grab the coins and be pulled up into the magenta wall's reverse gravity.

LEGEND

![1-Up Mushroom]	**1-Up Mushroom**
![Life Mushroom]	**Life Mushroom**

The yellow platform drops Mario off on a stone wheel. A fire trap rotates in the wheel's center. The wheel has enough gravity to hold Mario, so step off the platform and immediately jump over the first row of fireballs. Grab the 1-Up Mushroom and then walk straight up to the red carpet.

After jumping over the fire trap, Mario must head right until he's standing directly over a sliding red platform. The platform is in the blue area, so as soon as Mario leaves the magenta wall, he's pulled downward. If the platform slides away while Mario is in the air, he'll drop straight into the black hole. Ride the

Follow the red carpet as the path winds around a tall tower. There are several cannons that spray fire across the path, so be ready to move as soon as Mario ducks beneath the Thwomp at the wheel's top.

PRIMA Official Game Guide

This fire trap is tricky. Stand beneath it and duck, waiting for the moment all six arms are pointed away from the next step. Jump up and hurry away before the arms swing back and singe Mario.

When Bowser spots Mario advancing, he roars into action. The Koopa King starts spitting fireballs at Mario while he runs along the checkered path that leads straight to the tower's top.

The Koopa King is tired of Mario always interfering in his plans. He hopes to finally set him adrift in the cosmos, sending him far into the coldest reaches of space. Surely the great hero of the Mushroom Kingdom has the strength and cunning to stop Bowser's plans and avoid disaster?

No time to stand around—those fireballs are destroying the stairs. If Mario doesn't hurry, he'll fall into deep space.

Bowser pulls Mario up to the Star Reactor's core, a sphere that hovers in space. Beneath the glassy surface, the energy of the Grand Star pulses. That energy is Mario's chance for victory, if he can somehow turn it against Bowser. There are more pressing matters right now, though—namely, Bowser's stomping is sending shock waves around the sphere. Mario can either jump over the shock waves or stand on one of the green metal platforms to avoid the attacks.

There's a Life Mushroom encased in ice at the corner of the steps. Quickly spin to shatter the ice and grab the necessary power-up before charging up the remaining steps.

Bowser doesn't stop spitting fireballs until the moment Mario's at his doorstep.

Boss Battle: Bowser (cont.)

After the shock waves fail to shake Mario off the reactor, Bowser leaps high in the air.

He's about to come crashing down on Mario—now's the hero's chance. Use Bowser's shadow as a guide. His darkened outline on the surface reveals where he is about to land, so steer the tyrant to one of the blue plugs holding back the star energy.

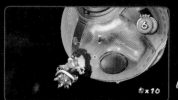

Bowser crashes through the surface, burning himself on the pure star energy. The Koopa King tucks tail and runs, leaving a trail of smoke in his wake.

Knowing he is vulnerable, Bowser runs away from Mario until he recovers from his injury.

Bowser is faster than Mario, so the hero cannot catch him. Instead, he must turn the tables and confront Bowser directly. When Bowser changes direction, Mario has just a few seconds to rush in and hit Bowser's tail with a spin attack.

The attack flips Bowser on his back, where he is completely helpless. He slides around the

reactor's surface, spinning out of control. Mario must intercept Bowser and hit him with a spin attack to launch him off the reactor. Mario must hit Bowser like this three times to win the fight.

When Bowser pulls himself together, he breathes fireballs across the planetoid, and he stomps several shock waves in hopes of knocking Mario off his feet.

TIP

Coins on the reactor will refill Mario's health. He must trick Bowser into crashing down on one of the green platforms to release a coin. Of course, now Mario can no longer use that green platform to avoid shock waves.

After the second successful attack on Bowser, the brute starts to get wise to Mario's trickery.

When his tail is on fire, Bowser manages to make faster turns while retreating and can run farther than before. Watch his position through the reactor's glassy surface. Again, hit Bowser when he changes direction. Bowser will turn to flee, but he's so tired he must stop almost immediately, giving Mario a clean shot at his tail.

(continued on next page)

Space Junk Galaxy

Battlerock Galaxy

Rolling Green Galaxy

Hurry-Scurry Galaxy

Sling Pod Galaxy

PRIMA Official Game Guide

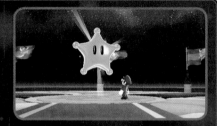

One last strike to Bowser while he's cooling his heels sends the tyrant crashing back to the tower.

Bowser crumples to the ground in front of Mario. He's down, but far from out. Bowser pulls himself up and retreats even farther out into the darkness of space.

Bowser abandons the Star Reactor, though, leaving Mario the Grand Star. This star energizes the Comet Observatory enough to open the Kitchen Dome. Mario flies back to Rosalina's starship, ready to continue his adventures across the heavens.

SLING POD GALAXY

If Mario feeds 400 Star Bits to the hungry Luma outside the Fountain Dome, it transforms into the Sling Pod Galaxy. This galaxy is a collection of the white pods first seen in Space Junk as Mario approached Tarantox's lair.

A Very Sticky Situation

Pitching Mario

BOWSER'S STAR REACTOR

A very sticky situation

Start

A

The Sling Pod Galaxy is a deep-space obstacle course that Mario must navigate, using the sticky Sling Pods to bounce between whirling obstacles and across dangerous empty expanses. If Mario can safely jump from pod to pod, he'll line up a perfect shot with the Power Star that lingers on this small galaxy's edge.

Mario touches down right in front of a white Sling Pod, ready to start this galactic game of catch.

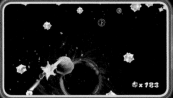

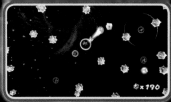

The Sling Pods soon give way to Pull Stars. Fling Mario into a minefield loaded with Pull Stars and grab hold of the closest star. Hold Mario in place to stabilize him and then carefully move from Pull Star to Pull Star in the minefield. If Mario even grazes a mine, it explodes and pushes him free of the Pull Stars.

Between each Sling Pod are at least two or three obstacles that Mario must avoid. Avoid the cannonballs streaking across the cosmos—wait until the moment before the coast is clear to pull back and release Mario, firing him to the next Sling Pod. Rotating metal plates serve to deflect Mario from reaching the next Sling Pod, so wait until the time is right and whip the hero through the gap.

Use inertia to let Mario drift past the Pull Star next to the 1-Up Mushroom. As soon as he grabs the power-up, immediately latch on to a Pull Star lest the hero simply float away.

Mario soon reaches two Sling Pods divided by at least six cannons. There is no timer on this stage, so watch the cannon patterns. Just as the cannon volley is about to stop, release Mario so he soars between the cannons as the bursts die down.

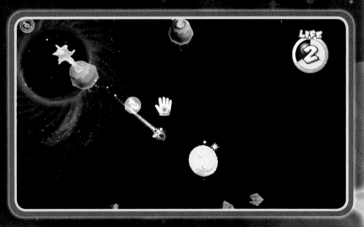

A giant coin fills the skies with Star Bits. Sling Mario to the coin and then catch him with a Pull Star just as he grabs it.

Space Junk Galaxy

Battlerock Galaxy

Rolling Green Galaxy

Hurry-Scurry Galaxy

Sling Pod Galaxy

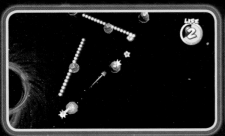

After exiting the minefield, Mario returns to a path of Sling Pods. Fire traps rotate between the Sling Pods, so wait until the incendiary lines are parallel with the lines between the Sling Pods before flinging Mario to the next one. A 1-up Mushroom lingers close to the edge of the fire traps.

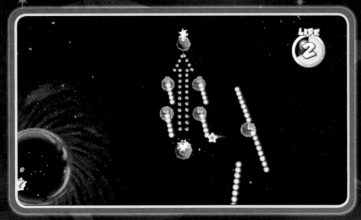

Follow the arrow, slinging Mario to a pod just beyond four small fire traps. From this Sling Pod, Mario has a straight shot at the Power star. Six metal plates circle around the stars going in different directions. Watch the patterns and time Mario's launch for the second before a clearing occurs. He sails right through as the plates are perfectly out of alignment, grabbing the Power Star and ending the mission.

Throwing Mario to the Mushroom sends him to a tough position, stuck trying to thread the needle between two fire traps spinning in opposite directions. Wait until the fiery lines are about to pass each other, then rocket Mario to the Sling Pod just next to the cosmic arrow formed out of carefully placed Star Bits.

TIP

Take your time in this mission. Just watch the patterns of the traps so you can perfectly time your throws with the Sling Pods.

KITCHEN GALAXIES

BEACH BOWL GALAXY

The Beach Bowl Galaxy is home of the penguins. These birds are just beginning swimmers, under the tutelage of the coach emperor penguin. Maybe Mario, too, can learn a thing or two about swimming in the sea from the coach.

Sunken Treasure

The coach is having trouble with his students—there's something sparkling underwater that is distracting the whole class. Would Mario mind getting his feet wet and cleaning up whatever is disrupting today's swim lessons?

BEACH BOWL GALAXY

Sunken Treasure

Start

A

Swimming for Stars

LEGEND

 1-Up Mushroom

▲ Star Chips

PRIMA Official Game Guide

SUPER MARIO GALAXY

Beach Bowl Galaxy

Ghostly Galaxy

Bubble Blast Galaxy

Buoy Base Galaxy

Bowser Jr.'s Airship Armada

Drip Drop Galaxy

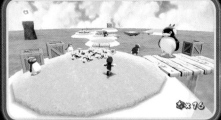

Shake the Wii Remote while looking at the wooden chest. Mario darts forward, shattering the crate and collecting the Star Chip hidden inside.

The Beach Bowl Galaxy is a peaceful place when Mario touches down on the sandy beaches full of sunbathing penguins. The little birds should be practicing their swim lessons, but the emperor penguin confides in Mario that some sparkling treasures underwater are distracting his pupils. If Mario could get rid of the distractions, the emperor penguin will be most pleased.

The goal of this mission is to assemble five Star Chips to create the Launch Star that vaults Mario close to the Power Star, but first make a detour. Swim away from the emperor penguin to the shallow ledge on the planet's opposite side. There is a trapeze above the ledge. If Mario jumps off the trapeze at the height of its arc over the water, he drops right down to a 1-Up Mushroom.

Watch out for the spiky fish rolling around the seafloor next to the nearby Star Chip. Swim around the fish to avoid damage and grab the Star Chip, which is also inside an air bubble.

> **TIP**
> If Mario keeps exploring dry land, he discovers coins tucked in the fronds of the palm trees. Walk up the trees' bowing trunks to grab the spare change.

The five Star Chips are underwater, so Mario must dive into the drink and start his search. He cannot breathe underwater, so watch his oxygen levels. When the meter above his head turns red, Mario must surface as soon as possible. If he fails to surface by the time the meter runs dry, he starts losing health. Within seconds, Mario must restart the mission.

There are bubbles in the water, though, that refill his air supply. Some bubbles gurgle up from little spouts. Most of the coins underwater are inside air bubbles, too, so if Mario picks up a coin, he also fills his lungs with oxygen.

A playful penguin points the way to a Star Chip. It's on a rock, next to the tall stone pillars.

That clam against the outer seawall snaps its shell open and shut, taunting the little penguins with its prize. Mario must swim over to the clam and wait for it to open up. When it does, swim forward and pick up the Star Chip.

Musical Interlude

The last Star Chip is located next to a dark cave in the corner, where the beach meets the seawall. As Mario closes in on the Star Chip, a Gringill pops out of the cave. Watch out for the toothsome monster.

After landing on the upper plateau, Mario spots a giant coin. Grabbing the coin starts a trail of musical notes that snake around the plateau, bringing Mario dangerously close to enemies like a Wiggler and Piranha Plant. Mario must dodge these baddies and keep chasing the notes. If they disappear, he misses the treasure revealed after grabbing the final note: a 1-Up Mushroom.

TIP

Before using the Launch Star to blast out of the ocean, collect the remainder of the coins to replenish any lost health.

But how is Mario to get that mushroom? It's too high and the water pool below it prevents him from executing a triple jump. There is a blue switch on the ledge just above the pool. If Mario pounds the switch, a walkway appears beneath the 1-Up Mushroom—but only for a few seconds. Mario must jump up and scurry across the walkway to grab the mushroom prize and reach the upper level.

After grabbing the 1-Up Mushroom, zero in on the next blue switch. Ground pound the switch to create another temporary structure: two wooden walls. These appear for an even shorter length of time than the walkway, so Mario must quickly wall jump to the ice crystal at the plateau's top.

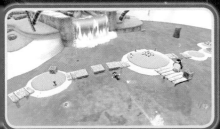

The Launch Star appears in the middle of the ocean floor. Swim to it and shake the Wii Remote to rocket out of the sea and zoom to a dry plateau high above the water. The Power Star is on a ledge up here, but the ledge is too high for even Mario's expert jumping skills. How will the hero ascend the ledge and grab the treasure?

The Power Star is stuck in the ice. Spin a few times to shatter the crystal and recover it.

Beach Bowl Galaxy

Ghostly Galaxy

Bubble Blast Galaxy

Buoy Base Galaxy

Bowser Jr.'s Airship Armada

Drip Drop Galaxy

SUPER MARIO GALAXY

PRIMA Official Game Guide

BEACH BOWL GALAXY
Passing the Swim Test

Start

Now that Mario has collected the shiny Star Chips that were distracting the penguin pupils, the emperor can now effectively teach his swimming lessons. In fact, Mario can even go in on the schooling, diving down to paddle with the penguins and seek out a golden win.

Before Test Time

The final test of swim school is to bring a golden shell to the emperor penguin. To start the lesson, Mario must cross to the emperor penguin and talk to him. He can dive into the ocean and follow the penguin packs, but he will not see a golden shell.

However, before class begins, look around the island for extra treasure, such as coins. Jump up the grassy hillside to reach a pool at the top of a waterfall. From this vantage point, Mario can see all the coins on the palm trees. Carefully walk up the bended trunk of the palm tree that extends over the water. Grab the coins from here and then jump out to the other palms for even more booty.

Look in the pool at the waterfall's top—there's a warp pipe under the rippling water. The pipe leads to a secret room with a wall covered with breakable bricks and a giant coin at the top. The giant coin turns all the bricks into Star Bits, but since gravity keeps Mario's feet on the room's floor, how can he reach that coin?

Break bricks by spinning next to them, essentially carving stairs out of them. The fewer bricks Mario shatters the better, since he wants to maximize the number of Star Bits collected.

At the wall's top, jump over the lone Goomba and make a dash for the giant coin. As soon as Mario touches the coin, the bricks turn into Star Bits, and he falls to the ground as the Star Bits quickly twinkle out of existence. Be quick with the cursor to scoop up as many Star Bits as possible before they vanish.

⭐ Shell Stealing

Before heading up to the emperor penguin, play with the shell and pick up the coins in the water. Mario can halt the shell by pressing ②. The brake light turns on, and he can point the shell in the direction he wants to travel before releasing ②. A beam of light is emitted from the shell's front that indicates which way the shell will go when you release the brakes.

After Mario talks to the emperor penguin and starts the lesson, he must dive into the water. A group of penguins is swimming laps around the bottom of the sea. The lead penguin pulls ahead by holding on to a golden shell, which acts as a makeshift engine (the shell even has brake lights).

Take the golden shell to the emperor penguin on the island. The coach is pleased with Mario's performance and awards him a Power Star.

To complete the test, Mario must lift the golden shell from the lead penguin. Since he cannot swim as fast as the penguins, he must cut the group off. Their traffic pattern is predictable—they keep swimming around the seafloor in a circle. Cut across and swim right up to the leader. Shake the Wii Remote to grab the shell.

THE SECRET UNDERSEA CAVERN

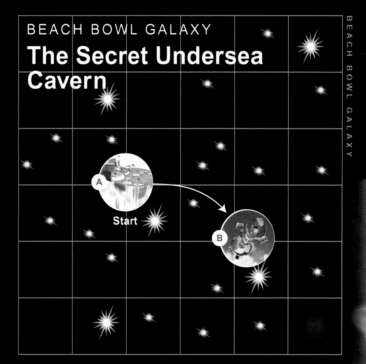

BEACH BOWL GALAXY
The Secret Undersea Cavern

Start

Snagged! Now Mario can use the shell to motor around the ocean.

Mario toured both land and sea during his first two excursions to the Beach Bowl Galaxy, and now he must explore a secret cavern that leads to an offshore planetoid.

Beach Bowl Galaxy

Ghostly Galaxy

Bubble Blast Galaxy

Buoy Base Galaxy

Bowser Jr.'s Airship Armada

Drip Drop Galaxy

BEACH BOWL GALAXY

PRIMA Official Game Guide

LEGEND

🍄 1-Up Mushroom

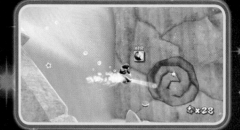

The shells regenerate after Mario throws them into treasure chests, so simply swim back to a previous spot and pick up an extra. Steer the shell toward the large circle in the rock wall. There's a penguin in front of it, checking it out. Just as Mario closes in on the wall, shake the Wii Remote to throw the shell.

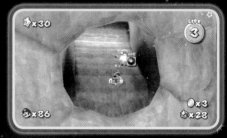

The shell shatters the stone circle, revealing the secret cavern. The penguin encourages Mario to explore what lies on the other side.

After collecting coins and Star Bits on dry land, Mario must dip into the ocean and find a green shell. There are multiple shells on the ocean floor; just swim into one to pick it up. Now, Mario can speed around the sea in style.

The waterlogged tunnel leads Mario to a hidden passage beneath the sandy beaches. There are several crates in the room that are full of goodies like Star Bits and coins, but watch out for bats. They flit around the ceiling, diving toward Mario when he gets too close. Shoot the bats with Star Bits to stun

To open the treasure chests on the ocean floor, throw a shell at them. Some of the chests just contain air bubbles…

…but the treasure chest directly in front of the secret cavern's entrance contains a 1-Up Mushroom.

them, then walk up and kick them into the wall to earn more Star Bits. After clearing out the bats, smash the wooden crate against the fence in the cave's rear. This reveals a small opening Mario can slip through.

There's a wooden plug in the cave floor just beyond the fence. Ground pound the plug to reveal a hidden Sling Star, but look out for a pair of bats.

Cyclone Stone

LEGEND

 1-Up Mushroom

⭐ Power Star

The Launch Star rockets Mario to the Cyclone Stone, a spinning aerial platform high above the penguin-filled beaches. It is covered with Thwomps. Mario must rush across the Cyclone Stone, negotiating its winding pathways while avoiding the crushing stones that rumble across the surface.

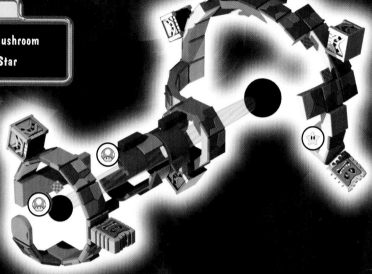

Beach Bowl Galaxy

Ghostly Galaxy

Bubble Blast Galaxy

Buoy Base Galaxy

Bowser Jr.'s Airship Armada

Drip Drop Galaxy

The main threat on the Cyclone Stone is the rolling rocks. These stones are hollow but are still heavy enough to squish Mario if he's caught underneath them. To survive these cube-shaped monsters and cross the Cyclone Stone, watch their movement patterns and head for the square on the path that matches the lone missing side of the cube. Mario can stand inside the monster safely as it slams its empty side down on the path. As soon as the stone moves on, he must run away because that monster always rolls back across the path.

When Mario lands, he immediately sees a 1-Up Mushroom on a platform that is too far away for a regular jump; however, a long jump vaults him right to it. Mario gets an extra life out of this, and after hopping across the shrinking step, he bypasses the first Thwomp entirely.

Jump to the rotating platforms in the Cyclone Stone's center. Carefully jump across each platform to reach the planetoid's other half.

PRIMA Official Game Guide

Hop on the sliding stones on the planetoid's center to pick up an extra 1-Up Mushroom.

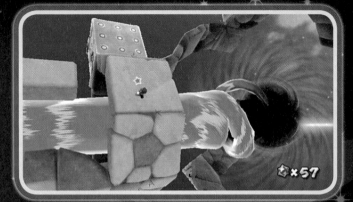

The winding path on the other side of the rotating platforms leads to the Power Star. There are several rolling rock monsters on this path, though, so watch for spaces where Mario can safely stand as the brute harmlessly rolls over him.

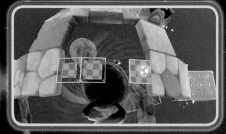

Use the shrinking platforms as shortcuts, avoiding the monsters as they roll and stomp across the regular path. Long jump across the gaps between the shrinking platforms. If Mario misses a jump, he falls straight into a black hole. If he's about to miss a jump, shake the Wii Remote to spin and try to salvage the jump.

The Power Star is inside an ice crystal at the Cyclone Stone's end. Smash the crystal to recover the Power Star.

WALL JUMPING UP WATERFALLS

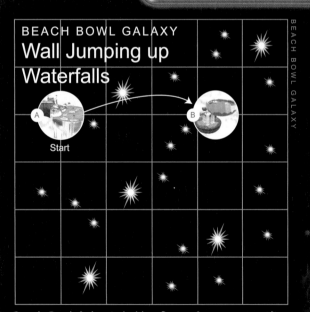

BEACH BOWL GALAXY
Wall Jumping up Waterfalls

A — Start → B

BEACH BOWL GALAXY

The Beach Bowl Galaxy's hidden Power Star requires Mario to slip into a new set of threads: the Ice Suit. Ice Mario's chilly feet create icy lily pads on contact with water, allowing him to run across lakes and pools to reach new areas. Ice Mario can even freeze a waterfall, turning two cascading chutes into a wall jumping opportunity. How cool is that?

Treasure Chest

The hidden Power Star is available from the "Passing the Swim Test" mission, so go see the emperor penguin and enroll in swim school. Now, slip beneath the waves and chase down the swimming penguins, cutting across the path of the leader to steal the golden shell.

Kitchen

Beach Bowl
Galaxy

Ghostly Galaxy

Bubble Blast
Galaxy

Buoy Base
Galaxy

Bowser Jr.'s
Airship
Armada

Drip Drop
Galaxy

Swimming Upstream

Swim back to the surface. Climb out of the water and head for the big beach. Cross the island to the right, seeking out a treasure chest near the planet's edge.

The Launch Star leads to a planetoid high above the beach, in the same orbit as the Cyclone Stone. The planetoid is dominated by a lake and several waterfalls. There's no apparent way to reach the ledges in the sky above the falls, but the giant coin in the sky offers a hint. How can Mario reach that coin?

TIP

Mario can fling the golden shell at the Gringill in the caves on the seafloor. The top Gringill releases Star Bits when popped with the shell, but the lower (and larger) eel leaves behind a 1-Up Mushroom when hit with the shell. After using the shell on the eels, Mario just needs to find the school of penguins again and re-steal the golden shell from the leader.

There's a Cataquack bumbling on the planetoid's other side. Cataquack's love to flow people around, so walk over to the friendly fella and get its attention. Lead the Cataquack back across the wooden bridges in the water. Stand under the shadow of the giant coin and wait for the Cataquack to catch up. When it reaches Mario, it bounces him high into the air with its bill.

The giant coin releases an Ice Flower. When Mario plucks the Ice Flower, he becomes Ice Mario. Now he can walk on water.

Throw the golden shell at the treasure chest on the beach to reveal a secret Launch Star.

Run across the lake's surface to the waterfalls. Wall jump back and forth between the two falls. When Mario touches one of the falls, he creates a frozen surface he can push away from. The falls are high and the Ice Flower's effects are not permanent, so wall jump as fast as possible.

There is another Ice Flower at the bowl's edge. Grab the Ice Flower to become Ice Mario again and start walking across the lake. Another Cataquack follows Mario on his trail of frozen lily pads. Guide the Cataquack to the small islands in the lake. There are shadows in the center of each island, revealing coins high in the air. When the Cataquack reaches Mario, it blasts him straight up to get the coins.

At the top of the falls, use the small Sling Star to bounce up to the next ledge. The camera pulls way back to show the icy bowl at the planetoid's top. The Power Star is up there! Still using Ice Mario's powers, jump to the next falls and wall jump into another Sling Star. Now Mario can jump straight up and spin to reach the final Sling Star. This shoots him to the frozen bowl with the Power Star.

Coax the Cataquack to the third little island. Let it rocket Mario right into the Power Star.

FAST FOES ON THE CYCLONE STONE

BEACH BOWL GALAXY
Fast Foes on the Cyclone Stone

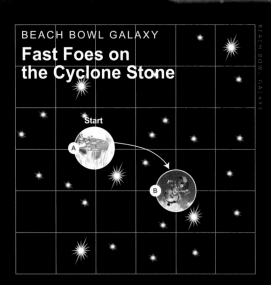

Start

A

B

BEACH BOW GALAXY

The Fast Foe Comet signals a return to the Cyclone Stone. Mario must again cross the winding path on the planetoid, but now the Thwomps slam down at double-speed. Avoiding the rolling rocks and crossing the rotating platforms was tough before—but the comet's influence makes this mission even more manic.

Cyclone Stone

LEGEND

1-Up Mushroom

Power Star

Chances are, Mario will stumble at least once on this course, so start the mission by jumping to the 1-Up Mushroom. After hopping back to the main path, start ducking and diving around the Thwomps and duck into the empty sides of the rolling cubes.

As before, jump out to the rotating platforms in the planetoid's center. Be mindful of the extra speed of the rocks on each side of the central platforms. Grab the 1-Up Mushroom on the sliding platforms and then cross to the Cyclone Stone's back half to run for the Power Star.

The Fast Foe Comet also affects the platforms—they move faster, too!

Use the shrinking platforms to bypass the rolling rocks.

Mario can safely stand under the "teeth side" of the cubes, but these monsters roll back across their routes twice as fast, so keep moving the instant the coast is clear.

Duck under the last Thwomp when it rises into the air, and smash the ice crystal to free the Power Star.

Beach Bowl Galaxy

Ghostly Galaxy

Bubble Blast Galaxy

Buoy Base Galaxy

Bowser Jr.'s Airship Armada

Drip Drop Galaxy

PRIMA Official Game Guide

GHOSTLY GALAXY

Deep in the darkest recesses of space lurks a galaxy haunted by restless spirits, but the pursuit of Power Stars trumps any fear of things that go bump in the night.

LUIGI AND THE HAUNTED MANSION

GHOSTLY GALAXY

Luigi and the Haunted Mansion

Luigi and his haunted mansions—Mario's brother just cannot get enough of them. However, without his Poltergust 3000, Luigi gets stuck in the depths of the haunted house and requires Mario's assistance. If Mario can spring his brother, Luigi will dedicate himself to helping Mario locate the Power Stars.

Three Goombas patrol the planetoid, but in keeping with the galaxy's theme, they wear jack-o'-lanterns on their heads. Mario cannot stun these Goombas with Star Bits—the pumpkins deflect any damage. To get rid of the little terrors, Mario must either spin into them, perform a ground pound on them, or pick up the hidden Rainbow Star inside the rock to the right. Spin to shatter the rock and pick up the Rainbow Star. Now Mario can run right through the Goombas, blasting apart their Halloween helmets.

While invincible, run through the arch and down the twisting path that leads to the haunted mansion. A Chomp rolls through the front door to greet Mario, but the Rainbow Star's power shatters it into a shower of Star Bits.

Planets A and B

Mario starts his initial approach on the Ghostly Galaxy from the Sling Star on the Toads' spaceship. The Launch Star launches Mario across space, dropping him down on a spooky platform in orbit of a giant, floating haunted mansion. Mario must find a way inside that mansion to rescue Luigi, but first—Goombas!

With the Chomp out of the way, pick up the coins on the bridge and enter the mansion's foyer.

As Mario climbs the stairs, a Boo pops out of the painting on the wall. Mario must turn around and lead the Boo into the pool of light on the ground floor. When the Boo is caught in the light, it vanishes, leaving behind the key to the upstairs door.

The house is indeed haunted—by Boos! When Mario's back in turned, the ghosts creep up on him. When he turns to face a Boo, it stops and disappears. To dispel the Boos, cast a little light on them. Spin to activate the blue switch near the front door. The swinging chandelier casts a pool of bright light on the floor. Lead the Boo into the light to make it permanently disappear.

Before leaving, pop the Prize Block on the landing to earn Star Bits.

The next room is under the spell of some wacky gravity. Ramps along the floor allow Mario to run up the walls, escaping the toddling Goombas wearing pumpkin helmets. To escape this chamber, Mario must collect five Star Chips. They float around the room, so Mario must cross all four walls to chase them down. Watch out for the windows—there's a black hole in each one.

Smash the wooden crates in the foyer's corner to pick up some extras coins.

There's a weak spot on this chamber's ceiling. Ground pound the spot to break through the ceiling and discover a secret room.

Beach Bowl Galaxy

Ghostly Galaxy

Bubble Blast Galaxy

Buoy Base Galaxy

Bowser Jr.'s Airship Armada

Drip Drop Galaxy

SUPER MARIO GALAXY

PRIMA Official Game Guide

What self-respecting haunted mansion wouldn't have a secret room? This tall library is equipped with a series of small Sling Stars that bounce Mario around the room—hit the switch on the wall to discover why. Coins appear in long columns between the Sling Stars. Mario has only about 10 seconds to rocket between the Launch Stars and pick up the coins before they vanish permanently. It's time to head back through the hole in the ceiling and keep collecting Star Chips to finish constructing the Sling Star to get out of this room.

The door reveals a narrow hallway containing two Boos. Each Boo has swallowed a coin, which is visible when Mario faces them and they disappear. While the Boos have stopped moving, jump over them. Turn away from the Boos so they float toward Mario. Lead the Boos into the pool of light at the hall's end.

The Launch Star appears over the black hole in one of the windows.

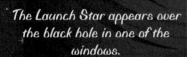

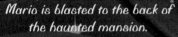

Mario is blasted to the back of the haunted mansion.

Inside the new room, Mario spots a giant coin. When he picks it up, a Boo Mushroom appears in a tiny alcove in the corner. This special power-up transforms Mario into Boo Mario. Now he can float through the air, temporarily disappear, and pass through solid walls, just like a Boo.

Luigi is behind bars, trapped in a tiny room inside the mansion. Mario must find a way inside to save his brother.

Use the three Pull Stars to cross the gap in the walkway to Luigi's right. Pull Mario to the middle Pull Star and then let him fall. Just as he grabs the key below the Pull Star, grab the Pull Star again so he doesn't fall on a bed of spikes. The key opens the door to the right.

It's Boo Mario!

Float to the room's top by repeatedly pressing Ⓐ and retrieve another giant coin. This frees the 1-Up Mushroom in the nearby portrait. Now Boo Mario can pick it up for an extra life.

To make Boo Mario disappear, give the Wii Remote a little shake. When he turns transparent, he can slip through the grating to the small library in the room's back corner. There is a spring next to a tall bookshelf, but without a solid physical form, Boo Mario cannot take advantage of it. Glide into the pool of light to dispel the Boo Mushroom's effects.

Use the spring to vault over the bookshelf and join Luigi. Mario's brother is sure glad to see him. Luigi shows Mario the Power Star he found while exploring the mansion. Together, with the Power Star, the two brothers escape the galaxy and return to the Comet Observatory.

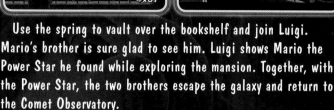

Now that you've rescued Luigi, he will help Mario find the missing Power Stars. Luigi searches out a single Power Star in three galaxies: Good Egg, Honeyhive, and Battlerock. When he finds the Power Star, he sends a postcard to Mario—not to brag about his accomplishments, but to request a rescue. The postcard shows a photo of where Luigi is in the galaxy, giving Mario a hint of where to start looking.

A VERY SPOOKY SPRINT

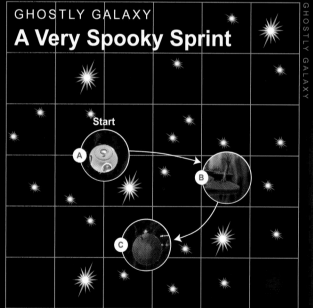

GHOSTLY GALAXY
A Very Spooky Sprint

Somewhere deep in the Ghostly Galaxy lurks a spirit with the need for speed. Mario must seek out this spectral thrill-seeker named Spooky Speedster and challenge him to a race through the cosmos. If he can best the Spooky Speedster, the zippy ghost will hand over its Power Star.

Beach Bowl Galaxy

Ghostly Galaxy

Bubble Blast Galaxy

Buoy Base Galaxy

Bowser Jr.'s Airship Armada

Drip Drop Galaxy

GHOSTLY GALAXY

PRIMA Official Game Guide

The start of this mission is largely the same as the Luigi rescue Mario just finished. A Launch Star on the base of the green Toad spaceship launches Mario to a platform haunted by bats and pumpkin helmet–wearing Goombas. The Rainbow Star is still in the rock formation, so shatter it to turn invincible and run roughshod all over the bats and Goombas.

The Launch Star blasts Mario through space, zooming by bomb-shaped planetoids. Star Bits glisten on the planetoids, so have that cursor ready to scoop them up.

After clearing the platform and picking up the resulting Star Bits, use the series of Pull Stars to drag Mario to the Sling Star in front of the mansion's imposing front door.

Planet C

Finish

Start

The Spooky Speedster waits for any challenger on a small planetoid decorated with some haunted trees. As soon as Mario talks to the Spooky Speedster, the ghost lowers his racing visor and gets ready for the run through a field of Pull Stars. The Spooky Speedster doesn't need the Pull Stars to fly through space, but with no Boo Mushroom in sight, Mario must rely on them to reach the finish line.

The race begins! The Spooky Speedster takes an early lead, but keep on the ghost by always reaching for the next Pull Star with the cursor.

When going into the first corner, watch out for the huge racks of meat. Mario bounces off these if he hits them, wasting precious seconds.

Sticking to the outside of the turns is safer, but it takes longer to get through the course.

Zip by the ribs when they tilt downward. If Mario bounces off a rib, he might lose his grip on the Pull Stars.

More racks of space meat present a challenge to Mario. Pull him as close to each Pull Star as possible so he doesn't accidentally float into a bone and bounce backward, giving the Spooky Speedster an insurmountable lead.

Shortcut alert! There is a small Sling Star on the course's outer edge, around the next corner. Float Mario into the Sling Star and shake the Wii Remote to blast ahead of the Spooky Speedster. Now it's just a matter of holding the lead to the finish line.

The next Pull Stars are inside spheres with their own shallow gravity fields. Shake the Wii Remote when Mario is close to the sphere so he drops to the surface without wasting any time.

Jump off the second sphere and pull Mario into the short minefield. Be careful here. If he touches a mine, he's rattled loose of the Pull Star path, giving the Spooky Speedster a chance to catch up.

Mario must drop to the finish line, located on the last planetoid, and run to the grassy patch on top to end the race successfully. The Spooky Speedster is a gracious loser and awards Mario the Power Star as promised.

Beach Bowl Galaxy

Ghostly Galaxy

Bubble Blast Galaxy

Buoy Base Galaxy

Bowser Jr.'s Airship Armada

Drip Drop Galaxy

Planet C

Beware of Bouldergeist

Beware of the Bouldergeist indeed. This phantom menace waits for Mario at the Ghostly Galaxy's edge, gathering its strength in anticipation of the battle. Before Mario can challenge the Bouldergeist, he must master the Bomb Boo, a special explosive ghost that roams the galaxy. Mario can turn these splashy spirits against the Bouldergeist and win the Power Star.

Several statues of Bowser decorate the foyer, but one is oddly placed inside the fireplace off to the left. These statues must be the key to leaving the room, but how can Mario break them apart? Step up to the portrait of the Boo on the wall. This is no ordinary Boo—it's a Bomb Boo, and when Mario gets too close to the portrait, it pops out to attack.

Planets A and B

Mario returns to the Toad spaceship in orbit at the Ghostly Galaxy's edge. The Launch Star underneath the vessel launches him to a rocky planetoid that is connected to the haunted mansion and that dominates the center of the galaxy. The platform is slightly different now, but there is one pleasant constant: A Super Star is still hidden inside the pointy rock.

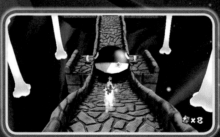

Spin to shatter the rock and pick up the Super Star. Invincible, Mario can plow through the bats and spiders that haunt the planetoid, and he can make a mad dash for the mansion's front door. If the Super Star's effects haven't worn off, Mario can run straight through the Chomp aggressively rolling down the bridge leading away from the front door.

Bomb Boos have incredibly long, elastic tongues that Mario can grab. To snatch up a Bomb Boo by the mouth and capture it, spin right next to it. Now, while holding the Bomb Boo's tongue, run around the foyer, smashing the Bomb Boo into statues. The statues explode, releasing Star Bits. After emptying out the room, grab a fresh Bomb Boo and sling it into the statue in the fireplace to reveal a Launch Star.

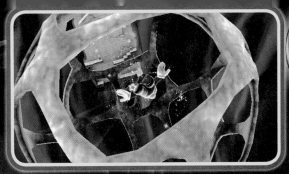

Before rocketing away from the mansion with the Sling Star, empty the Prize Block in the back.

Mario soars across the galaxy, zooming through the center of a hollowed-out planetoid before touching down at the bottom of a giant, floating wall.

Beach Bowl Galaxy

Ghostly Galaxy

Bubble Blast Galaxy

Buoy Base Galaxy

Bowser Jr.'s Airship Armada

Drip Drop Galaxy

✦✦ Planet D ✦✦

The wall doesn't suffer the effects of odd gravity—down is always down on this planetoid. Mario must fling himself up the wall's side with the Sling Pods, dodging enemies and picking up Star Bits. Beware of spiders waiting for Mario on the wall's bottom level, followed by pumpkin-wearing Goombas a little farther up.

Pull back and aim carefully. If Mario misses a Sling Pod, he'll float away into space.

Launch Mario around the four Sling Pods to pick up Star Bits and reach the Sling Star.

The Sling Star points directly to a Launch Star. Zip to the top Launch Star to blast off for the wall's back side.

PRIMA Official Game Guide

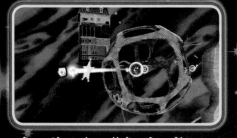

A Bomb Boo flits around the wall's bottom. Grab the Bomb Boo and fling it into the Bowser statue here to discover a hidden 1-Up Mushroom.

Once Mario has all five Star Chips, a trail of Pull Stars leads him away from the wall. Drag him through the center of another hollowed-out planetoid. There is a large Sling Star on the planetoid's far side that rockets Mario toward the Bouldergeist's lair.

Use the spring to the right of the Bowser statues to bounce up to a Sling Pod. Mario must collect five blue Star Chips to construct a series of Pull Stars that get him off this wall and closer to the Bouldergeist. Sling Mario between the pods to pick up four of the Star Chips. The fifth Star Chip is directly above the small Sling Star. Aim for the Launch Star, but be ready to shake the Wii Remote so Mario's captured by the Launch Star and doesn't just fly off into space.

Planets E and F

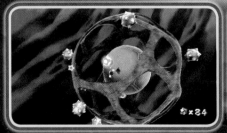

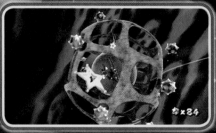

Mario lands softly on a rubber ball squeezed into the center of a hollowed-out planetoid. Bounce across the ball's surface to find a 1-Up Mushroom. Watch out for the mines on the planetoid's surface. The ball can bounce Mario high enough to hit a mine. Keep bouncing Mario against the web-work of the planetoid's surface until he reaches the Sling Star.

The Launch Star sends Mario down to a splintered avenue that leads to the Bouldergeist's lair. There is a blue Luma on the road selling power-ups. For 30 Star Bits, Mario can buy either a Life Mushroom or a 1-Up Mushroom. Unless Mario is dangerously low on extra lives, purchase the normal red Mushroom. Mario needs the extra health to take on the Bouldergeist.

Boss Battle: Bouldergeist

The Bouldergeist is a specter with the power to control stone. The apparition is actually quite small, but it can construct an imposing stone body, complete with giant fists, to ward off intruders. Mario must break the Bouldergeist's shell twice and hit its true form with a Bomb Boo twice to win the Power Star.

During the battle's first half, the Boulder-geist does not manifest its huge fists. Instead, it peppers the arena with rocks. The Bouldergeist raises the rocks from the

floor, letting them hover in the air for a second before throwing them down at Mario. To avoid the rocks, keep moving. The black rocks turn into Bomb Boos when they strike the ground. Run to the Bomb Boo and shake the controller to grab the ghost's tongue. Spin the Bomb Boo into the Bouldergeist to damage its stony armor.

After suffering one attack, the Bouldergeist goes on the offensive. Watch for flashes of black to appear on the ground, then immediately run away from them—spiky stones are about to pop out of the floor, creating walls that seal off parts of the arena.

TIP

Trapped? Mario can spin into the walls to break them.

Golden boulders are rare, but sometimes the Bouldergeist is feeling charitable. When a golden boulder hits the ground, it shatters and reveals a coin.

After smashing the Bouldergeist three times with a Bomb Boo, its exterior crumbles. The actual spirit is revealed—and it's tiny! The Boulder-geist tries to keep its distance from

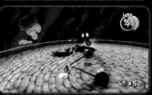

Mario, leaving a trail of explosive Bomb Boos as it retreats. Capture a Bomb Boo and spin it into the Bouldergeist's small form to damage the boss.

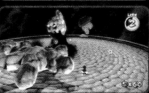

Now the Bouldergeist is furious. It conjures up its giant stone fists and immedi-ately slams them to the ground, trying to squish Mario with one fell swoop. Watch for the hands'

shadows to appear on the ground and then run away. The Bouldergeist will also try to smash Mario with a flying fist attack. Sidestep the fist and capture a Bomb Boo as soon as possible so Mario can shatter this suit of stone armor with three more direct hits.

(continued on next page)

Beach Bowl Galaxy

Ghostly Galaxy

Bubble Blast Galaxy

Buoy Base Galaxy

Bowser Jr.'s Airship Armada

Drip Drop Galaxy

SUPER MARIO GALAXY

NOTE

The Bouldergeist will try to put its hands between its body and the Bomb Boos. Just two hits from a Bomb Boo shatters a hand, but the Bouldergeist is powerful enough to quickly regenerate it.

Try to grab two Bomb Boos with one spin. Now Mario has two chances to smash the Bouldergeist's body in just one attack run.

In the battle's second half, the Bouldergeist raises the walls closer together, narrowing Mario's room to maneuver.

After three hits, the Bouldergeist's armor disappears. Get in close and capture a Bomb Boo as it rises from the ground. Now,

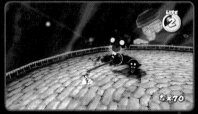

spin it into the ghost to finish the battle and earn the Power Star.

MATTER SPLATTER MANSION

Planets A and B

GHOSTLY GALAXY

Matter Splatter Mansion

GHOSTLY GALAXY

Start
A
B
C

This mission leads Mario to the hidden Power Star in the Ghostly Galaxy, accessible from the "A Very Spooky Sprint" mission. Mario must find a secret Launch Star that vaults him away from the Spooky Speedster's race and to a bizarro world where floors and walls are only temporary constructs.

Mario soars through space, slowing his descent before landing on the rocky planetoid overlooking the haunted mansion. As before, break the stone on the right of the starting point to earn a Super Star. Use your invincibility to clear the planetoid of ghastly nasties.

However, instead of using the Pull Stars to approach the Launch Star next to the haunted house, walk to the glowing rock spire on the planetoid's upper level. Spin to splinter the rock and check out the sources of the sparklies. It's a Launch Star—and it's pointing away from the haunted mansion. Step into the Launch Star and shake the Wii Remote to see where it leads.

Mario rockets far, far away from the haunted mansion to a strange dimension where not everything is as it seems.

⭐ Planet C ⭐

Mario lands inside the remains of a crumbling mansion. When Mario steps forward, the floor seems to move. Actually, there is a strange spotlight that makes the mansion visible, but only

Kitchen

Beach Bowl Galaxy

Ghostly Galaxy

Bubble Blast Galaxy

Buoy Base Galaxy

Bowser Jr.'s Airship Armada

Drip Drop Galaxy

a little bit at a time. Mario must follow the mansion's floor as it appears before him, but keep moving so he's not caught standing over empty space when the spotlight moves on.

Follow the floor to the right, facing the Boo floating in the ether. As long as Mario is looking at the Boo, it doesn't move. However, he must eventually glance away, as the visible section of floor doesn't slow. Keep pace with the floor, bouncing into the Prize Block as long as the ground beneath it remains solid. Then follow the floor down to the key, which unlocks to door to the right.

Walk through the door and head for the giant coin to get the floor moving again.

Follow the stairs to the north and hop across a fractured hall to the right.

⚠️ CAUTION

Pound the Prize Blocks to earn goodies, but don't get greedy. The floor moves quickly, and it's easy to get left behind.

Follow the stairs down to another door. Breeze past the Boo, occasionally glancing over to make sure it stays put.

SUPER MARIO GALAXY

Mario reaches a section of the invisible mansion that has multiple floors. As soon as he grabs the key to open the doors in front of him, the mansion's visible area starts moving again.

The giant coin behind the left door makes several Star Bits appear. These show the way up to the next level. Jump from the nearby piano to the bookcase. Wall jump to a ledge to the bookcase's right just as it appears out of thin air.

Wall jump on the right wall as it appears to reach a platform with four doors. This is the mansion's top, but the floor keeps moving. Grab the key quickly to fling open the doors and spot the Power Star before the ground vanishes.

TIP

If you keep up with the floor as it appears, you can catch glimpses of what's behind the doors before they materialize. There's a 1-Up Mushroom behind the rightmost door here, for example. So, once Mario grabs the key, go directly for that door before scurrying farther up the mansion.

If Mario has time, grab the coins from the other closets before snagging the Power Star and ending the mission.

BOULDERGEIST'S DAREDEVIL RUN

The Daredevil Comet signals that Mario must return to the Ghostly Galaxy and challenge Bouldergeist in a second showdown. However, this time, Mario has only one wedge of health and no means of recovering additional vitality. With just this one wedge, Mario must smash the boss with no fewer than eight Bomb Boos.

Boss Battle: Bouldergeist

When the battle begins, the Bouldergeist casts down stones from the sky. Mario can rarely stand still in this battle, lest the boss draw a bead on his position and smack him with a falling stone. Follow the black rocks as the Bouldergeist drops them, because these turn into Bomb Boos on impact. Get those Bomb Boos as quickly as possible, lessening Mario's exposure to Bouldergeist's attacks.

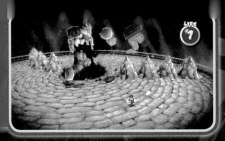

The Bouldergeist segments the arena with stone walls. When the black outlines appear on the ground, run to avoid getting speared by the rising rock.

After three hits, Mario shatters the Bouldergeist's stone shell. Now, zoom in and grab one of the rising Bomb Boos with a quick shake. Smash it into the Bouldergeist's weakened form.

After the monster recovers, he always immediately attacks with a flying fist. Run to the side to dodge the attack and then start looking for black rocks to shatter against the floor to create Bomb Boos. The fist attacks are troublesome, but they can actually sometimes help Mario. The Bouldergeist will smash his own walls just to get at Mario, and this reopens the entirety of the arena, giving Mario the means to escape.

TIP

Mario can swing the Bomb Boos into the Bouldergeist's hands to stop an attack. If he hits one of the hands two times with a Bomb Boo, it temporarily disappears.

Watch for those rising hands. When their shadows appear on the ground, run. If Mario has a Bomb Boo, go for the shot to stop the attack.

When the Bouldergeist's shell collapses for the second time, quickly rush in to grab a Bomb Boo as it materializes from the floor. Hit the Bouldergeist one last time to end the fight.

Beach Bowl Galaxy

Ghostly Galaxy

Bubble Blast Galaxy

Buoy Base Galaxy

Bowser Jr.'s Airship Armada

Drip Drop Galaxy

SUPER MARIO GALAXY

BUBBLE BLAST GALAXY

The Bubble Blast Galaxy gurgles with sludge so poisonous that nobody dares set foot in the swamp. However, the Toads have crashed in the swamp while seeking Power Stars, so Mario must travel to the treacherous galaxy to help his friends and see if they did uncovered the location of another much-needed Power Star.

Through the Poison Swamp

BUBBLE BREEZE GALAXY

Through the Poison Swamp

BUBBLE BREEZE GALAXY

This is the only mission in the Bubble Blast Galaxy. Mario cannot touch the swamp sludge, so he must travel over it in a series of bubbles. These bubbles are far from invincible, so if Mario catches a sharp corner or is pinched in a rotating block, he drops face-first in the muck.

Mario lands on one of the few safe islands in the swamp, right next to the Toads' crashed craft. While the Toads attempt to repair their ship, they implore Mario to explore the galaxy and retrieve the Power Star. After spinning in the stone circle to retrieve some Star Bits, Mario must quickly find a bubble.

First Half of Swamp

LEGEND

🔺 Star Chip

There is a bubble machine near the crashed spaceship. Jump into the bubble to be captured inside of it. The bubble floats safely above the sludge, but without any breeze, it just hangs in the air. The cursor that scoops up Star Bits is now a portable fan. Aim the little horn at the bubble and press Ⓐ to release a blast of air. This pushes the bubble along.

Mario must locate five Star Chips to create the Launch Star that bounces him to the swamp's back half, closer to the Power Star.

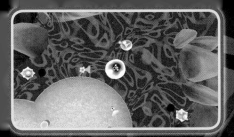

The first Star Chip is just off the island's coast, where the ship crashed. Blow the bubble north to locate the Star Chip, then push the bubble into an air current that rushes it farther north.

The next Star Chip is in the winds generated by the fans to the starting island's east.

After navigating through the winds, blow the bubble farther north to enter a canyon. The third Star Chip is to the west.

The canyon leads to another torrent of air currents. Push the bubble down the current's center to snag the fourth Star Chip.

The fifth Star Chip is in the canyon's corner, guarded by two floating mines. Ease up to the mines when trying to get the Star Chip, then blow the bubble to the Star Chip when the coast is clear.

TIP

To inch the bubble up to the mines, gingerly tap Ⓐ to release limited blasts of air. To correct any overshot, move the cursor to the bubble's opposite side and press Ⓐ to push against the current flow and stabilize the bubble.

After collecting the five Star Chips, the Launch Star appears on the sandy island to the canyon's south. Nudge the bubble to the Launch Star, then shake the Wii Remote to drop Mario onto the star. The Launch Star blasts Mario high over the swamp, through several rings of Star Bits, before depositing him in an even more dangerous part of the galaxy.

Second Half of Swamp

LEGEND

🍄 1-Up Mushroom

Beach Bowl Galaxy

Ghostly Galaxy

Bubble Blast Galaxy

Buoy Base Galaxy

Bowser Jr.'s Airship Armada

Drip Drop Galaxy

SUPER MARIO GALAXY

When entering the swamp's second half, there is a bubble machine on the island Mario lands on. This area is decidedly more perilous, filled with mines and revolving doors that can pinch the bubble until it pops, dropping Mario into the slime. There is a path through the swamp, though, that splits only toward the end.

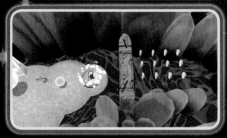

Blow the bubble gently down the first canyon to a rotating stump. Two alcoves are carved into the wood. Hover next to the log until the large alcove rotates into view and then nudge Mario into it.

When Mario reaches the next island, shake the Wii Remote to pop the bubble. Open the door to the west by ground pounding the blue switch on the island. The door doesn't stay open for long, so immediately jump to the bubble machine and hitch a ride. Blow the bubble through the door before it closes and pinches the fragile bubble.

There is a giant coin in a nook on the stump's opposite side. Blow Mario to the coin. Several Star Bits appear outside the swamp's walls; pick them up with the cursor.

Blow Mario into the air currents, but don't let the bubble move too fast. Temper its speed by blowing in the opposite direction as it rides the larger current.

Nudge Mario farther along the canyon, avoiding the mines. There is a 1-Up Mushroom in the canyon's middle, but two mines revolve around it. This is a trap—the mushroom is not worth the risk. Just keep moving, picking up coins to earn that extra life instead.

NOTE

This half of the swamp is loaded with coins. Push Mario's bubble into the coins carefully—picking up 50 earns him an extra life. However, overshooting the coins and hitting a mine completely negates the gain.

The Power Star is on the island just after the mine that moves in a diamond-shaped orbit.

Psst!

There is a plethora of coins in a secret passage to the Power Star's east, but it's quite risky going after them. If you want to try, float the bubble over the blue switch next to the Power Star and ground pound it. This opens the door next to the switch, but Mario has only a few seconds to reach the bubble machine next to the Power Star, hitch a ride, and then blow the bubble through the door before it shuts. It took me a few tries to make it, but once I successfully slid through the door, I earned an extra life with all the coins tucked back there.

Beach Bowl Galaxy

Ghostly Galaxy

Bubble Blast Galaxy

Buoy Base Galaxy

Bowser Jr.'s Airship Armada

Drip Drop Galaxy

BUOY BASE GALAXY

The Buoy Base Galaxy consists of a giant tower looming above a deep pool of water. The tower is inactive at the mission's start—Mario must discover the mechanism that brings the tower to life so he can recover the Power Star at the planet's top. Even though most galaxies hatched from orbiting Prize Blocks contain only one Power Star, the Buoy Base has a very special hidden star. Can Mario find it?

The Secret of Buoy Base

Mario should go after the hidden star first, so when dropping down on the island, ignore the whirring robots bumbling about. Slip under the waves and check out the underwater world below the tower. There are coins and Star Bits everywhere. Swim around the water, scooping up the Star Bits. The hidden star is through the green warp pipe located at the pool's bottom.

The warp pipe is encased in a steel-and-glass cage. Fortunately, there is a Bullet Bill torpedo tube nearby. Swim up to the tube and wait for

a projectile to emerge. Swim in front of it to get its attention, then lead it straight down to the cage. Swim around the cage at the last second, tricking the projectile into smashing the cage. Slip down the pipe to appear on the Buoy Base's exterior.

The Power Star is inside another cage at the hill's top. Numerous Bullet Bill cannons face away from the cage. Get one of the Bullet Bills to follow Mario to the cage to free the Power Star. Run to the left, popping the Prize Block to earn coins—just don't linger too long or a Bullet Bill will blast Mario off the path.

PRIMA Official Game Guide

> **CAUTION**
> If Mario slips off the path and falls into the water, he's pulled back inside the Buoy Base and must return to the warp pipe to get back outside.

Run up the path leading to the hilltop, pausing only to get a few Bullet Bills to lock on to Mario. Lead the Bullet Bills up the remainder of the path to the cage. Four electrically charged spheres rotate around the cage, so jump over them if necessary and lead at least one Bullet Bill to the cage. When the cage explodes, Mario can grab the special green Power Star.

This is one of the three green Power Stars Mario needs in order to activate the green Launch Star back on the Comet Observatory. After flying back to the hub, check out the green Launch Star. There's now a green Luma next to it, encouraging Mario to seek high and low for its remaining hidden friends. After you recover the three green Power Stars, this Launch Star will lead to a new galaxy.

THE FLOATING FORTRESS

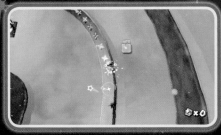

The robots on the small island next to the tower tell Mario that he must kick-start the looming contraption to find the Power Star. Since there is no way to get up the tower as is, Mario must slip beneath the waves to find some secret "switch" for activating the tower's many mechanisms. The seabed glistens with Star Bits and coins, so swim around to collect the goodies before focusing on the tower's submerged section.

BUOY BASE GALAXY
The Floating Fortress

Start

A

BUOY BASE GALAXY

After retrieving the hidden star, Mario must return to the Buoy Base Galaxy to ascend the center tower and claim the second Power Star from the planet.

A massive weight hangs from the tower's bottom. This holds the tower in place. Mario must somehow remove the weight. There is a torpedo tube in the side of the sea bowl. Swim over to it to catch the eyes of a Bullet Bill as it blasts into the water. Then, swim toward the weight with the Bullet Bill in tow. Quickly paddle to the weight's other side so the Bullet Bill crashes into it. The explosion drops the weight, allowing several floating devices to rise. Now Mario can climb to the tower's top.

★★ Ascending the Tower ★★

A pressure valve is on the tower's next tier. Spin on the valve to free a green Topman. The Topman has a springy head Mario can use to launch himself farther up the tower. Knock the Topman silly with a spin. Then, spin it into the corner (look for the white circle) and jump on its head to bounce to the next ledge. Spin on the blue bolt up here to activate the rest of the tower.

The tower is now alive with activity. Mario must swim to the bright yellow floats at the tower's bottom. Jump to the floats and check out the ? Block to the right for some extra Star Bits. Now, wall jump up the alcove next to the bubble cannon. There are several bubble canons on the tower; if Mario is caught in the cannon's volley, the bubble pushes him off the tower and down to the water.

TIP

Look for shadows on the ground to detect out-of-reach goodies, like coins. Push the stunned Topman into the shadow and then bounce off its head to grab some coins.

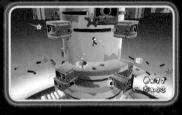

Wall jump farther up the tower's side. Several monsters toddle around next to a row of Thwomps. Stun the monsters with Star Bits and kick them off the tower before dodging the pile-driving Thwomps. There are bubble cannons between the Thwomps, so watch the path ahead. Wait for the cannon to fire and then slip by unharmed.

Spinning the bolt also generates five blue Star Chips. Collect all five to create a path of Pull Stars that extends from the tower's top to a small planetoid in a higher orbit. The five Star Chips are on the ledges and moving platforms between the blue bolt and the tower's top. Look for one on top of the Thwomps before continuing up the tower to retrieve the remainder.

Long jump to a platform several feet away from the tower to recover a 1-Up Mushroom.

Beach Bowl Galaxy

Ghostly Galaxy

Bubble Blast Galaxy

Buoy Base Galaxy

Bowser Jr.'s Airship Armada

Drip Drop Galaxy

PRIMA Official Game Guide

The last blue Star Chip is over the springy robot at the tower's top. Bounce off its head to rocket up and grab the Star Chip.

Psst!

That planetoid over the tower looks familiar. The top housing is made of two red panels, and the bottom half is definitely lighter than the red panels. The screws on the planetoid's sides also seem familiar. Wait a second. Mario's on a Pokeball!

Break free of the tower's gravity and drag Mario up the Pull Star path to the spherical planetoid in the sky.

Shock waves ripple across the planetoid's surface, so jump over them as soon as Mario lands.

There is a single golden bolt on the planetoid's roof. Jump on the bolt and spin to unlock the planetoid. The interior is full of water, but gravity keeps it from spilling out. Dive into the water and swim to the Power Star in the planetoid's middle.

BOWSER JR.'S AIRSHIP ARMADA

Hovering at the edge of the Kitchen Galaxies is Bowser Jr. and his fleet of airships. Bowser's flunky has watched Mario systematically collect all the Power Stars from this region of the cosmos, and unless he stops it, he's going to get an earful from Bowser. And that's not a good thing from a brute who can breathe fire.

BOWSER JR.'S AIRSHIP ARMADA
Sinking the Airships

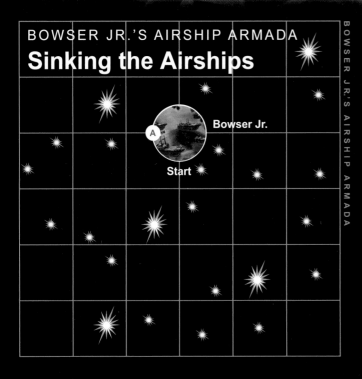

Bowser Jr.

A

Start

After his minions previously failed to stop Mario, Bowser Jr. takes matters into his own hands and launches a direct attack on the hero of the Mushroom Kingdom. Mario must intercept the airships as they circle the galaxy and take the fight to Bowser Jr.

Beach Bowl Galaxy

Ghostly Galaxy

Bubble Blast Galaxy

Buoy Base Galaxy

Bowser Jr.'s Airship Armada

Drip Drop Galaxy

✦ Crossing the Cosmos ✦

Aim for the flagpole on the next ship and press Ⓐ to fire. Mario soars through space, threading a needle of two rotating mines and grabbing the flagpole.

...ario must cross several airships before ...e reaches Bowser Jr., but with few ...ngplanks connecting the vessels, the ...ero must find other means of transpor-tion. To start the search, board the first ...rship and clear out the crew. There is ...crystal full of Star Bits on the ship's ...w; grab those and use them to stun the ...emies. A cannon is on the airship's aft. ...fter defeating the crew, drop into the ...annon and get ready to blast off.

Two robots and a Magikoopa guard the next vessel. Mario can stun the robots by jumping on their heads. The Magikoopa on the aft, patrolling the cannon, casts spells as fast as it can. Mario can spin into the Magikoopa to eliminate it, then jump down into the cannon.

Aim for the flagpole's top on the next ship. If Mario misses, use the Pull Star to recover before the hero flies off into space.

Three spiders block the way to the next gangplank. Shoot the spiders with Star Bits to stun them so Mario can just kick them out of the way when the dingy slides beneath them.

Two Wigglers circle the flagpole's bottom. Gently lower Mario to the deck and jump over the Wigglers. There is a Mandibug on the gangplank that leads to a small dingy, but before setting off to the next section of the mission, spin on the pressure valve to free several Star Bits.

Mario won't hold on to those new Star Bits for very long—there's a blue Luma on board. For 30 Star Bits, the Luma sells Mario either a 1-Up Mushroom or a Life Mushroom. Take the red Mushroom. The gauntlet Mario must survive is brutal.

Another Magikoopa tries to ambush Mario before he boards the next airship. Avoid the Magikoopa's spells and use the Sling Star to hop on the airship's deck.

⭐ The Gauntlet ⭐

After bopping the Mandibug, jump on the dingy and spin next to the lever. The dingy detaches from the airship and starts gliding between two rows of parked airships. All cannons are trained on Mario. The sky fills with flak. Mario must either jump over the exploding cannonballs or weave between them as they streak across the dingy's deck. If Mario is tagged, the lip on the dingy's aft helps keep him from falling off.

Boss Battle: Bowser Jr.

then run toward the ship's edge, facing Bowser Jr. Stand back so your shots clear the electrical barrier and spin again to hurl the shell across space and smash Bowser Jr.'s ship.

Bowser Jr. responds by firing Bullet Bills at Mario and sending forth a Magikoopa. Eliminate the Magikoopa as soon as possible by jumping on its head. Mario has enough to worry about dodging Bullet Bills and cannonballs without having to also avoid fireballs from a Magikoopa's wand.

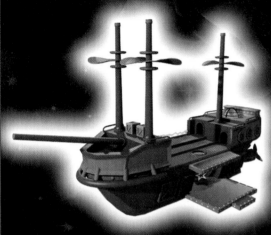

When Bowser Jr. fires a Bullet Bill at Mario, jump in front of it to get its attention and then lead it to the  *cage on the ship's aft. The cage contains three coins and a 1-Up Mushroom.*

Bowser Jr. brings his personal airship about, lowering it so he can taunt Mario from the safety of cold space and a nasty buzzing electrical barrier. The airship is armed with six cannons, so Mario must do a lot of ducking, dodging, and diving to avoid the volleys and return fire on Bowser Jr.

Bowser Jr. opens fire as he sails alongside Mario's airship. Cannonballs roar across the deck. Fortunately, Mario's airship has a steady supply of Koopas tromping about the deck. Spin next to a Koopa to grab its shell,

After three successful shell strikes, Bowser Jr. pulls out all the stops. He turns his airship to face Mario, making it a smaller target.

(continued on next page)

Beach Bowl Galaxy

Ghostly Galaxy

Bubble Blast Galaxy

Buoy Base Galaxy

Bowser Jr.'s Airship Armada

Drip Drop Galaxy

Bowser Jr.'s ship sports a giant Bowser head, and it shoots three blistering fireballs at a time! Step between the fireballs and recover another Koopa shell from the wandering creatures. Fling the shell at Bowser Jr.

TIP

Running low on health? Shoot a Star Bit on the lamp on the airship's bow to retrieve a coin.

When Mario finally sinks Bowser Jr.'s airship, he frees another Grand Star. This majestic star allows Mario to visit the newly opened Bedroom Dome on the Comet Observatory, linking him to a new array of exotic galaxies.

When Mario has only one hit to go, Bowser Jr. usually unleashes a torrent of six Bullet Bills and three fireballs. Avoiding this volley is tough, so move quickly to throw a shell at the ship before all the projectiles reach the deck.

DRIP DROP GALAXY

The Drip Drop Galaxy is a mysterious planetoid hovering at the far reaches of the known universe. The world is primarily water, held into a perfect sphere by the incredible gravity of the planet's small core.

Giant Eel Outbreak

DRIP DROP GALAXY
Giant Eel Outbreak

DRIP DROP GALAXY

Start

A

The penguins wait to enjoy this watery paradise, but an outbreak of Gringills under the waves has them cornered on a teeny-tiny island. The penguins ask Mario to please swim down into the deep and get rid of the eels so they can play freely in the waves.

164

Eel Exterminator

There are several treasure chests on the ocean floor that Mario can also open with the shells. Not all the chests contain useful goodies. This chest actually contains a harmful puffer fish.

The treasure chest next to the sunken ship's bow contains a 1-Up Mushroom.

The penguins on the small island ask Mario to please get rid of the Gringills below, offering him a nice green shell to start the mission. Mario can use the shells to speed through the water and as projectiles against the giant eels. When Mario spins underwater, he throws the shell in a straight line. If he can hit all three Gringills with shells, the penguins will show their thanks.

There are a few red shells on the seafloor that Mario can use to easily eliminate the Gringills. Look for the crashed Toad spaceship. There is a red shell on its exposed undercarriage and the rock formation just next to it. Swim down and grab the red shell with a little spin. Now, swim after a Gringill. Get behind the beast and aim for its tail. Spin to throw the red shell. It rockets through the drink, tagging the giant eel right on the backside.

Stop under the water and watch the Gringills' swim patterns. When they power overhead, aim with the beacon at the shell's front and then throw it.

CAUTION

There are many dangers in the deep, including running out of air while chasing down the Gringills. However, there are several air bubbles on the ocean floor Mario can pick up so he doesn't have to always surface and refill his lungs. There is also a Bullet Bill cannon that releases homing projectiles into the water, so watch for the red eyes of a Bullet Bill locked on to its quarry.

After blasting all three Gringills out of the ocean, the Power Star appears on the sunken ship's bow.

Beach Bowl Galaxy

Ghostly Galaxy

Bubble Blast Galaxy

Buoy Base Galaxy

Bowser Jr.'s Airship Armada

Drip Drop Galaxy

SUPER MARIO GALAXY

BEDROOM GALAXIES

GUSTY GARDEN GALAXY

The Gusty Garden Galaxy is a collection of vibrant, grassy planetoids all connected by the fierce wind currents that rip across the heavens. The galaxy's inhabitants are the star bunnies that Mario met at the beginning of his galactic adventure, but some nasty moles have recently moved in. If Mario can help save the bunnies, he can earn several Power Stars.

Bunnies in the Wind

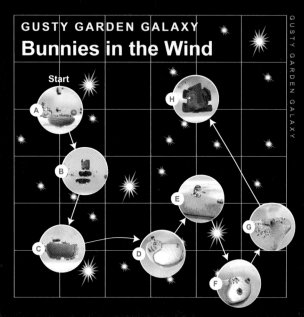

GUSTY GARDEN GALAXY
Bunnies in the Wind

The bunnies of Gusty Garden are hiding a Power Star. If Mario wants it, he must cross the galaxy and play hide-and-seek with a bunny on a giant cube. With so few Launch Stars in this galaxy, Mario must find another means of transportation to reach the cube.

Before grabbing a Floaty Fluff, check out the planetoid's underside. There are Star Bits down here, as well as Goombas.

Walk to the Floaty Fluff path at the planetoid's edge and shake the Wii Remote to hitch a ride on the winds.

Planets A and B

The locals of Gusty Garden, the star bunnies, greet Mario when he lands on this galaxy's outer planetoid. The bunnies explain that without many Sling Stars, Mario must use little blooms called Floaty Fluffs to planet-hop. Like a dandelion seed, Floaty Fluffs travel on the winds. Fortunately, there are plenty of howling winds to help push the Floaty Fluffs across space, but there are breezeless voids Mario must worry about. If there is no wind to propel Mario along, shake the Wii Remote to rattle the Floaty Fluff and get some extra altitude. You can shake Floaty Fluffs only three times, though, before they lose all their petals. With a stripped Floaty Fluff, Mario earns a one-way ticket straight down.

Watch out for Piranha Plants when Mario lands on the next planetoid. The snappers sometimes hide Sproutles in the Gusty Garden, so always clear them out. (There are no Sproutles on this planetoid, however.) Rustle through the grass and flowers to find hidden coins and Star Bits, then step over the side to check out the southern hemisphere.

Planet C

 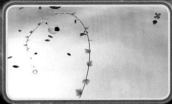

Three ice crystals with Star Bits are on the planetoid's underside, guarded by a mole. The mole pops out of its hole to throw a wrench at Mario if he's far away. (The mole hides when Mario is close.) When the mole peeks out, ground pound to flip it upside down and kick it off the planetoid. When the coast is clear, drop down the warp pipe.

More Piranha Plants! Weed them out of this garden. The Piranha Plant closest to the Floaty Fluffs releases a Sproutle that grows out to a 1-Up Mushroom hanging in space. Don't go for it just yet. If Mario winds around the Sproutle, he drops to the 1-Up Mushroom but then keeps dropping. Instead, walk to the planetoid's bottom half and investigate.

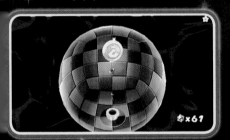

The warp pipe leads to a secret room with a giant coin. When Mario nabs the coin, the room fills with Star Bits. Scoop them up and return to the surface.

Another mole waits for Mario next to a couple of crystals. Eliminate the mole and then free the Star Bits from the crystals. Mario should have a pretty solid collection of Star Bits by this point, but he can earn even more if he has a sharp eye. There are footprints in the nearby dirt patch. Sneak up on the invisible creature and spin to stun it. Now that it's visible, Mario can kick it to shower the planetoid in Star Bits.

 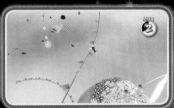

Use the Floaty Fluffs to move on the next planetoid. There is a giant coin between the planetoids. If Mario grabs it while soaring through the air, several rings of Star Bits appear.

Walk to the opposite side of the planetoid from the dirt patch. There is a Sproutle seed on the ground, next to the tall grass. Hit the seed with a spin attack. A Sproutle grows upward, slithering out beneath the 1-Up Mushroom. Now Mario can use the Sproutle on the planetoid's top to grab the 1-Up Mushroom. He falls to this new Sproutle and slides back down the planet's surface.

Gusty Garden Galaxy

Freezeflame Galaxy

Dusty Dune Galaxy

Honeyclimb Galaxy

Bowser's Dark Matter Reactor

Bigmouth Galaxy

PRIMA Official Game Guide

Use the Floaty Fluffs to keep moving, flying through the giant coin between the planetoids to earn more Star Bits.

Smack this Piranha Planet to reveal another Sproutle. It leads to the planetoid with the Launch Star.

Planets D, E, F, and G

The next four planetoids are very small and are connected by a series of Sproutles. Use the Sproutles to bound between the planetoids, but the ultimate goal is to reach planet H, where the large purple Piranha Plant guards a Launch Star.

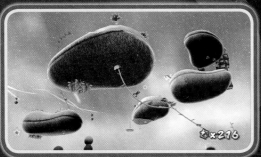

Eliminate the Piranha Plant next to the stones to start the Sproutle chain. It drops Mario on the yellow planetoid, next to a mole and a Piranha Plant. The Piranha Plant on the yellow planetoid's top hides a Sproutle that extends to the lower purple Piranha Plant planetoid.

The purple Piranha Plant snaps at Mario as soon as he touches down. Hang back and taunt the Piranha Plant until it lunges forward and slams its head on the ground. Now jump on its head. The Piranha Plant vanishes, leaving behind the Launch Star that links the tiny planets to a giant cube with a very well-manicured garden.

A seed on the yellow planetoid's bottom extends a Sproutle to a tiny bean-shaped planetoid.

Planet H

Gusty Garden Galaxy

Freezeflame Galaxy

Dusty Dune Galaxy

Honeyclimb Galaxy

Bowser's Dark Matter Reactor

Bigmouth Galaxy

When Mario reaches the cube, a happy little bunny hops up to him. The bunny has the Power Star, but he's too playful to just hand it over. If Mario plays a little game of hide-and-seek, the bunny will give up the prize.

TIP

There is a 1-Up Mushroom in the tunnel that goes through the heart of the cube. The bunny won't always duck down here, though, but Mario should always pick it up no matter what.

The bunny takes off across the cube. When it gets almost out of Mario's direct line of sight, a beacon indicates where it went. Gravity holds Mario down no matter what side of the cube he's on, so keep running after the bunny. It bounds through hedges and under bridges, so Mario must keep right on top of it. It's easiest to corner the bunny next to the thick bushes at the cube's corners.

After Mario finally catches the bunny, the Power Star bounces over to the fountain.

SUPER MARIO GALAXY

PRIMA Official Game Guide

GUSTY GARDEN GALAXY
Dirty Tricks of Major Burrows

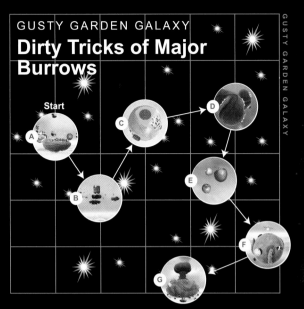

Major Burrows is the leader of the moles that infested the bunnies' Gusty Garden Galaxy paradise. Mario must get rid of the militant mole before he roots out all of the bunnies and lays claim to the entire galaxy.

Bunnies in the garden stand near a patch of Floaty Fluffs, but don't let these cottontails distract Mario into immediately setting sail. Slip to the planetoid's bottom half to discover a slick secret. There's a circle of prickly plants around a warp pipe. Avoid the pointy leaves for now and slip into the pipe.

Planets A and B

Before using the Floaty Fluffs on the first planetoid to start the cross-galaxy journey to Major Burrows, check the underside. There are several stone circles down here to ground pound for Star Bits. Mario can ground pound the wooden pegs, too, but they release Goombas. Of course, Goombas can always be stunned and swatted for Star Bits too.

Ride the Floaty Fluff through the winds to reach the next planetoid.

Mario drops into a spherical chamber overrun with prickly plants. Carefully walk around the plants and grab the giant coin to earn a Rainbow Star. Now invincible, Mario can blast through the prickly plants, filling the spherical chamber with Star Bits. Before the effects wear off, return to the planetoid's surface and power through the rest of the prickly plants.

After picking up all the Star Bits from the prickly plants, ride the Floaty Fluff to the next planetoid. Shake the Fluff to rise up and get the coins in the air.

More dirt trails! Moles are tearing up this planetoid too. Three moles crisscross the planetoid, burrowing just beneath the surface. Follow the trails of disturbed soil to hunt the moles. Ground pound as they pass to pop them out of the dirt. When the mole is exposed, finish it off with a spin attack. There are three moles on the planetoid, so Mario better get to work.

Planets C and D

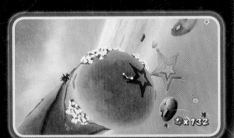

After exterminating all three moles, a Launch Star appears on the planetoid's far end.

This planet is marked with several dirt paths—something's been tearing up the garden. It's a mole, but unlike the moles that hang out in the metal holes, this mole burrows through the ground, leaving a rocky trail behind it. The mole's spiky helmet hurts Mario if it rams him. Ground pound the mole to push it to the surface. Now that it's exposed, spin to smack the mole off the planetoid.

The Launch Star rockets Mario to the apple-shaped planetoids. The journey takes him right through the center of a ring-shaped world. There are four Launch Stars along the hole in the planetoid's center. Grab one as Mario flies past to drop down to the planetoid's surface.

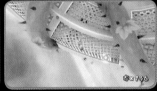

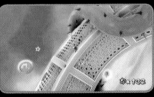

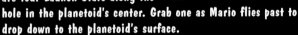

The surface is covered by a thorny vine that Mario must avoid. There are several coins on the ground; if Mario picks up the giant coins, the planetoid soon sparkles with Star Bits. Walk the ring, avoiding the thorns, to pick up all the treasure.

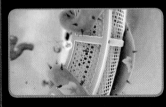

After pocketing all the coins and Star Bits, wind around the planetoid until reaching a Launch Star. This Launch Star shoots Mario over to the apples.

Use the Launch Star on the planetoid to fly over an elongated planetoid that looks like a question mark from a distance.

Gusty Garden Galaxy

Freezeflame Galaxy

Dusty Dune Galaxy

Honeyclimb Galaxy

Bowser's Dark Matter Reactor

Bigmouth Galaxy

Planet E (or An Apple a Day Keeps Bowser Away)

The Gusty Garden is so fertile it grows apples that are as big as a house. When Mario lands on the first apple, he's greeted by a Wiggler that was just minding its own business. However, it is none too pleased when Mario ground pounds the wooden peg in the surface, which flips the Wiggler over. When the Wiggler flips back onto its feet, it stomps around the apple, steaming mad.

The wooden peg disturbs another resident of the apple: a giant worm. The worm pops out of the core and burrows into the nearby Granny Smith apple.

Mario must ground pound the wooden peg on the Granny Smith to make the worm burrow around the galaxy. The worm digs into the Red Delicious, the largest of the three apples. Mario runs across the worm's body to reach the apple, which is currently being bruised by a few rumbling boulders. Keep ground pounding the wooden pegs on the surface to rattle the worm. Soon, it pops out of the apple, but the big guy has run out of segments—only its head appears!

Fortunately, the worm's head leads right to the Launch Star over the surface of the big red apple.

I have a short list of favorite moments in Super Mario Galaxy and the worm in the apple scene is definitely on it. This is a wonderfully clever sequence, something I've never seen before in any other game. When crawling across the worm between the apples, use the camera control to check out the detail— the bright colors, the expression on the worm's face. Very cool.

Planets F and G

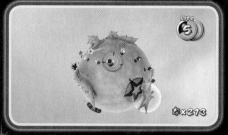

The worm points the way to a small planetoid covered with thorns. Watch out for the thorns while stomping the wooden pegs to earn Star Bits, and pick up a Mushroom that boosts Mario's health to six.

When the hero is ready to confront Major Burrows, use the Launch Star to rocket to his lair.

Boss Battle: Major Burrows

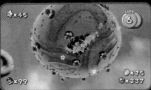

Mario must strike Major Burrows three times to defeat him. However, after the first hit, the major makes himself a harder target. He burrows under the surface and chases Mario. When Mario keeps his distance, the main mole stays so deep all Mario sees is a slight disturbance in the soil. Major Burrows rises to expose his spiked helmet and tries to ram Mario with it. To stop the major, run away from his helmet until the major pops his head and arms above ground. Now, ground pound next to him. The mole bounces out of the ground and starts running away. Like Bowser, chase down the major and spin-attack his little tail.

Gusty Garden Galaxy

Freezeflame Galaxy

Dusty Dune Galaxy

Honeyclimb Galaxy

Bowser's Dark Matter Reactor

Bigmouth Galaxy

How mean is Major Burrows? When Mario arrives, the big bully is chasing after a tiny star bunny. The bunny begs for Mario's help—and that's the prodding Mario needs to leap into action. Like the other tunneling moles on the previous planetoids, Major Burrows must be brought to the surface with ground pounds before Mario can directly attack.

The planetoid's surface is covered in prickly plants and frozen coins. Mario can 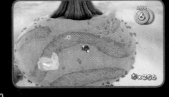 *free the coins himself, but Major Burrows's tunneling breaks the ice and turns the prickly plants into Star Bits.*

A quick ground pound as the major chases the bunny stops the hunt. The Major pops out of the ground, dazed. Spin-attack to know the brute backward. Major Burrows now has his eyes set on a juicer target: Mario.

After the second hit, Major Burrows loses his temper.

(continued on next page)

173

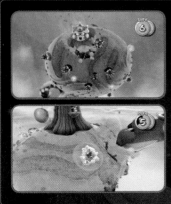

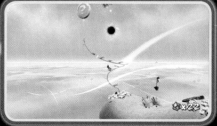

Major Burrows pursues Mario again. Major Burrows keeps his helmet aboveground when Mario is at a distance, but rises out of the soil with both arms flailing as he closes in. If Mario doesn't keep a few steps ahead, the major's claws dig in and cause damage. Sidestep the mole and ground pound. Major Burrows pops out of the soil and runs away from Mario. Mario must now chases down Major Burrows before he can burrow back underground. Spin attack Major Burrows' tail to finish the fight. He is blasted off the planetoid, and the bunny rewards Mario with a Power Star.

The second planetoid is small and occupied by both Piranha Plants and a mole. After ground pounding the mole, spin-attack the Piranha Plants to reveal a Sproutle. The vine creeps up to the next planetoid in the chain, leading straight to another giant coin.

GUSTY GARDEN GRAVITY SCRAMBLE

After defeating Major Burrows, Mario must return to the galaxy for the third Power Star. An entire corner of the galaxy remains unexplored—a series of gravity-altering contraptions.

⭐⭐ Planets A, B, and C ⭐⭐

The mission begins on the same first planetoid, but footprints on the underside demand investigation. Mario can immediately collect almost enough Star Bits for an extra life if he follows and smacks the two invisible creatures walking in the planetoid's shadows. After earning the Star Bits, return topside to hitch a ride on a Floaty Fluff to the next planetoid.

The journey to the next small planet requires Mario to shake the Floaty Fluff three times to cross the windy void. Shaking the Floaty Fluff too many times too soon results in disaster. Wait until Mario almost dips below the wind gust, then shake the Wii Remote to stay aloft.

There are also three giant coins between Planets A and B, but they appear one at a time and only if the previous one has been collected. The result: Star Bits.

The giant coin reveals a circle of Star Bits that ring the planetoid. A mole on the planetoid's bottom is quickly dispatched with a ground pound and a swat. After collecting the Star Bits, head topside and bop the Piranha Plant to extend another Sproutle. Before using the Sproutle, grab the giant coin floating above the stone.

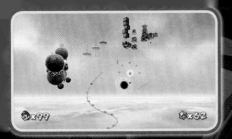

After pushing across the surface, Mario can use the Launch Star to vault to the strange contraption in orbit around the galaxy.

The Sproutle leads to a Luanch Star—and a Rainbow Star. Mario touches the Rainbow Star before blasting off, making him invincible against the rogues of the next planetoid.

Gusty Garden Galaxy

Freezeflame Galaxy

Dusty Dune Galaxy

Honeyclimb Galaxy

Bowser's Dark Matter Reactor

Bigmouth Galaxy

⭐ Planet D ⭐

It's a good thing Mario is invincible—the planetoid rumbles under the weight of several rolling boulders. The planet is also ringed with prickly plants. With the invincibility of the Rainbow Star, Mario can run from one end of the planet to the other, leaving nothing but Star Bits in his path. Keep the cursor close to Mario as he plows through the obstacles—collecting all those Star Bits helps earn extra lives.

⭐ Planet E ⭐

Mario lands on a yellow disc, the first in a series of three. There is no Launch Star to get off these discs just yet—the plumber must find five Star Chips to assemble his getaway means. Tall poles stick out of the discs, allowing Mario to climb up and jump to the next disc. Each disc has its own gravity field.

Shinny up and down the poles, jumping off to grab the Star Chips. To grab a Star Chip behind Mario, face away from the Star Chip and jump. He pushes away from the pole and nabs the prize, and he propels himself close enough to be grabbed by the low gravity of a nearby disc. After collecting all five Star Chips, the Launch Star appears on top of the green disc.

NOTE

That gold Chomp on the planetoid is the same color as a Power Star. Hmmm.

SUPER MARIO

The blocks here have sharp edges—a sure sign that Mario will fall off the block if he doesn't watch his step.

Walk up the blocks, carefully crossing the rotating ones so Mario doesn't slip off, and hit the switch at the column's top. The gravity changes, dropping Mario to a new column of blocks.

Mario lands on a series of blocks. The gravity here is controlled by a series of arrow-shaped switches. Depending on which way the switch is pointing, gravity pushes "down" in that direction. Since the green arrows on top of the first set of blocks points down, Mario's feet stay on the floor.

Climb up this column of blocks. A Life Mushroom is on the pillar's side. To get it, hop to one of the blocks as it rises beneath the power-up. Continue to the column's top and hit the next gravity switch.

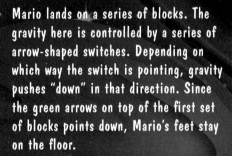

When Mario reaches the green arrow, stand between the two cannons so he's not blasted off the blocks. Spin next to the green arrow. The arrow turns pink and points directly at the cannons. That's the new direction for gravity! Mario falls to the blocks, his feet now sticking to the sides of the blocks.

Run down this column until Mario reaches the drum, which he can walk all the way around. Run to the switch and hit to reorient gravity again.

Walk down the column and follow the square blocks as they extend to the right. Step around the cannons carefully, lest Mario be blasted off the machine. The Power Star is encased in an ice crystal on the last block.

MAJOR BURROWS'S DAREDEVIL RUN

The Daredevil Comet rises over the Gusty Garden Galaxy, allowing Major Burrows one more chance to tackle Mario. The comet tips the odds in Major Burrows's favor too. Mario has only one wedge of health to get the job done.

★ Mean Mole ★

Gusty Garden Galaxy

Freezeflame Galaxy

Dusty Dune Galaxy

Honeyclimb Galaxy

Bowser's Dark Matter Reactor

Bigmouth Galaxy

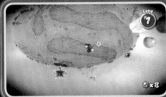

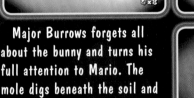

Major Burrows forgets all about the bunny and turns his full attention to Mario. The mole digs beneath the soil and crisscrosses the planetoid, chasing him down. Run from Major Burrows as he tears up the prickly plants. Switch back as Major Burrows gets close and ground pound just as he surfaces. The ground pound jolts the major out of the soil, and he runs off. Now it's Mario's turn to chase him. Follow Major Burrows and spin-attack his tail.

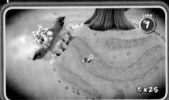

After the second hit, Major Burrows gets angry, putting out his claws and chasing Mario. Run from Major Burrows, but then veer off and ground pound as close to him as possible. The ground pound rattles the major. When he pops out of the ground, chase after him one last time. A spin attack to the tail sends the major flying for the last time, revealing the Power Star.

Somebody! Anybody! He

Major Burrows starts the battle by chasing the helpless bunny yet again. Mario can use this as a distraction, getting close to Major Burrows and delivering a teeth-chattering ground pound. While the major is stunned, a quick spin kicks the battle into high gear.

Mario is indeed pleased with the latest addition to his growing Power Star collection.

SUPER MARIO GALAXY

PRIMA Official Game Guide

THE GOLDEN CHOMP

Mario passed the hidden star of the Gusty Garden Galaxy on an earlier mission: Gusty Garden Gravity Scramble. Remember that lone gold Chomp? Perhaps that gilded monster deserves a closer look.

To the Chomp!

Start the mission the same as before—use the **Floaty Fluffs** to soar through the wind currents. Cross the planetoids as before, getting closer to the long planetoid with the gold Chomp.

To break the gold Chomp, just run into it. The Power Star then appears at the planetoid's top. The mission isn't over yet, though. The planetoid is still covered with prickly plants and boulders. Race through them before the invincibility wears off and claim the Power Star.

When Mario reaches the bean-shaped planetoid, take out the mole on the bottom and collect the gold coin on the topside. Now, bop the Piranha Plant to extend the Sproutle into the sky, leading straight to the Sling Star with the Super Star right in front of it.

Golden Goodies

After turning invincible and crashing down to the planetoid, run straight for the gold Chomp. Mario cannot defeat it without the Rainbow Star's power. If he runs out of invincibility before reaching the gold Chomp, just return to the Comet Observatory and try the mission again.

FREEZEFLAME GALAXY

The Freezeflame Galaxy is frozen solid on one side and searing hot with molten lava on the other. Mario must survive the harshest elements to take the galaxy's coveted Power Stars and continue making his way to Bowser at the edge of the Bedroom galaxies.

The Freezy Peak of Baron Brr

FREEZEFLAME GALAXY

The Freezy Peak of Baron Brrr.

After teaching Mario about skating, the penguin shows how it's done. Chase after the penguin now, avoiding the boulders. If Mario can catch the penguin, the feathered friend will release the Launch Star that points to Freezy Peak.

Skate to the Launch Star and pirouette right into it to rocket down to the base of the icy crag.

Baron Brr is the coldhearted ruler of Freezy Peak, an ice-covered crag that dominates the Freezeflame Galaxy's core. The baron's throne is only halfway up the mountain, though. If just getting to Baron Brr is tough, imagine the trials Mario will face to reach the summit.

Planet B

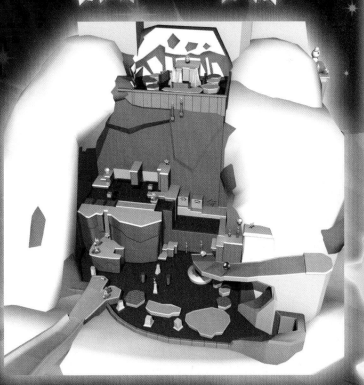

Planet A

Mario begins this mission on a frozen ring high above Freezy Peak. Several boulders roll around the ring; just trying to run from them is difficult. Mario's feet have no traction on the ice, so he must learn how to skate. The penguin on the ring is more than happy to help. It explains that if Mario just spins, he starts sliding across the ice like a pro.

Gusty Garden Galaxy

Freezeflame Galaxy

Dusty Dune Galaxy

Honeyclimb Galaxy

Bowser's Dark Matter Reactor

Bigmouth Galaxy

PRIMA Official Game Guide

A Goomba patrol welcomes Mario to Freezy Peak. Skate to the little nasties and spin to knock them off the planet. After collecting the frozen coins, Mario must grab the giant coin to the right. He has to cross on the frozen platforms, though. Mario knows how to swim, but this water is just too cold. If he falls in and doesn't immediately climb out, he loses health.

Jump across the water spigots. Ice Mario freezes the water under his feet, creating temporary platforms.

Grabbing the giant coin causes an Ice Flower to appear on the water spigot to the left. Jump across the rest of the icy platforms to grab the Ice Flower. Watch out for the Ice Bubbles that bounce around. A spin attack may stun them, but if they fall into the water, they come right back out at full strength. The Ice Flower turns the hero into Ice Mario.

TIP *Ice Mario must triple jump up these water spigots to reach the 1-Up Mushroom.*

Ice Mario can walk on water, so hop down to the lake's surface and run to the stone stairs in the far corner. Jump to the small Sling Star to bound up to a frozen ledge above the lake. Mario can slide down the ledge on his behind. Aim for the two power-ups up here—the Life Mushroom and the 1-Up Mushroom. If Mario misses either of them, just reclaim the Ice Flower and try again.

As Ice Mario, run across the lake to the ledge on the left. Spin to thaw the Ice Bubble, but kick it into the rock, not back into the cold water.

By now, the Ice Flower's effects have worn off. No matter—there are plenty of Ice Flowers on Freezy Peak. Run to the right, past the sliding rocks, to reach another chilly lake. Dash across the frozen platforms to reach a series of wooden boxes that sink into the water under Mario's weight. Empty the Prize Blocks up here to earn Star Bits and then grab the Ice Flower at the far end of the wooden boxes.

As soon as Mario grabs the Ice Flower, he must rush to the mountain's next level before the effects wear off. Run across the water to the ledge opposite the wooden boxes. Leap across the sliding stones and into the small Sling Star.

Hop up the two water spigots before Ice Mario reverts back to normal.

Boss Battle: Baron Brr

Baron Brr is the regal king of Freezy Peak—but he doesn't take too kindly to outsiders. Mario must teach the Baron a lesson in manners by melting his cold exterior three times. Like any nobility, Baron Brr keeps plenty of lackeys around, so watch out for the Ice Bubbles.

The Ice Flower's effects are gone, so Mario must seek out a new one. While Baron Brr throws ice balls down from his throne, hop across the little platforms in the frozen lake. There is a small cave below Baron Brr's throne. The cave's left side contains an Ice Flower; the right side contains coins.

As Ice Mario, dash across the lake to the alcove leading straight to Baron Brr. Wall jump to ascend to the throne.

Baron Brr slams to the ground, sending out a shock wave. If Mario doesn't jump over the shock wave, he's tossed back down to the water.

Spin next to Baron Brr to rattle the coldhearted boss. Baron Brr loses his icy exterior, revealing a small, stony heart.

Now is Mario's chance to inflict some damage— spin into Baron Brr before he rolls around in the snow and recovers his icy armor. Attack Baron Brr three times to dethrone the boss.

After Mario attacks Baron Brr twice, the boss calls for backup. Two Ice Bubbles appear on the throne, running interference for the baron. Spinning next to the Ice Bubbles turns them into useless rocks; run into them to destroy them. Even if they land in the water and recover their icy shells, they still have to float back up, giving Mario a few seconds to concentrate solely on Baron Brr and fight him off. After defeating Baron brr, the Power Star appears.

Gusty Garden Galaxy

Freezeflame Galaxy

Dusty Dune Galaxy

Honeyclimb Galaxy

Bowser's Dark Matter Reactor

Bigmouth Galaxy

FREEZEFLAME GALAXY
Freeze Flame's Blistering Core

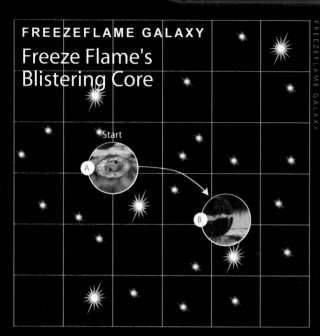

Start

A

B

FREEZEFLAME GALAXY

The Freezeflame Galaxy runs hot and cold—and Mario's about to discover just how steamy this galaxy gets near the center. The galaxy's core is a sea of boiling lava. In order to dive into the core and retrieve the Power Star, Mario must pluck his first Fire Flower.

 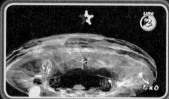

Planet A

At the mission's start, no playful penguin waits to greet Mario on the icy ring world. To get off this planetoid and rocket to the core, Mario must skate around the ring and collect five Star Chips encased in ice crystals. Check both sides of the ring to recover the five Star Chips.

The Launch Star appears in the ring's center. Watch out for the boulders as Mario uses the Pull Stars to cross to the center and blast off via the Launch Star.

Planet B

Planet overview

first area

Check the alcove behind the arrow sign on the wall. There's a Life Mushroom back there. Smash the wooden box to retrieve it.

The Freezeflame Galaxy's molten core is a treacherous place. One misstep and Mario burns his feet in bubbling lava; this makes him temporarily lose control as he runs around to cool himself off. Be careful during these few seconds. If Mario doesn't get back to solid ground, he'll burn off his remaining health.

Next, climb the pole to the Life Mushroom's left to reach the high ledge.

After jumping to the ledge, look down the slope. A giant coin is at the bottom, but there are four fire monsters between it and Mario. Carefully step around the monsters and walk to the ramp's bottom. Collect the giant coin, and a Fire Flower appears between two torches on the slope. Get it!

Walk across the rock platform, avoiding the spiky fire monsters that roll across the ground. These beasties can be defeated with Fire Mario's fireballs, but there's no Fire Flower in sight—yet. Give these monsters a wide berth as Mario empties Prize Blocks for Star Bits and smashes open wooden crates for coins.

Spin the Wii Remote to unleash fireballs at the monsters. After the ramp is clear, walk down and light the torch at the door to open it.

NOTE

If the Fire Flower's effects wear off, return to the twin torches to pick up another one. Mario sure looks hot in those white overalls!

NOTE

Some of the wooden crates hold back fire monsters, so after smashing the box, back up. Let the monster roll forward, then dash around it to collect the coin.

Light the two torches next to the arrow signs with a fireball. When both are lit, a set of stairs rises from the lava.

Gusty Garden Galaxy

Freezeflame Galaxy

Dusty Dune Galaxy

Honeyclimb Galaxy

Bowser's Dark Matter Reactor

Bigmouth Galaxy

SUPER

Hop up the stairs. At the top, jump straight up and spin to be caught by the gravity field of the platforms on the ceiling. Now Mario's view of the whole planet switches. The floor is the ceiling and the ceiling is the floor. Crazy!

Getting Warmer

Second area

Run up the platform. There is a Fire Flower on the ledge to the left. Fire Mario's fireballs make short work of the monsters rolling around the area, so take care of them first and pick up the Star Bits they leave behind. Now it's time to use those fireballs to light some torches around the tower on the platform's far side.

Jump at the platform's edge to throw a fireball far enough to light the darkened torches on each side of the tower.

TIP

Before lighting the torches, sneak around the tower's rear. Carefully hop down the ledges in the lava falls. A giant coin is in the alcove behind the tower. After picking up the coin, musical notes stretch up the alcove. Wall jump back and forth to collect the notes. If Mario grabs them all before they disappear, he earns a 1-Up Mushroom.

Lighting the torches makes the tower rise. Another alcove is revealed when the tower stops moving. There are several coins in the alcove, so wall jump to the top and close in on the Power Star.

★ Very Hot ★

Third area

...an across a series of rolling platforms ...the lava. As soon as Mario reaches ...able ground, he can see the Power ...ar—but it's behind bars. There are ...o darkened torches flanking the bars, ...ough. This is a job for Fire Mario, ... run up to the door's right side and ...uck the Fire Flower from a bubble. ...atch out for the Lava Bubble, though. ...in next to the Lava Bubble to snuff ...s flame. The Lava Bubble then drops ...the ground like a stone. Kick it to ...nish it off.

Use the sliding platform in the lava as a staging ground for throwing fireballs. Lighting the torch on the left is easy. The lava slopes down in front of the right torch, so Mario must aim a little left so the fireball bounces into the torch. When both are lit, the bars swing open and Mario can run across a ledge to grab the Power Star.

 Gusty Garden Galaxy

 Freezeflame Galaxy

 Dusty Dune Galaxy

 Honeyclimb Galaxy

 Bowser's Dark Matter Reactor

 Bigmouth Galaxy

HOT AND COLD COLLIDE

FREEZEFLAME GALAXY
Hot and Cold Collide

The temperature is so mixed up in the Freezeflame Galaxy that ice and lava can actually coexist. Mario must bounce between these extremes as he explores the galaxy to find the next Power Star.

FREEZEFLAME GALAXY

★ 185 ★

PRIMA Official Game Guide

Planet A

The Launch Star blasts Mario down to a planet with a split identity. One side is cold as ice while the other seethes with fire.

Fire and ice mingle on the starting planetoid, a ring world. Blasts of fire streak across the icy ring, singeing Mario as he accidentally skates in front of one. Should he take damage from the fire, check for coins in the ice crystals. Skate to the end of the ring's topside, then break through a crystal wall to slide underneath the planetoid. The Launch Star off this chaotic planetoid is in a giant ice crystal at the end of the ring track.

Planet B

The planet's chilly side suffers from fast-rising tides. When Mario lands, the near-freezing water is filling the chamber, so he'd better seek high ground before he's frostbitten. Mario lands near two unlit torches, but there are no Fire Flowers around to ignite them. To exit this chamber, spin on a faucet valve on the opposite side of the torches; however, if Mario leaves, he'll miss out on some valuable goodies.

Ice Side

Fire Side

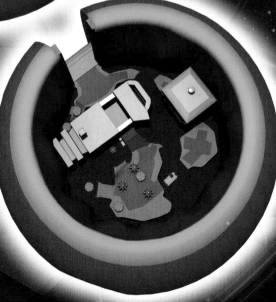

When the water is low, follow the little rounded path to an alcove containing a Life Mushroom.

There is a 1-Up Mushroom below the ledge with the Prize Block. Ground pound the stack of stone wheels to open the way to the extra life.

Stand on an unlit torch and backflip. At the height of the jump, spin Mario so he clambers on the archway above the torches. Bop the ? Block up here for Star Bits.

After collecting the treasure, spin on the faucet to lower the wall dividing the hot and cold sides of the planet.

The Fire Flower is just beyond the door between the planet's two sides, but it's behind bars. Like the cold water in the other chamber, boiling lava ebbs and flows. When the lava is on the way down, walk out and ground pound the exposed stone wheels for Star Bits.

Follow the path around the caged Fire Flower to the entrance's left. Several fire monsters roll about, but without the Fire Flower, Mario cannot hurt them, so avoid them. There is another faucet handle on the opposite side of the Fire Flower's cage. When the lava is low, jump down and spin on the faucet. Be quick about it—the lava will rise and consume the handle. Spinning this handle lowers the bars around the Fire Flower.

Before plucking the Fire Flower, wall jump to reach the ledges above it. There is another 1-Up Mushroom on a nearby rock. Mario must long-jump to clear the gap, though. If he misses the jump, he topples right into lava—so don't long jump until Mario's at the wall's edge.

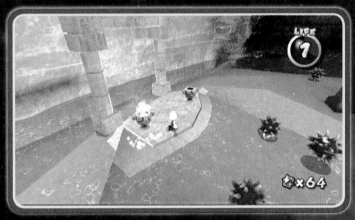

After grabbing the Fire Flower, make a beeline for the planet's chilly side. Run across the room if the water is low. If the tide is high, just wait it out. Mario can always go back and get another Fire Flower. Sprint across the room when it's dry and ignite the two torches. A Launch Star then appears right next to Mario. Use it to soar to a patchwork of lava and ice above the planet.

Gusty Garden Galaxy

Freezeflame Galaxy

Dusty Dune Galaxy

Honeyclimb Galaxy

Bowser's Dark Matter Reactor

Bigmouth Galaxy

To reach the Power Star, Mario must skate across a series of squares floating in space. Half the squares are composed of ice, the other half of lava. The only way to get across is to crack open the crystal that contains an Ice Flower. Ice Mario's frozen touch is so potent, it even freezes lava. But the power doesn't last forever, so as soon as Ice Mario is in effect, start skating across the squares.

At the end of the first track, Mario can jump between to snow-covered surfaces to access the course's second part.

This course is primarily lava. There is another Ice Flower near the snow, so grab it before skating over the molten earth. There's a 1-Up Mushroom out here, but it's slightly off course. Pirouette to the Mushroom, then zigzag back on course to the next snowy patch.

After jumping between two more snowy surfaces, Mario's ready for the final stretch. Skate across the lava squares, pausing for nothing. Skate between the Ice Bubbles and jump through the air to clear the squares that are connected at the corners. Wind around the final bend, then jump right into the Power Star to end the mission.

Reaching Baron Brr's throne was an accomplishment, but that was only halfway up Freezy Peak. If Mario wants to retrieve the hidden Power Star of Freezeflame Galaxy, he must ascend the rest of the treacherous mountain.

Base Camp

To retrieve the hidden Power Star, Mario must start the "Freezy Peak of Baron Brr" mission again. Follow the previous route up the mountain. Skate down to the Goomba that stands near the chilled lake, then jump across the frozen platforms to grab the giant coin. The Ice Flower pops up in the lake's center again, allowing Mario to walk across the water unscathed. Bounce to the frozen ramp and grab the Mushroom and 1-Up Mushroom before continuing up the path.

Mario can also recover another giant coin on the lake. It's to the Ice Flower's left, between four pillars. Grabbing the giant coin causes a plethora of regular coins to appear over the ice for several seconds. Skate through the coins, grabbing as many as possible before the Ice Flower wears off or the coins vanish.

Gusty Garden Galaxy

Freezeflame Galaxy

Dusty Dune Galaxy

Honeyclimb Galaxy

Bowser's Dark Matter Reactor

Bigmouth Galaxy

After clearing out all the goodies at the lake, use the Ice Flower to ascend the mountainside, using the water spigots as temporary platforms. When Mario reaches the two spigots beneath the 1-Up Mushroom, he must use a triple jump to reach the ledge above the extra life. A Sling Star up there sends Mario farther up the peak, into new territory.

Mario lands on a snowy ledge next to a trio of friendly looking snowmen. Those button eyes are actually Star Bits, so wave the cursor over the frosty fellows to collect some goodies. After harvesting the Star Bits, smash the ice crystals to the left to unveil a Fire Flower. Now Mario can melt the snowmen to clear the path and continue up the mountain.

Further Ascension

After melting the first two snowmen, jump to the ledge at the area's rear and hop up the stones that slide in and out of the mountainside. Ice bats flutter around the remaining snowman, but they can be melted with a fireball too. Melt the last snowman in the area with a fireball to reveal a Launch Star.

LEGEND

 Fire Flower

There are three sliding stones in the mountain's face that push Mario onto shrinking platforms. The middle platform has a 1-Up Mushroom on it. Grab the extra life, then hop on top of the sliding stones to keep from falling off the mountain.

LEGEND

🍄 **1-Up Mushroom**

🌻 **Fire Flower**

Round the corner and continue up the frozen peak. Watch out for more ice bats in the skies over an extra Fire Flower. After plucking the flower, jump to the ramp on the left and continue up the peak. A boulder may rumble out of the cave along the ramp. Step on the small ledge to let the boulder roll by.

Use fireballs to melt the snowman over the cave. The melted snowman reveals another Sling Star. Use the Sling Star to reach another narrow ledge. Follow it up the remainder of the peak.

Mario is vaulted to Freezy Peak's next tier. Smash the nearby ice to retrieve another Fire Flower. Wait for a boulder to rumble out of the cave to the right and follow it down the ramp. Hop in the air and blast the snowman across the gap with a fireball to clear the path.

The Power Star marks the summit of Freezy Peak.

Gusty Garden Galaxy

Freezeflame Galaxy

Dusty Dune Galaxy

Honeyclimb Galaxy

Bowser's Dark Matter Reactor

Bigmouth Galaxy

FROSTY COSMIC MARIO RACE

Freezy Peak is bathed in the bluish glow of the Cosmic Comet, beckoning Mario to return to the mountain one last time for a race. Another Power Star is on the line, so Mario must accept the invitation.

Cosmic Mario falters at the jump! Now Mario can pull ahead. Shake the Wii Remote to make him immediately skate. If Mario tries to run on the ice, Cosmic Mario easily overtakes him again.

Frozen Race

Mario sidles up to the starting line with Cosmic Mario, ready for a chilly run through a frozen course. Instead of running, Mario must now outskate this spacey challenger.

Skate to the end of the course's second leg and jump as soon as Mario passes under the ice ceiling. He flips up to the last third of the track.

At the race's start, Cosmic Mario takes off like a rocket. Mario must jump into the air and land to start skating across the frozen surface. Cosmic Mario usually gets an early lead on Mario, but this course offers Mario a few places to make up the difference and pull ahead.

Pirouette over the gaps in the ice squares to close the gap between Mario and Cosmic Mario.

A 1-Up Mushroom is near the first snowy patch, but pass it by. Mario must stay on Cosmic Mario. Jump at the snow patch to move on to the next leg of the course.

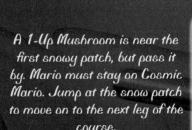

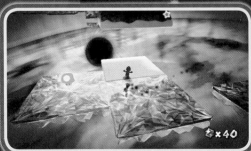

The course's end is especially tricky—a bad jump is cataclysmic. Unless Cosmic Mario is breathing down Mario's neck, play it safe and take little hops between the ice squares. The Power Star is on the last square. Jump into the Power Star to claim it. If Mario misses, he might skate right off the square. How embarrassing to lose right at the finish line!

DUSTY DUNE

Many secrets are choked beneath the sun-scorched sands of Dusty Desert. Hidden planetoids in orbit around the galaxy's blazing star contain forgotten treasures, and when triggered, entire towers rise out of the sands. To survive this treacherous galaxy, Mario must watch his step on the deadly quicksand—one false move over the shifting dunes and it's game over.

Soaring on the Desert Winds

DUSTY DUNE GALAXY

DUSTY DUNE GALAXY
Soaring on the Desert Winds

Woe to the poor soul who tries to trek across Dusty Dune's loosely packed sands. The only way to cross the dangerous desert is by air, so Mario must sniff out the means for flight.

Gusty Garden Galaxy

Freezeflame Galaxy

Dusty Dune Galaxy

Honeyclimb Galaxy

Bowser's Dark Matter Reactor

Bigmouth Galaxy

Planet A

Mario must fly from one tornado to the next, careful not to ever touch the dunes. Just one toe in the sand spells trouble, so don't be too ambitious with travel paths. Just hop from one tornado to the next, always choosing the closest one. The goal is a green warp pipe sticking out of the dunes.

Feeling gutsy? There is a 1-Up Mushroom among the tornados and it's within reach—but just barely.

Without any Launch Stars to cross the desert safely, Mario must turn to unconventional means for travel: tornados. The dust devils that swirl across the dunes pull Mario off his feet and spit him high into the sky. However, Mario spins with his arms outstretched, slowing his descent like a helicopter landing.

PRIMA Official Game Guide

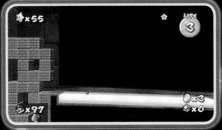

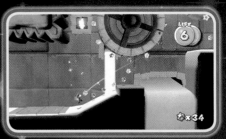

The warp pipe leads to an underground tunnel beneath the dangerous dunes. Mario must ground pound through a stack of bricks to reach the chamber's bottom. Walk to the pile's right and ground pound so a ledge stops Mario. Duck and squeeze into a narrow passage that leads to a shortcut. The tunnel's bottom floor definitely offers more trouble but without as much reward.

Step on the two switches beneath the Thwomp to release a series of Star Bits around the spindles to the right.

Jump across a Thwomp that crashes against the bottom floor. After hopping to the solid ledge, wait for a trio of Thwomps to crash to the ground. As the Thwomps rise back into the air, run beneath them to grab a Life Mushroom. There is a giant coin directly above the Life Mushroom. Collecting it causes several Star Bits to appear in the vertical shaft Mario must slide down.

The spindles are large enough to have their own gravity. Run around the spindles to pick up the Star Bits.

TIP

The giant coin is entirely optional, but wall jumping off the Thwomps reveals a 1-Up Mushroom along the ceiling. To grab the extra life, wall jump on top of the Thwomps when they hit the floor.

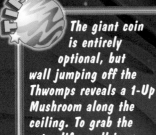

Jump from the spindles to the Thwomp over the switches. There's a 1-Up Mushroom on top of the Thwomp.

After dropping to the tunnel's bottom floor, run to the right. Empty the Prize Blocks for Star Bits and watch out for rivers of quicksand.

Jump across the bricks to avoid slipping and sliding in the rivers of sand. The giant coin over the third brick reveals a Fire Flower.

Planet B

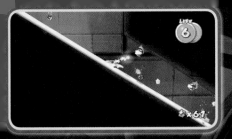

Use the Fire Flower to incinerate the Piranha Plants on the floor and ceiling of a fast-moving ramp.

The excitement is far from over. After surviving the Piranha Plants, Mario must run from a boulder that crashes down the ramp.

⭐ A Sling Star at the ramp's bottom launches Mario out of the underground chamber. Nudge him into the lines of Star Bits while flying through the air.

Use the Launch Star outside the warp pipe to blast off to the giant tower in the background. The Power Star is at the top of the looming tower of sand and brick.

LEGEND

⭐ Power Star

To start Mario's journey up the tower's sides, he must jump into the tornado's heart and start spinning. A flying rooster tries to drop explosive eggs on Mario, but he easily sidesteps the yolks.

Soar to the tower's next level. Steer toward the ledges sticking out of the tower's side, then jump up to the sandy river. Watch it up here; those fast-moving sands can whisk Mario right off the tower and into the quicksand below.

CAUTION

So, which sand is safe to walk on and which spells instant doom? Light yellow sand is safe. The orange sand is the real bad stuff Mario must avoid at all costs.

Gusty Garden Galaxy

Freezeflame Galaxy

Dusty Dune Galaxy

Honeyclimb Galaxy

Bowser's Dark Matter Reactor

Bigmouth Galaxy

PRIMA Official Game Guide

he must slide down a wall until he's right across from where he needs to land. Be careful—slide down too far and Mario will miss the jump.

The Power Star is in a crystal at the tower's top, just beyond the maze.

Backflip up the stones sticking out of the sand falls to reach the tower's next tier.

Jump into the tornados to flutter up to a giant coin. When Mario grabs the coin, a new tornado appears. Soar over to that tornado to get some extra lift. This propels Mario up to a ledge just below a glass wall. A giant coin is on that ledge that throws some extra Star Bits on the tower's side.

Now Mario must wall jump to navigate through the three-columned route that winds around the tower's side. Sometimes

BLASTING THROUGH THE SAND

DUSTY DUNE GALAXY

Blasting through the Sand

Start

A
B

C

DUSTY DUNE GALAXY

The Power Star is located on a sandy disc in orbit around the Dusty Dune Galaxy's main planetoid. Mario must somehow find the series of Pull Stars that yank him to the disc. From there, it's a matter of maintaining balance to keep from falling into the sinking sand while finding the secret switch that leads to the Power Star.

★ ☆ Planet A ★ ☆

From where Mario stands at the mission's start, the coast looks fairly clear. However, stepping out onto the circular platform's center to grab a lone coin leads to trouble. Five creatures pop out of the sand and wobble about the platform. Stun the creatures one at a time with spins, then kick them off the platform into the sand. Kicking each creature off the platform results in Star Bits, which Mario can use to daze the remaining monsters.

This hungry Luma leads to this galaxy's hidden star. If you wish to pursue the star now, check the mission strategy for "Sand Capsule and the Silver Star."

When all five creatures are gone, a red Pokey pops out of the ground. Jump and spin into the head of the Pokey, causing a Launch Star to appear.

The Launch Star blasts Mario off the ring covered with rolling boulders— and a few hidden surprises.

Jump to the ring, watching out for the boulders. The Sling Star that leads to the next part of this planetoid is on a small platform in the ring's center. A Rainbow Star is under the platform with the Sling Star, so grab it and tear around the ring to get rid of the boulders and collect Star Bits.

Planet B

Mario lands so hard on the sandy platform next to the ring that he sinks up to his waist. Jump to free him from the sand, then investigate the area. There are coins in ice crystals on this platform with rounded edges. Rounded edges? That means Mario can walk to the other side and be held down by gravity! Sure enough, there's a surprise waiting for him on the bottom—a hungry Luma

TIP

Before leaving the ring, jump out to the small platform to the north. There is a Life Mushroom on its underside that raises Mario's health to six.

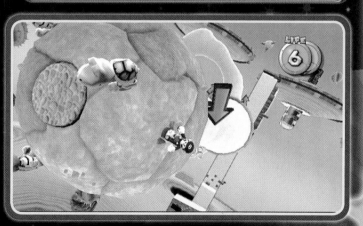

The Sling Star bounces Mario to a small planetoid with a Dry Bones. Jump from this planetoid to the next one in the chain, a snaking ring.

Gusty Garden Galaxy

Freezeflame Galaxy

Dusty Dune Galaxy

Honeyclimb Galaxy

Bowser's Dark Matter Reactor

Bigmouth Galaxy

SUPER MARIO GALAXY

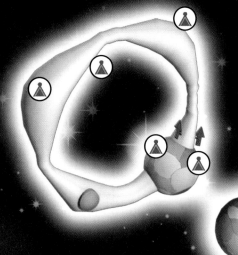

Finding all the Star Chips creates a set of Pull Stars that leads to a small planetoid with moving sand.

To get off this sandy ring, Mario must collect five blue Star Chips. Collecting these is complicated by the moving sand that whooshes Mario around the ring, giving him only brief opportunities to grab the Star Chips before he must go around again for a second (or third) shot. The first Star Chip is on a small hump just beyond the starting point, a rocky bulb with a Dry Bones and a shell.

There is a warp pipe on the planetoid's far side, but to reach it, Mario must jump across a series of moving platforms in the sand. Searing sun rays bear down on the planetoid, too, so be careful not to step in their focused energy. While jumping across the platforms, grab as many coins as possible—especially if Mario gets zapped by a ray.

One of the Star Chips is encased in a crystal on one of the few sturdy platforms.

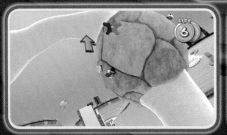

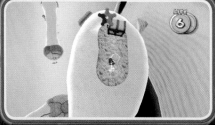

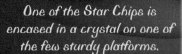

Grab the shell on one of the passes and steer Mario to a platform with a treasure chest. Break the chest with the shell to reveal another Star Chip.

The warp pipe leads to a familiar-looking secret room—it's just like the one Mario found on the other side of the orange pipe in the Good Egg Galaxy.

Follow the same steps, collecting the giant coin to start a trail of musical notes. Picking up all the notes, though, results in three 1-Up Mushrooms instead of just one. After grabbing the Mushrooms, use the pipe in the ceiling to leave.

Planet C

Gray Side

Tan Side

LEGEND

 1-Up Mushroom

Gusty Garden Galaxy

Freezeflame Galaxy

Dusty Dune Galaxy

Honeyclimb Galaxy

Bowser's Dark Matter Reactor

Bigmouth Galaxy

The warp pipe spits Mario out onto the sandy disc. Almost the entire surface is covered with deadly quicksand, so stay on the stonework. The stone paths wind around jaggedly—be careful. There are rings in the disc that let Mario slip between the planetoid's two sides. One side has tan-colored bricks; the other side has dark gray bricks. When walking across the path, keep an eye on the tornados. Getting swept up here isn't necessarily beneficial, especially if Mario stops flying right over the quicksand.

There are two 1-Up Mushrooms on the disc's tan side. The first is on a ledge directly across from the massive Thwomp. Mario can reach the ledge via long jump or tornado. The second 1-Up Mushroom is on top of the Thwomp. The only way to reach it is to use the tornado to flutter high enough to grab the edge of the Thwomp and hoist Mario up.

Use the ring at the walkway's end to switch back to the disc's gray side. More tornados twirl along the bricks. Avoid them as Mario heads right, to the next ring that connects the two sides. There is a 1-Up Mushroom on a single brick between a tornado and a Dry Bones. Mario can grab it with a single jump, but watch that the tornado's winds don't accidentally grab him.

DUSTY DUNE GALAXY
Sunbaked Sand Castle

Return to the disc's tan side. Mario must run between two tornados that have picked up some debris. If the tornados strike him, he's bounced right into the quicksand. On the far side of the tornados is a tower. Climb the tower and ground pound the blue switch at the top. This flattens the tower—on this side of the disc. The tower is now on the disc's other side, giving Mario a way to reach the Power Star.

CAUTION

The switch's effects are temporary. A ticking clock speeds up when the tower is about to drop to the disc's other side. If Mario misses the Power Star, he must return to the disc's tan side and hit the blue switch again.

Planet A

Mario starts the mission on a stable sand disc—no worries of quicksand here—but there's seemingly nowhere to go. A series of blocks hang high above him, but how can Mario get them down? Ground pound the nearby red switch to make the blocks fall from the sky and sink into the sand. A Launch Star is at the top of the block column, but before Mario can use it, he must dodge all the incoming bricks.

Run back through the ring and over to the disc's gray side. Jump up the tower to nab the Power Star.

A rooster sails down with the blocks and starts peppering the floor with exploding eggs. Dodge the eggs and the blocks. If Mario is caught under a brick, he is squished and must start the mission over. A 1-Up Mushroom comes down the column's right side, followed shortly by a Life Mushroom on the left. There are lots of Star Bits between all the blocks, so wave the cursor over the falling bricks to pocket the goodies.

When the last of the blocks sinks into the sand, the rooster leaves and the Launch Star is available for use.

★ Planet B ★

The Launch Star drops Mario on another barren-looking disc of sand. But looks are again deceiving. He must collect five Star Chips to create a new Launch Star, but only one Star Chip is currently visible in the disc's center. To make the rest of the Star Chips appear, Mario must ground pound the blue switch. However, before pounding the switch, swipe the shell off the nearby Koopa's back.

There is an alcove on one side of the tower. Run to it and grab the Star Chip

Use the shell to break open the treasure chest on the tower's ledge. If Mario misses the chest, the Koopa regenerates, so he can try again later.

There is a Star Chip behind four Dry Bones on a long ledge.

Once the tower finishes rising from the sand, wall jump up the alcove to the roof (the Koopa is up here). Grab the final Star Chip from the triangular ledge to make the Launch Star appear on the roof.

NOTE: The blue and red switches control the rise and fall of the tower (the blue switch raises the tower, the red switch lowers the tower). If Mario missed a Star Chip, pound the switch to lower the tower and grab it as it drops toward the sand.

Gusty Garden Galaxy

Freezeflame Galaxy

Dusty Dune Galaxy

Honeyclimb Galaxy

Bowser's Dark Matter Reactor

Bigmouth Galaxy

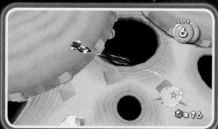

Mario lands on the northern planetoid in a pair of tiny spherical worlds. A huge Pokey dominates the upper planetoid. Grab the 1-Up Mushroom in its shadow, then retreat to the upper planetoid's bottom to find a small Sling Star. This drops Mario down to the lower planetoid, which is loaded with coconuts.

The next planetoid is a small, sandy sphere covered with coconuts. The sand level rises and drops, revealing a couple wooden plugs. There are a few crabs on the planetoid too. Spin into a crab's rear to dispatch it. To get off this planetoid, kick one of the coconuts into the giant prickly plant. After Mario pops the plant, the Launch Star appears.

Stand behind a coconut and look up at the upper planetoid. Spin to boot the coconut into the air. The upper planetoid's gravity snares the coconut and pulls it down to the surface. Now, return to the upper planetoid via the small Sling Star. Roll the coconut in front of the Pokey and spin. The coconut strikes the Pokey, popping it and revealing the next Launch Star.

NOTE

There is a hidden star accessible from this planetoid: *Sparkling Treasure of the Sand.* To learn how to find it, check that *"Sparkling Treasure of the Sand"* mission's strategy.

Mario blasts off for a disc with a giant glass-enclosed tower.

Bedroom

Gusty Garden Galaxy

Freezeflame Galaxy

Dusty Dune Galaxy

Honeyclimb Galaxy

Bowser's Dark Matter Reactor

Bigmouth Galaxy

Planet E

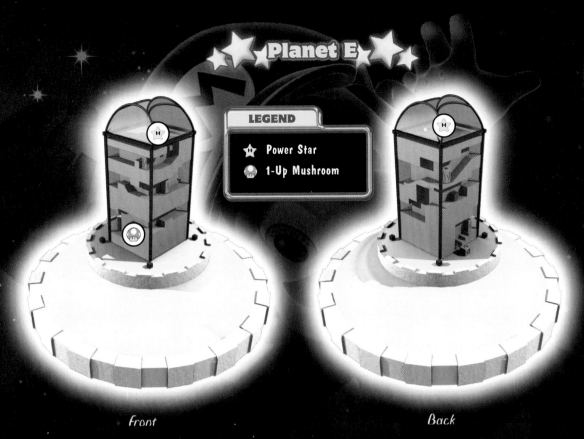

LEGEND

⭐ Power Star
🍄 1-Up Mushroom

Front   Back

At the tower's bottom, a warp pipe leads Mario inside. As soon as he's deposited within the tower's glass walls, it begins to sink. Although, from this angle it looks like the tower is rising. It's a visual trick—marvel at it later, because now it's time to run.

When Mario lands on the tower, he's close to the Power Star—it's right under the glass ceiling. However, there's no way into the tower from the roof. Mario must step off the roof and drop to the disc below, grabbing Star Bits as he falls.

Mario must run through the tower as it drops, rounding corners and jumping up on new ledges. Look for a 1-Up Mushroom around a corner, right below

a ledge. If Mario doesn't step out of the way, that ledge will squash him.

PRIMA Official Game Guide

After a few turns, wooden crates start blocking Mario's ascent. Spin to smash through crates, leaving only splinters behind. The passageways get narrower as he approaches the tower's roof, so try to stay as far ahead as possible.

If Mario survives the falling tower, he can grab the Power Star from under the glass ceiling.

SAND BLAST SPEED RUN

Sand Blast Speed Run is a zipper of a trip through the "Blasting through the Sand" mission. Mario has only 4:30 to cross the planetoids and reach the final disc. If he fails to reach the Power Star in time, he's sent all the way back to the beginning with one less life.

The sandy run through the Star Chips is another time sink. To hurry through the area, grab the shell at the start before stepping into the sand. This way, Mario can try to get all five Star Chips on the first trip around the ring. Aim for the sturdy platforms in advance, because if Mario isn't right there, he'll slip past. If he has to go around the ring more than twice to get all the Star Chips, he'll be hard-pressed to finish the mission in time.

Trouble Spots

One of the easiest places to lose precious time is at the mission's beginning. The five Pokey heads love to bounce just out of the way as Mario tries to spin and stun them. To speed things up, use any collected Star Bits from the first Pokey head to stun the rest, then just run through the mass of dazed heads. The red Pokey loves to back away just as Mario spins too. If it backs up to the wall, it drops into the sand and reappears in the center—with all of its segments, no matter if Mario has smacked the Pokey down to just its head.

Quickly pull Mario across the Pull Stars—forget about collecting all the coins. Hurry!

Don't worry about power-ups on the ring. Just jump straight to the Sling Star.

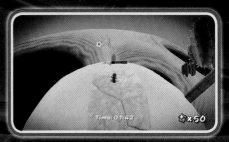

Rush to the warp pipe on the sandy planetoid so Mario has enough time to negotiate the two-sided disc puzzle.

Time: 01:32 ✦ x119

Time: 00:51 ✦ x157

Fortunately, there are no tornados on the disc in the speed run. Just run across the pathways, watching out not to accidentally slip off the side, and keep using the holes to switch between the disc's two sides.

Time: 00:34 ✦ x158

Time: 00:24 ✦ x158

Rush to the tower on the disc's tan side and hit that blue switch to transfer the tower to the disc's other side. Now, book it back across the pathway to the blue switch and duck through the hole in the disc.

Time is almost up! Run for that Power Star and leap up the tower to snag it before the clock hits zero.

Time: 00:12 ✦ x158

TREASURE OF THE PYRAMID

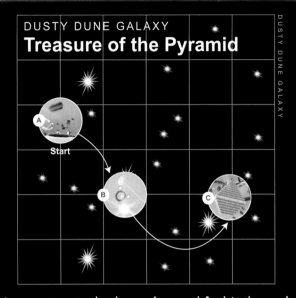

DUSTY DUNE GALAXY
Treasure of the Pyramid

A — Start
B
C

DUSTY DUNE GALAXY

It's time to return to that hungry Luma and feed it the snack it so richly deserves. Satiating the Luma's rumbling tummy makes the little star so happy it turns into a new planetoid. Mario must investigate this new planetoid for a hidden Power Star.

Hungry Luma

Return to the ring world with the crashing boulders. The hungry Luma is on the bottom of the sandy ledge right next to the ring; walk over the edge to spot it. This Luma wants to snack on only 20 Star Bits—which isn't difficult to gather. Grab the Super Star under the Sling Star in the ring's center and smash the boulders to free dozens of Star Bits. After feeding the hungry Luma, it blasts off and creates a new pyramid-shaped planetoid. Use the Luma's Launch Star to rocket to the pyramid and drop through the warp pipe on the bottom.

Gusty Garden Galaxy

Freezeflame Galaxy

Dusty Dune Galaxy

Honeyclimb Galaxy

Bowser's Dark Matter Reactor

Bigmouth Galaxy

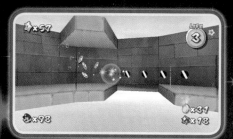

The pyramid's interior is largely covered with sand. To craft the Power Star, Mario must somehow find five Silver Stars stuck in the sand. The first one is locked in a crystal near the warp pipe entrance. After freeing the Silver Star, walk to the green line on the chamber's left side. Touching the green line starts a mechanism that raises the sand ceiling, revealing the rest of the Silver Stars. The only catch is the floor rises right along with it!

The rest of the Silver Stars are caught in crystals too. Shatter the crystal with a spin before the moving sand swallows it up again.

Areas safe from the sand become few and far between. When the sand gets close to the floor, Mario has only a small alcove to duck into before he's smashed. Fortunately, the alcove's floor is the switch that moves the sand. As the sand starts climbing, head up the next column to the right to rescue the final Silver Star from its crystal prison.

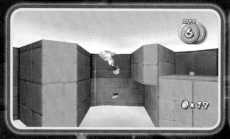

When Mario reaches the chamber's top, he spots a red line. This line turns green when the sand reaches the top. If Mario steps on the green line again, the ceiling starts dropping back down. After grabbing the Silver Star below the wooden crates, run to the line and move the sand again. As the sand comes crashing back down, head down the next open column in the wall to keep seeking out the Silver Stars.

The Power Star that appears at the chamber's bottom is green. This is one of the green Power Stars needed to activate the special Launch Star on the Comet Observatory.

BULLET BILL ON YOUR BACK

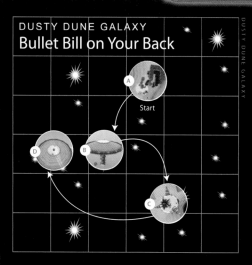

DUSTY DUNE GALAXY
Bullet Bill on Your Back

Start

DUSTY DUNE GALAXY

The second hidden star in the Dusty Dune Galaxy (this is one of the rare galaxies with seven total Power Stars) requires that Mario return to a tiny planetoid from the "Sunbaked Sand Castle" mission. What are those little crabs trying to obscure?

Mario lands on a bowl-shaped planetoid. The sandy surface is stable, so he can run around. That's a good thing, too, because there are two Bullet Bill cannons in the bowl's center. The cannons are atop a large tower that's buried in the sand. Also under the sand is a Power Star. To reveal it, Mario must ground pound the blue switch to raise the tower. While the tower rises, collect coins in tiny alcoves carved into the structure.

Gusty Garden Galaxy

Freezeflame Galaxy

Dusty Dune Galaxy

Honeyclimb Galaxy

Bowser's Dark Matter Reactor

Bigmouth Galaxy

Cross the galaxy as before, stopping on the small planetoid with the crab infestation. The sand level on this world rises and falls, revealing two wooden plugs when the sand is at its lowest. To clear up the planetoid, smack a coconut into the giant prickly plant. This reveals a Launch Star, but don't use it. Instead, wait for the sand to ebb, then ground pound the wooden plugs. A trail of musical notes appears on the planetoid, but the sand starts to rise at the same time. Mario must follow that tune, picking up all the notes before they vanish.

The Power Star is stuck in a cage. And the tower's base is crawling with Dry Bones!

Other cages rise with the Power Star, one of which contains a Rainbow Star. Mario can jump off one of the switches high enough to get a Bullet Bill's attention, then lead the projectile down to the cages. Free the Rainbow Star and run through the horde of Dry Bones. After eliminating the skeletal Koopas, lure another Bullet Bill to the cage with the Power Star.

After grabbing the final note, a new Launch Star appears over the tiny planetoid. Wait for the sand to rise to its highest level to reach it.

The Power Star bounces to the tower's top. Ground pound the red switch to lower the tower back into the sand and bring the Power Star within reach.

HONEYCLIMB GALAXY

The Honeyclimb Galaxy stretches into the cosmos as far as the eye can see. Only Bee Mario can traverse the giant walls covered with sticky honeycombs, so seek out that Bee Mushroom and start buzzing to find the next Power Star.

Wall 1

The first of the three walls Bee Mario must scale is obstacle-free—save for gravity. After grabbing the Bee Mushroom at the starting platform, Bee Mario can buzz up to the first batch of honeycombs and begin the big climb.

The second wall is definitely more dangerous—meteors streak down the honeycombs to knock Bee Mario to his doom. Since he isn't exactly fast while crawling across the sticky honeycombs, it's often smarter just to buzz away from the wall and avoid the meteors.

There are many coins on the walls, including giant ones that make Star Bits appear on the walls' edges. To gather the Star Bits, buzz Mario over to one side or the other and wave the cursor over the newly appeared goodies. Not all the honeycombs are connected. Mario must fly between the gaps, landing on the sweet stuff before his Flight meter runs out.

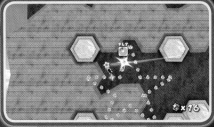

This giant coin between four separate honeycombs creates a star of Star Bits. Buzz to one of the four honeycombs and scoop the Star Bits up with the cursor.

Be careful buzzing to the 1-Up Mushroom on the lone honeycomb. The gap between the spaces is wide, and if a meteor strikes Mario, it's tough to find purchase before completely falling off the wall. Grab the giant coin near the wall's top to make a slew of Star Bits appear around the honeycombs. After collecting the Star Bits, fly to the Launch Star to rocket to the last wall.

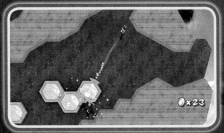

At the first wall's top, Bee Mario finds a Launch Star. Buzz over to it and shake the Wii Remote to blast off to the second wall. Mario flies through rings of Star Bits while soaring to the next wall, so wave that cursor along his path to stuff his pockets with stardust.

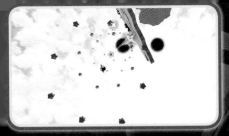

As Bee Mario blasts through the sky, pick up Star Bits with the cursor.

The Power Star is at the wall's top, just beyond the grid of honeycombs overrun with Mandibugs. Fly from one honeycomb to the next, recovering flight power while resting on the sticky spots. Wave the cursor over any Star Bits to collect them while resting. When the coast is clear and the Mandibugs are inching back to their starting positions around the Power Star, buzz up to claim the prize and return to the Comet Observatory.

Gusty Garden
Galaxy

Freezeflame
Galaxy

Dusty Dune
Galaxy

Honeyclimb
Galaxy

Bowser's Dark
Matter Reactor

Bigmouth
Galaxy

★ Wall 3 ★

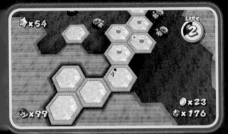

Oh no, Mandibugs. These bugs skitter across the honeycombs, trying to knock Bee Mario off the wall. Bee Mario can push away from the wall and ground pound on their backs to earn coins, but sometimes it's safer just to avoid the bugs as they crawl about. Keep crawling up the wall, inching in front of the Mandibugs so they rush forward. As the Mandibugs slowly retreat back to their original positions, press ahead.

BOWSER'S DARK MATTER REACTOR

Bowser's first defeat at the hands of Mario was only a minor setback. The Koopa King is back to work, tinkering with even more menacing machines that could drastically alter the fabric of the universe. Mario must follow Bowser to his next outpost, the Dark Matter Reactor, and stop the tyrant before he irreparably damages the galaxies. If Mario can best Bowser again, he can take back the stolen Grand Star that powers the Dark Matter Reactor and return it to Rosalina.

★ Dark Matter Reactor ★

Another 1-up Mushroom hangs in front of a lone honeycomb. Ride the sliding honeycombs over to it.

SUPER MARIO GALAXY

Bowser's Dark Matter Reactor spews forth some icky, horrible gunk that is deadly to the touch. The journey to the reactor and another battle with Bowser requires Mario to avoid the purplish goo at all times. Unlike falling in chilly water or lava, Mario doesn't bounce out of the dark matter with just one less health wedge. One touch and he must start over.

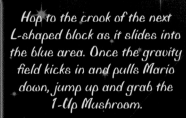

The green area pulls Mario to the right, so jump on top of the L-shaped block, then leap to the next sliding platform.

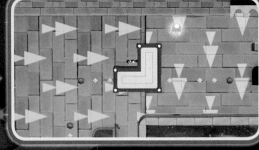

Hop to the crook of the next L-shaped block as it slides into the blue area. Once the gravity field kicks in and pulls Mario down, jump up and grab the 1-Up Mushroom.

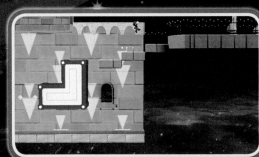

Jump from the blue area to the ledge with the Goomba patrol. Dispel the Goombas with spin attacks, then climb the pole to reach the reactor's next level.

Dark matter is everywhere in this mission. Mario must ride moving platforms up entire walls of the stuff, as well as carefully jump across rotating ledges over a giant cylinder of dark matter. After crossing the cylinder, Mario enters a field with crazy gravity. Whatever way the arrows on the wall point is "down." There are dark matter walls everywhere, so Mario must stand on the right sides of the moving blocks so he's pulled to safety, not to his doom.

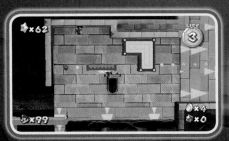

Jump across the pink wall to be pulled to the sliding platform. Then hop to the L-shaped block, but stay in the crook as it passes into the green area.

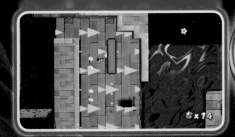

Jump to the blue platform that slides through the green field.

Drop down to the purple block in the blue field. Hop over the block and drop to the block shaped like a plus sign (+). Stand in the northwest crook of the "+" when the block starts moving toward the next gravity field.

Dark matter also eats through any surface. At the pole's top, Mario must hop down to a ledge that's being consumed by "moving holes." If Mario stands still and a hole passes under his feet, he falls through. Jump over the holes onto a series of pink sliding platforms. These platforms slide across a giant block of dark matter. There are holes in these platforms, too, so jump back and forth across the platforms to avoid the dark matter and pick up a 1-Up Mushroom.

Jump over the top of the "+" and prepare for gravity to pull Mario up in the pink field.

After riding the pink platforms, jump to a series of sliding yellow squares on a pulsing block of dark matter. The dark matter holes on these squares are stationary—the square slides over them instead. Jump across the squares to ascend the dark matter cube and reach a safe walkway. A 1-Up Mushroom is in a crystal at the dark matter cube's top. After claiming the power-up, walk to the next field of switching gravities.

Jump off the "+" and stand in the crook of the L-shaped block as it slides into the white field. Ride the block to the blue field, then jump out of the odd gravity area.

Run up the stairs to grab a Life Mushroom and find a frozen Luma. Once freed, the Luma thanks Mario.

Gusty Garden Galaxy

Freezeflame Galaxy

Dusty Dune Galaxy

Honeyclimb Galaxy

Bowser's Dark Matter Reactor

Bigmouth Galaxy

SUPER MARIO GALAXY

Bowser keeps applying the pressure. After getting back up, he unleashes a three-pronged attack. First, he covers the reactor with fireballs. While trying to avoid the fireballs, Mario must then jump over Bowser's shock waves. The king even lets fly with a few punches before he resumes jumping high over the reactor in an effort to stomp out Mario. Again, lead Bowser to a glass plug so he burns himself in the process.

Bowser isn't necessarily surprised to see Mario again, but he's not too happy about it either. The Koopa King roars into action, pulling Mario to the heart of his Dark Matter Reactor. This battle unfolds similarly to Mario's first encounter with Bowser. The hero must avoid Bowser's shock waves and fireballs long enough to trick him into crashing into one of three glass plugs that contains the pulsing star energy within the reactor's heart.

Bowser begins his attack by stomping on the reactor, sending shock waves rippling over the surface. Avoid the shock waves by hopping on the circular green platforms. As before, these green platforms contain hidden coins if Mario tricks Bowser into smashing one while he's throwing one of his infamous tantrums. After stomping out a few shock waves, Bowser starts patrolling the planetoid, throwing wild punches. Back off to avoid the swings.

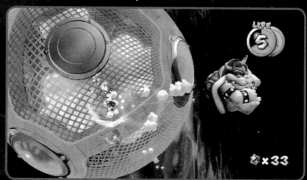

Mario must strike Bowser three times while he's on his back.

After several punches, Bowser leaps high above the reactor. Mario must run to one of the glass plugs. When darkened by Bowser's shadow, get out of the way. The tyrant crashes down to the reactor, shattering the glass and burning himself. Bowser then flees from Mario while his tail cools off. Mario must give chase for a little bit. If Bowser spots Mario, he runs in the other direction. After several seconds of running, Bowser stops to recover. Mario must then strike Bowser's tail. This flips the king on his back, which makes him totally vulnerable. Deliver a spin attack to Bowser as he slides around the reactor on his shell.

After pounding Bowser three times, the brute relents. He escapes to another corner of the universe, leaving behind the Grand Star that powered the Dark Matter Reactor. Mario takes the Grand Star back to the Comet Observatory, fueling the space station. The Engine Room Galaxies are now available.

BIGMOUTH GALAXY

The hungry Luma outside the Bedroom Dome is craving Star Bits. Feed it 600 Star Bits, and the little star blows up like a balloon and blasts off into space, transforming into an entirely new galaxy: Bigmouth Galaxy. Mario must follow the trail to the Bigmouth Galaxy and investigate—there's surely a Power Star here to recover.

Deep Diving

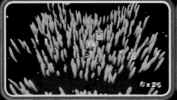

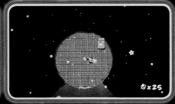

In deep space, an old penguin makes his home in a whale-shaped planetoid. However, his personal paradise is threatened by monsters, such as giant jellyfish and crabs. If Mario can help the elder penguin and recover a golden shell from beneath the waves, the penguin will let him return to the Comet Observatory with another Power Star.

After slipping into the water, swim straight down to the kelp gardens. The seaweed obscures another 1-Up Mushroom. Then, swim forward and blast through the brick wall to enter a giant chamber.

Golden Shell

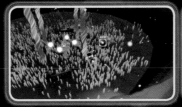

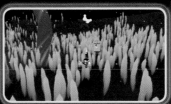

Beyond the brick wall, four jellyfish dance around something sparkling. Swim down for a closer look—it's a Star Chip. Four more are hidden in the kelp around the jellyfish.

Before leaving the beach, gather all the available goodies. There are rings of shells in the sand. If Mario spins in the middle of the rings, the shells turn into Star Bits. Smash the nearby rock pillars to recover Star Bits too. Spin the soft backsides of the blue crabs on the beach; they release a 1-Up Mushroom.

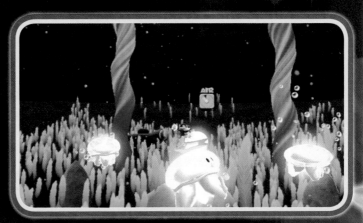

The Star Chips create a Sling Star in the center of the four jellyfish.

Gusty Garden
Galaxy

Freezeflame
Galaxy

Dusty Dune
Galaxy

Honeyclimb
Galaxy

Bowser's Dark
Matter Reactor

Bigmouth
Galaxy

PRIMA Official Game Guide

The Sling Star sends Mario up to a strange pool of water on the chamber's ceiling. The golden shell is here, so swim into it to collect the prize and then swim back down to the lower sea.

NOTE

Mario can use the golden shell to pop either the giant jellyfish or the four little ones in the large chamber for coins. New golden shells regenerate in the upper sea every time Mario fires one off into an enemy.

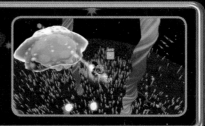

Take the golden shell back to the beach. Swim through the hole in the brick wall and skirt around all the waiting Boos just below the coastline.

On the beach, throw the golden shell at the gilded chest to crack it open. The Power Star rises from the chest, ready to be claimed and returned to the Comet Observatory.

ENGINE ROOM GALAXIES

GOLD LEAF GALAXY

The Gold Leaf Galaxy looks remarkably like the Honeyhive Galaxy at the onset of autumn. The main planet is set up almost exactly the same, except in reverse. However, once Mario leaves the main planet and explores the Gold Leaf Galaxy's outer worlds, he discovers strange new planetoids of all shapes and sizes.

Searching for Blue Star Chips

GOLD LEAF GALAXY

Searching for Blue Star Chips

Start

A

B

The first Power Star in the Gold Leaf Galaxy is on a spherical planetoid high above the main world. To reach it, Mario must assemble five blue Star Chips to create a Pull Star chain that points directly at the Power Star's resting place.

Planet A

LEGEND

Star Chip
Bee Mushroom
1-Up Mushroom

Gold Leaf Galaxy

Sea Slide Galaxy

Toy Time Galaxy

Bonefin Galaxy

Bowser Jr.'s Lava Reactor

Sand Spiral Galaxy

SUPER MARIO GALAXY

PRIMA Official Game Guide

A friendly bunny greets Mario when he arrives in the Gold Leaf Galaxy, telling him about the five Star Chips that the other bunnies have been gawking at—a hint to look for wide-eyed bunnies in order to spot the Star Chips. The planet is infested with bugs, so as Mario peeks around for the bunnies, stomp out the insect problem for extra Star Bits.

The fourth Star Chip is directly behind the large waterfall in the planet's middle. Break the wooden crate near the bunny.

> **NOTE**
>
> Before setting off to explore, look out to space. Just like the Honeyhive Galaxy, there are Star Bits in the sky, but this time they form a giant "L." And that ledge with the 1-Up Mushroom in Honeyhive? It now holds coins.

The first Star Chip is on the ledge directly ahead of Mario's starting position. Follow the bunny seen near the planet's edge and step around the ledge's rear. Wall jump up the alcove to reach the ledge's top. The Star Chip is in the middle of a trio of Piranha Plants.

To retrieve the fifth and final Star Chip, return to the starting position on the planet. There is a large flower near the fence that lines the planet's edge. Swing up the flower stem to vault to the big ledge containing the massive tree. There is a line of coins on the ground that leads to a Bee Mushroom on a lily pad.

Jump down from the ledge to another bunny standing in the middle of three wooden pegs. The bunny is looking directly at the next Star Chip. It's too high to reach without aid, so ground pound each wooden peg. A small Sling Star appears that bounces Mario up to the Star Chip.

Next, head back down the ramp and hop up to the trapeze. Swing back and forth until Mario arcs right into another small Sling Star. Spin into the Sling Star to fly up to a ledge with a fountain. Break all the crystals around the water to earn Star Bits. Wait for the geyser in the fountain's center to stop, then backflip into the middle of the water. Mario jumps up and grabs the third Star Chip.

Buzz up to the next ledge, stopping on the purple flower petals to restore the Flight meter. Ground pound the wooden peg in the hollow stump's middle to release a bevy of Star Bits.

x

x

x

The fifth Star Bit is above the nearby spring. Ground pound the spring to recover it.

The Star Chips create a chain of Pull Stars at the starting spot on the planet. Pull Mario across the Pull Stars to reach a Launch Star that rockets him to the next planetoid.

 **Planet B**

Gold Leaf Galaxy

Sea Slide Galaxy

Toy Time Galaxy

Bonefin Galaxy

Bowser Jr.'s Lava Reactor

Sand Spiral Galaxy

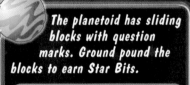

TIP The planetoid has sliding blocks with question marks. Ground pound the blocks to earn Star Bits.

When Mario lands on the planetoid, a bunny hops right up to him. It wants to play hide-and-seek. If Mario can catch the bunny as it runs around the spherical planetoid, it will hand over the Power Star.

Chasing down the bunny is tricky. Without any ledges or fences to get caught on, the bunny has free rein of the planet. Mario can almost always see where the bunny is because of the beacon over its head, but gaining on the little fella isn't easy. Stomp on the red button to raise several platforms, which slow the bunny down. Now, corner the bunny and get that Power Star.

After catching the bunny, grab the Power Star to finish the mission.

SUPER MARIO

CATAQUACK TO THE SKIES

GOLD LEAF GALAXY
Cataquack to the Skies

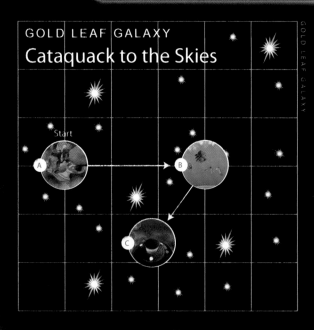

Those silly Cataquacks have one-track minds—they just love to chase things down and then flip them into the air with their giant bills. Mario can use this talent to his advantage, though, to reach the second Power Star in the Gold Leaf Galaxy.

When Mario arrives back on the main planet, the boulders are really thundering across the countryside. Weave between the rolling rocks and follow the main road to the cave that all the boulders are coming from. Quickly spin the stone circle near the cave to get some extra Star Bits.

Mario must play with the Cataquack that is next to the cave. It is penned up and cannot run away. Look on the ground in the little corral. There's a shadow of a small Sling Star. Lead the Cataquack near the shadow and let it toss Mario into the air. Spin when he closes in on the Sling Star.

★★ **Planet A** ★★

LEGEND

🍄 Bee Mushroom
🍄 1-Up Mushroom

After picking up the nearby Bee Mushroom, buzz across the planet to find two more corralled Cataquacks. Let them bounce Mario up to the next ledge.

Another corralled Cataquack? These creatures must have a tendency to roam! Let the Cataquack bounce Mario up one more level to a ledge with a red button.

Ground pounding the red button releases a string of Star Bits along the narrow path behind the waterfall. Walk across the path—don't get Bee Mario wet—and walk to the ledge with the fountain. Before taking off to the next planet via the Launch Star, shatter the nearby crystal full of Star Bits.

Planets B, C, and D

Mario lands on a small planetoid occupied by a Wiggler and a Cataquack. Leave the Wiggler alone and concentrate on the overly friendly Cataquack. Lead it to the flat spot at the planetoid's top. There's even a Cataquack symbol on the ground marking where Mario must lead the creature. Let the Cataquack bounce Mario up to a large cube-shaped planetoid.

The Cataquack here is sleeping. Wake it by smashing the wooden crates on the cube. (Many of the crates contain Star Bits and coins too.) When the Cataquack is awake, let it chase Mario around the cube. Lead it between the bushes, staying close enough to keep it interested, but not so close that it flings Mario into the air.

Lead the Cataquack to the launchpad marked with its symbol.

The Cataquack flips Mario up to a long, narrow planetoid covered with crawling Cataquacks. There is a Launch Star at the planetoid's far end, but it's too high to reach without the aid of a friendly Cataquack. Lead a Cataquack across the planetoid and let it bounce Mario right into the Launch Star.

After Mario dons the Bee Suit, lead the Cataquack to the wooden tower's base. Let it bounce Mario up the tower's side, then buzz the rest of the way to the top.

The Cataquack launches Mario to a spherical planetoid, sectioned off into different parts by short walls. Jump over the first wall to the right to clear out the little monsters splashing in the water. Spin in the shell circle to collect some Star Bits. After emptying out the watery area, jump back over the wall and look for a mole's trail in the dirt.

Buzz to the round pedestal next to the flower garden. There's a Wiggler making the rounds on the pedestal, so fly over its head and land safely in the center to pick up some Star Bits and recover Bee Mario's flight power. After a brief rest, jump to the flowers. Several insects spoil the serene scene. Buzz over them and ground pound to clean off the flowers.

The Power Star rests on the last bloom in the flowerbed. Buzz over to it and retrieve the prize.

The mean mole has corralled that poor Cataquack. Ground pound next to the mole to stun it, then kick it off the planetoid. Smooth out the disturbed soil with a spin, clearing a path for the trapped Cataquack. Lead it to the small grassy mound and let it bounce Mario straight up to a Bee Mushroom.

WHEN IT RAINS, IT POURS

GOLD LEAF GALAXY
When It Rains, It Pours

Start

A little rain is always good for the flowers and trees—but not for Bee Mario. He must use the Bee Suit to climb the tall tower above the main planet and wrest a Power Star from a mole.

Rainy Day

Use the nearby trapeze to vault Mario on top of a collection of rain clouds. Buzz from the clouds to a large wooden ledge.

Use the rain clouds to reach a series of wooden walkways.

When Mario lands on the main planet, the storm clouds have already set in. Find a Bee Mushroom immediately so he can start buzzing through the skies to reach the tower. Run around the boulder cave's rear. Wall jump up the alcove to reach the ledge that overlooks the trapeze. (Watch out for the Piranha Plant up here.) The Bee Mushroom is atop the gray cloud. Fortunately, Mario is light enough to walk on clouds, and the precipitation doesn't affect Bee Mario as long as he's on the cloud's top.

Crossing this walkway wouldn't normally be a problem for Bee Mario, but the showers complicate things, and those Mandibugs aren't helping either. Buzz across the small gaps in the walkways, but wait patiently between storms before continuing on. If even a single drop gets on Bee Mario, he loses the suit.

Use the spring at the walkway's end to bounce to a trapeze. Swing on the trapeze as high as Mario can go, then fling him to a ledge that circles the giant tree trunk.

Buzz across the gray clouds to start crossing the gap in the middle of the planet. Finish crossing on top of the pretty purple flowers.

As soon as Mario lands, duck into a small alcove to avoid the passing rain cloud.

Gold Leaf Galaxy

Sea Slide Galaxy

Toy Time Galaxy

Bonefin Galaxy

Bowser Jr.'s Lava Reactor

Sand Spiral Galaxy

The Sproutle shoots through the air, connecting Mario to the arena at the tower's top. Grab the Sproutle and shake the Wii Remote to swing Mario along the vine and land right in front of the Power Star's guardian, a mean mole sitting in the cockpit of a bubble cannon.

When Mario buzzes up to the next ledge, immediately duck into the alcove to avoid the rain. If he ever gets wet and loses his Bee Suit, he must drop back down to the last available Bee Mushroom.

The Star Bits in the alcove are a big hint. Duck into the alcove and wait for the next rain cloud to drift by. After it passes, buzz out and fly up to the next level.

The giant coin next to the spring creates a batch of Star Bits. Scoop up the goodies, then use the spring to bounce up to the tower's top. There is a stone wheel on the ledge. Ground pound it to release a Sproutle.

Boss Battle: Bubble Cannon

High atop the tower that overlooks Gold Leaf Galaxy, a mole with a nasty temper rules all. Seated in the cockpit of a bubble cannon, the mole fills the air with bubbles that whoosh away any encroachers. Mario must somehow buzz in close to the mole and smash through the glass that covers the cockpit. Three hits are all it takes to send this mole packing for another galaxy.

When Mario first arrives, the mole doesn't consider him much of a threat. He fires only one bubble every few seconds. It's easy to duck behind the gray wall near the arena's center and dodge the attacks. Right after a bubble pops against the wall, buzz out and fly to the cannon. Climb to the cockpit's top and ground pound right on the glass. The mole shakes Mario free and steps up the frequency of the attacks.

With the mole shooting more bubbles, Mario could use more cover. Fall back to the red button on the long walkway, protected by two small walls. Ground pound the button. Several platforms rise out of the arena. Use these platforms as cover while closing in on the cannon. If a bubble has already hit Mario and he's lost the Bee Suit, he must use these platforms to reach the cannon's top and deliver the second blow.

Boss Battle: Bubble Cannon (cont.)

Now the mole fires with wild abandon. Mario must use cover to close in on the cannon. If a bubble strikes him, he flies across the arena, slamming into the fence. If Mario drops on the ground, he's unharmed. However, if the bubble pushes Mario over the spikes in parts of the arena, he takes damage. Bounce up the ledges to reach the cannon cockpit and smash it one last time.

The Power Star appears at the arena's edge. Carefully jump to it, avoiding the spikes.

Gold Leaf Galaxy

Sea Slide Galaxy

Toy Time Galaxy

Bonefin Galaxy

Bowser Jr.'s Lava Reactor

Sand Spiral Galaxy

THE BELL ON THE BIG TREE

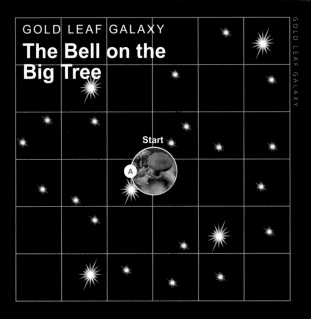

GOLD LEAF GALAXY
The Bell on the Big Tree

A hidden Power Star in Gold Leaf Galaxy—that's music to Mario's ears. To retrieve it, Mario must return to the "Cataquack to the Skies" mission and seek a series of musical notes. If Mario can follow a tune long enough, he'll hear the sweet sounds of a Power Star falling into his hands.

Music Lover

When Mario returns to Gold Leaf, use the Cataquacks to reach the large tree with the moat around its massive trunk. However, instead of continuing up the ledges with the corralled Cataquacks, walk toward the bubble machine next to the tree trunk. Jump in the bubble.

Hit the bell hanging off the tree with the cursor to release musical notes. The swirling notes circle the tree trunk twice—but they do not hang in the air forever. Mario must collect all the notes before they vanish. If he misses a single note, the Power Star will not appear.

Before grabbing the Power Star, blow Mario into the giant coin at the tree's top. This releases a trail of Star Bits that leads straight to a 1-Up Mushroom. After collecting the Mushroom, blow Mario back around the tree to pick up the Power Star.

The two Marios hunker down at the starting line. As soon as the race begins, Cosmic Mario takes off like a rocket. Mario must keep pace, bolting up the well-worn path to the set of blocks that span the gap in the planet's middle. Try to cut off Cosmic Mario right in front of the blocks, making a sharp right turn at the log.

Colliding with the Power Star may burst Mario's bubble—but for once, that's music to his ears.

COSMIC MARIO FOREST RACE

When the Cosmic Comet rises over the Gold Leaf Galaxy's edge, Mario must return to challenge his rival, Cosmic Mario, to a spirited race across the planet. This race is quite a contest, as Cosmic Mario no longer makes mistakes. He has his eyes on the prize, so Mario cannot afford any false moves on the way to the finish line.

Cosmic Mario flawlessly executes his jumps up the blocks. If he pulls ahead here, not all is lost. However, if Cosmic Mario is well in advance by the time Mario reaches the ledge above the blocks, just grab the 1-Up Mushroom so losing the race isn't a wash. If Mario is in the lead, though, don't be tempted by the 1-Up Mushroom. Just concentrate on keeping ahead of Cosmic Mario.

This is the second place where Mario can get the lead over Cosmic Mario. Cosmic Mario usually plays it safe, opting to head right and hop across the short gap, even though he must run down a longer path to reach it. Long-jump across the wider gap to the pair of blocks sticking out of the middle walkway (occasionally Cosmic Mario will take this route too). From there, it's a straight shot to the finish line and the Power Star.

SEA SLIDE GALAXY

The Sea Slide Galaxy is a huge watery ring floating in space, peacefully inhabited by the penguins. These playful birds are harboring a collection of Power Stars, so Mario must blast off for the wet world. If he shows the penguins some winning moves, they'll award him with their precious Power Stars.

★★★ Going After Guppy ★★★

SEA SLIDE GALAXY

SEA SLIDE GALAXY
Going After Guppy

It's shark week in the Sea Slide Galaxy. The great predator of the deep has moved into Sea Slide and is currently making life difficult for the penguins. Can Mario restore balance to the ecosystem?

★ Out of the Pool ★

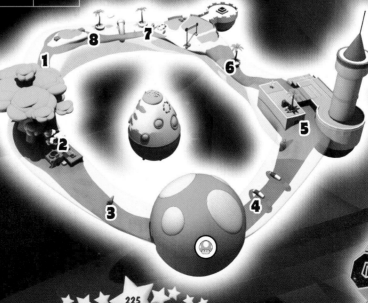

LEGEND

1-8 Guppy's Rings

🍄 1-Up Mushroom

Gold Leaf Galaxy

Sea Slide Galaxy

Toy Time Galaxy

Bonefin Galaxy

Bowser Jr.'s Lava Reactor

Sand Spiral Galaxy

Why are all the penguins on the beach? Shouldn't they be laughing and playing in the water? It turns out that a big bully of a shark named Guppy has moved into Sea Slide Galaxy and has scared all the penguins on to land. This simply cannot stand. Dive into the water and swim to Guppy, who lingers underneath the stone arch to the right of the beached penguins.

> **TIP**
>
> Before going to Guppy, swim around the ring and wave the cursor over banks of Star Bits to pad Mario's pockets. He needs all the Star Bits he can get—so many Lumas need to be fed.

Guppy freely admits that he's taken over the waves, but he loves a good challenge, so he tells Mario that if he can keep up with his master swimming skills, he will consider letting the penguins back into the water. Mario must follow right behind Guppy and pass through eight rings. If Mario misses a ring or Guppy makes a full loop before Mario crosses the eighth ring, the penguins must remain permanently landlocked.

The first ring (labeled 8 on the map—you will work toward 1) is close to the starting point. Mario isn't a bad swimmer, but he cannot keep up with Guppy just by kicking his feet. Between the 8 and 7 rings, pick up the shell between two rocky pillars. The shell helps Mario keep pace with Guppy so the shark doesn't get too far ahead.

Ring 7 is on the inside of the Sea Slide Galaxy track.

Pass through the school of fish to close in on ring 6.

Thread the needle at the gate near the tower to zero in on ring 5.

Ring 4 is between the two caves that run beneath the grassy hill. Take the left cave after passing through the ring. There is a 1-Up Mushroom on the seafloor.

Ring 3 is between these two rocks. It's a tight fit, but Mario can squeeze through the hole between the rocks to keep on Guppy's tail.

FASTER THAN A SPEEDING PENGUIN

Ring 2 is on the water filter's other side. The cage drops down just as Guppy passes, so swim low to avoid getting bonked by the machine.

The last ring, 1, is at the brick wall. Avoid hitting the bricks with the shell and pass through the ring.

Guppy is a shark of his word. He surfaces on the beach next to the penguins and apologizes for his brutish behavior. The penguins are now more than welcome to cool their beaks in the water again. As a reward for reaching a peaceful resolution, Mario is given the honor of a Power Star.

SEA SLIDE GALAXY **Faster Than a Speeding Penguin**		

Start

Now that the seas are safe again, the penguins are busy frolicking in the water. It isn't long before their love of swimming leads to a race. First place gets something shiny, so Mario better sign up for this race.

★ Swim Meet ★

Start/Finish

Gold Leaf Galaxy

Sea Slide Galaxy

Toy Time Galaxy

Bonefin Galaxy

Bowser Jr.'s Lava Reactor

Sand Spiral Galaxy

PRIMA Official Game Guide

If Mario ever hits a breakable wall or one of the Gringill, he loses his shell. There are other shells on the course, but it's tough to catch up with the leader unless Mario holds the same shell for the entire race.

The penguins are milling about the beach, getting ready for a big race around the Sea Slide Galaxy's watery ring. Five entrants can join the race, but only four penguins have signed up so far. That leaves one empty spot for Mario. To enter the race, talk to the purple penguin on the beach. Mario then appears at the starting line with the four penguins. After a quick countdown, the race begins. The current record for the race is 1:30, but surely Mario can beat that?

Just as Mario needed a shell to keep up with Guppy, he needs one to stay competitive with the sleek penguins. Mario will remain in fifth place until he picks up a shell. The first one available is just under a small island in the river's middle. Spin to grab the shell as he approaches. Within seconds, Mario catches up with fourth place.

There is one last speed boost after Mario passes through the brick wall. Steer for it to gain a lead that the penguins can never capture.

The penguins in the lead are pretty far ahead, so Mario must seek out a boost. When he reaches the twin caves, veer left. There is a ring next to a Gringill's gaping maw. Swim through it to enjoy a speed boost.

Mario cannot breathe underwater, so steer through bubbles to get some fresh air.

Running into the penguins slows Mario down, so carefully glide by the other racers.

The large red-and-white banner marks the finish line. If Mario crosses the finish line before the other penguins, he earns the prize. The Power Star appears on the beach, next to the Toads that enjoyed watching the race. Pick up the Power Star to return to the Engine Room Dome.

SEA SLIDE GALAXY
The Silver Stars of Sea Slide

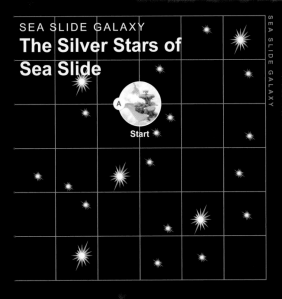

Start

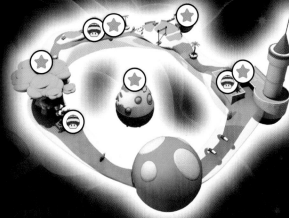

LEGEND

⭐ Silver Star

🐝 Bee Mushroom

...he penguins actually don't have the third Power Star of the Sea Slide ...alaxy—but they can point the way to it. Five Silver Stars are on the great ...ng. Mario must collect them all to assemble the Power Star.

Silver Stars 1 and 2

...he search for the five Silver Stars on ...ea Slide requires Mario to take to the ...kies—none of the stars are underwater. ...ortunately, there are Bee Mushrooms ...n the ring. In the Bee Suit, Mario can ...uzz above the waves and seek out his ...uarry. As always, watch those toes when ...ear the water. If Bee Mario gets even ...e tip of his shoes wet, the Bee Suit ...elts away.

Once Mario has the Bee Suit, the first Silver Star is within reach. Fly to the top of the small puffy cloud directly ahead. Mario can stand on the cloud, so take a breather and regain any spent flight power. Then, buzz over to the stone arch and pick up the first Silver Star.

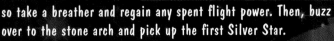

CAUTION

There are no invisible walls that prevent Mario from flying outside the ring. If he's buzzing over empty space when his Flight meter runs dry, he falls straight down. And keeps going.

Always spin in the middle of the shell circles—this reveals Star Bits.

Gold Leaf Galaxy

Sea Slide Galaxy

Toy Time Galaxy

Bonefin Galaxy

Bowser Jr.'s Lava Reactor

Sand Spiral Galaxy

Aim with Ⓒ and press Ⓐ

To reach the second Silver Star, Mario must blast off from the Sea Slide ring for a few moments. A Toad has built a cannon on the ring's edge that can launch Mario out to the Toad spaceship, where he can retrieve the Silver Star. (Hey, that's a hungry Luma next to the cannon.) Jump in the cannon and aim for the Toads' spaceship. Mario zooms through the air and is caught by the small gravity field surrounding the spaceship.

The Silver Star is above the ship. Use the Pull Stars to drag Mario off the spaceship and to the Silver Star. To return to the ring, use the Sling Star at the end of the Pull Star chain. A 1-Up Mushroom is out here, though. To get the power-up, pull Mario to the last Pull Star but release Ⓐ right away so inertia carries him over to the 1-Up Mushroom. As soon as he has the Mushroom, immediately pull him back to the Pull Star before he floats away.

The fourth Silver Star is on top of the giant mangrove that provides shade for the Sea Slide Galaxy inhabitants. Fly across the ring, stopping on stones and clouds to recover spent energy, until Mario closes in on the mangrove. Several spiders reside in the mangrove, so watch out for them. Star Bits stun the spiders long enough for Mario to kick them off the tree with a spin attack.

Silver Stars 3 and 4

The third Pull Star is on the palm tree next to the tall tower. After dropping out of the skies, use Bee Mario's flight to cross the water and land on the tower's front lawn. If Mario loses the Bee Suit, there is a Bee Mushroom right in front of the tower. Use the Bee Suit to buzz up to the palm tree's fronds and grab the Silver Star. Use the blocks on the ground next to the tree if Mario lacks the Bee Suit, then just backflip up to the fronds.

Take the red shell off that Koopa near the castle and break open the treasure chest behind the tower. It's full of Star Bits.

Four spiders guard the Silver Star at the mangrove's top. Stun those spiders with Star Bits so they harmlessly swing on their webs while Mario closes the deal with spin attacks. After the spiders are off the tree, jump to the mangrove's top and snag that fourth Silver Star.

Mario splashes down on the island's lower half. There's suffi-cient gravity to hold him to the ground, so walk up the island's side and grab the giant gold coin. The coin unleashes a symphony of musical notes that circle the island. To pick up an extra 1-Up Mushroom, avoid the crabs and capture all the notes before they vanish.

TIP

Use the branches to rest. Watch Mario's shadow to see when he's hovering directly over a branch and won't slip off when he tries to land.

Silver Star 5

The fifth Silver Star is on the island in the ring's exact center, but it's much too far to reach with the Bee Suit (Mario would make it halfway before dropping out of the galaxy). To reach the island, drop off the mangrove and land on the water-filter machine at the tree's base. Toads, penguins, and even Guppy have gathered here, all staring at a special valve.

The last Silver Star is on the island's summit, right next to an elder penguin seeking solace from the ring's hustle and bustle.

Spin on the valve to unleash a blast of water from the filter station. The water snakes across the empty space and splashes against the island in the ring's center. Jump in the water and let the current whisk Mario safely to the island.

The Power Star appears, but it's all the way back on the first beach. Leave the island via the Launch Star, then use a network of smaller Sling Stars to land on the Power Star's beach. Grab the Power Star to end the mission. Mario's not done with the Sea Slide Galaxy yet, though. There's still a hungry Luma out there, so return to this mission to locate the galaxy's hidden Power Star.

HURRY, HE'S HUNGRY

The hungry Luma that was hanging out by the cannon in the "Silver Stars of Sea Slide" section needs some Star Bits soon so it can transform into a new planetoid.

Hurrying and Scurrying

New planetoid

To earn the Power Star, Mario must pick up every musical note on the planetoid. However, as soon as he lands, the ground beneath him starts to vanish. He better get moving if he is to cover every square inch of the planetoid and gather all the musical notes.

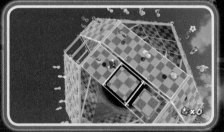

Start by running all the way along one line of the planetoid. Pick up every musical notes on this single line—don't step off it. When Mario finally wraps around the planetoid once, move to the next line and follow it all the way around the planet's circumference.

When Mario returns to the galaxy, he must collect 40 Star Bits before feeding the hungry Luma. Spin in the shell circles to pick up Star Bits. Swim around the island, waving the cursor over signs and clouds to pick up additional goodies. If Mario still needs more Star Bits, swim to the castle tower and use the Koopa shell to break open the nearby treasure chest. This should be enough to feed the Luma.

The Luma transforms into a planetoid made entirely of shrinking platforms. But it's too far to reach with the Bee Suit. Use the Toads' cannon to blast off from the ring and land on the new planetoid.

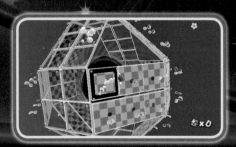

After clearing the planet's center, start picking up the musical notes on the "arms."

Run to the end of an arm on one side, then come back down the other and move on to the next arm.

The Power Star appears in the center of the now-barren planetoid. Stand on the final platform as it shrinks so Mario falls right to the Power Star.

Run across the platforms in lines to collect the remaining musical notes. Snake down the various arms to grab the notes, then move back and continue on to the next arm. The ultimate goal is to use up every space on the planetoid, grabbing the final musical note off the last platform.

UNDERWATER COSMIC MARIO RACE

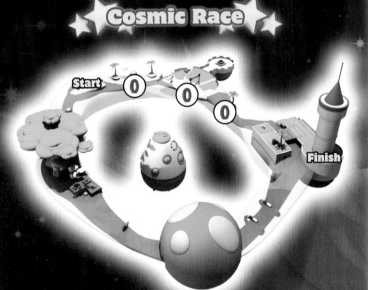

Cosmic Race

Start

Finish

The Cosmic Comet rises over the Sea Slide Galaxy. The ring world is bathed in the comet's blue hue, indicating the return of Cosmic Mario. Still sore after losing to Mario in Gold Leaf Galaxy, Cosmic Mario challenges Mario yet again for another Power Star prize.

LEGEND

○ Speed Boost

Gold Leaf Galaxy

Sea Slide Galaxy

Toy Time Galaxy

Bonefin Galaxy

Bowser Jr.'s Lava Reactor

Sand Spiral Galaxy

233

PRIMA Official Game Guide

Mario and Cosmic Mario line up at the beach's edge, ready to sprint to the water. Cosmic Mario executes a solid dive under the waves, and unless Mario can dive right in after him, Cosmic Mario gets an early lead. Just as Mario jumps out and touches the water, press ② to dive. Accidentally ground pounding in the air just brings Mario crashing down while Cosmic Mario slips away.

Follow the arrow signs to the beach below the tower. When Mario surfaces, spin to dispose of the shell and make a beeline for the tower.

Grab the red shell near the starting line. If Mario misses it, he can stay competitive with Cosmic Mario by constantly spinning, but it's harder to control.

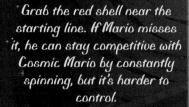

Use the speed boosts to rocket through the water. Again, Cosmic Mario knows where these boosts are, too, and will use them.

Cosmic Mario may gain on Mario, but there's one last trick to ensure Cosmic Mario stays in second place. The Power Star is on the tower's other side, closer to the right side than the left. So as Mario approaches the tower, veer right. Cosmic Mario always takes the right route, so if Mario goes around to the left, Cosmic Mario wins because Mario must take an extra four or five steps to reach the Power Star.

Whoops—Cosmic Mario makes a critical mistake that Mario can capitalize on. Don't follow Cosmic Mario out of the water. Instead, stay in the river and swim toward the speed boost that Cosmic Mario bizarrely ignores. While Cosmic Mario trudges over land, Mario can power ahead and take the lead.

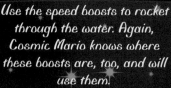

Don't let that 1-Up Mushroom tempt Mario away from the speed boost.

TOY TIME GALAXY

The ultra-playful Toy Time Galaxy is alive with bright colors and sugary sweets, but terrible toys and menacing monsters are threatening to spoil playtime. Mario must climb about the toy train and blast off to rid the playroom of these nasties before they put everybody down for a long nap.

⭐ Heavy Metal Mecha-Bowser ⭐

TOY TIME GALAXY
Heavy Metal Mecha-Bowser

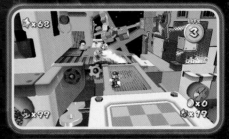

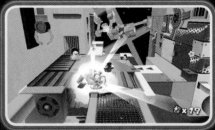

TOY TIME GALAXY

Who doesn't love to play with toy robots? Unfortunately, Mecha-Bowsers—little wind-up versions of the Koopa tyrant—have taken over the metal plaything in the Toy Time Galaxy. Mario must get the drop on these menaces, and discovering the Spring Mushroom is the best way to do so.

Mecha-Bowsers toddle around the planets until they spot a target and then breathe fire at it. Mario cannot stun them with regular means by spinning into them. To dispose of a Mecha-Bowser, Mario must ground pound it square on the head or back. The pieces of the Mecha-Bowser fly apart, revealing a coin.

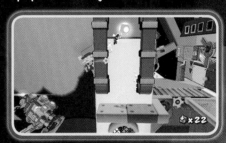

Before exploring the planet, wall jump up the alcove to the left to fetch a 1-Up Mushroom.

⭐ Planets A and B ⭐

Mario arrives in the Toy Time Galaxy just in time to catch the first train to trouble. Jump on one of the boxcars and ride the train to the Launch Star on the track's opposite side. The Launch Star blasts Mario straight to the first major planet in the system, which is currently crawling with Mecha-Bowsers.

Gold Leaf Galaxy

Sea Slide Galaxy

Toy Time Galaxy

Bonefin Galaxy

Bowser Jr.'s Lava Reactor

Sand Spiral Galaxy

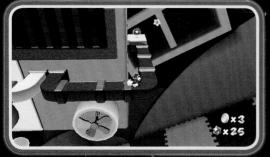

x3
x25

x77

Cross the planet to the right and follow the yellow and red pipes around to a Life Mushroom. Mario will need that extra health to survive this galaxy's trials.

x68
x99   x7
             x82

After gathering the power-ups, it's time to explore this planet—and more importantly, find a way off of it. Gravity here pulls Mario straight down, but he defies it by walking along bright pink surfaces. Mario adheres to this sticky stuff and can walk along or straight up walls.

x5
x25

Mario crashes down to another planet constructed of children's blocks. Bash the Mecha-Bowsers that are milling about before they can turn on Mario. There is a giant coin over an orange circle. Grabbing the coin releases a brand-new Mushroom—the Spring Mushroom.

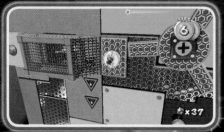

x37

Mario must walk to a rotating arm and spin on the blue screw in the center to stop it. Once the arm grinds to a halt, jump to the yellow screw next to the blue cage. The Launch Star is behind the grating. Spinning unscrews the cage, allowing it to fall away. But there is no way to reach the Launch Star—gravity will not permit it.

x82

The Spring Mushroom gives Mario the Spring Suit, wrapping a coil around him that lets him make fantastically high jumps.

x52

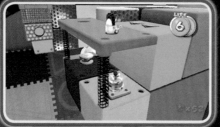

x52

Return to the planet's main level—do not try to jump away from the arm or Mario will stumble into space. Bop the Mecha-Bowsers to clear a path, and look for a long blue block. There is another yellow screw here. Spin on the screw, then fall down the resulting hole. Spin on the blue screw next to the spring. This extends an arm across the gap in front of the Launch Star.

x82

x52

Walk up the pink wall and spin on the Launch Star to achieve escape velocity.

Spring Mario can bounce across the blocks' surface, punching otherwise-unreachable Prize Blocks. Sweep up the resulting Star Bits, then smash any remaining Mecha-Bowsers. Ground pound while springing through the air to ruin the nasty little toys.

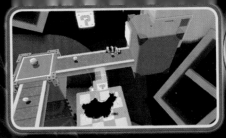

Bounce on top of the blue checkered block. Smash the stone circle up here for Star Bits. There are more Mecha-Bowsers rolling around. If the Mecha-Bowser's flames hit Mario, he loses the Spring Suit. (There are extra Spring Mushrooms littered around the galaxy for this reason.) Mario must cross the series of conveyor belts to find a Launch Star.

There are Prize Blocks on top of Prize Blocks in this level. If Mario pops the lower tier of Prize Blocks, he may earn Star Bits, but he can then never reach the highest Prize Blocks.

Bounce up the blue checkered ramp to the conveyor belts' right. A warp block sticks out of a large green block. Drop down the warp pipe to find a secret room.

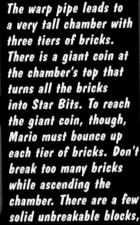

The warp pipe leads to a very tall chamber with three tiers of bricks. There is a giant coin at the chamber's top that turns all the bricks into Star Bits. To reach the giant coin, though, Mario must bounce up each tier of bricks. Don't break too many bricks while ascending the chamber. There are a few solid unbreakable blocks, so spring off these as Mario goes higher. Once Mario touches that giant coin, though, it's a long way down. However, the spring prevents Mario from taking any damage. Sweep the cursor around the chamber to pick up the Star Bits before they vanish. Return to the planet's surface via the warp pipe.

Bounce up the tall stack of colored blocks in the planet's corner to find the Launch Star.

The Launch Star blasts Mario to a small plate hovering in space. There is a Launch Star inside a glass bottle; Mario must bounce on top of the bottle and shatter the stopper with a ground pound in order to access it. The Launch Star puts Mario on a crash course with a toy robot—a very large toy robot.

Gold Leaf Galaxy

Sea Slide Galaxy

Toy Time Galaxy

Bonefin Galaxy

Bowser Jr.'s Lava Reactor

Sand Spiral Galaxy

SUPER MARIO GALAXY

Planet B) to climb up the toy's face and somehow stop it. Mario must spin on the screws to slowly dismantle the machine. The first blue screw opens a warp pipe that leads to the robot's other leg.

Spin on the next blue screw to create a small Sling Star, which bounces Mario up to the robot's large chest plate. There are four golden screws on the chest plate, one in each corner. Spin on each screw while avoiding the fire trap to detach the plate and expose the two cavities in the toy's chest.

The upper cavity contains coins—and a Mecha-Bowser. The lower cavity has a warp pipe that leads to the robot's right arm.

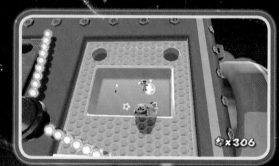

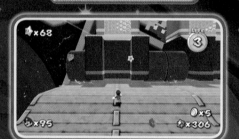

Two more Mecha-Bowsers are waiting for Mario when he emerges from the warp pipe. Dismantle the Mecha-Bowsers with ground pounds before jumping to the sticky green surface on the robot's arm. Walk across the green surface and jump to the robot's elbow joint. Jump from there to the shoulder joint.

Spin on the gold screw in the robot's shoulder joint. This creates a Launch Star that vaults Mario to a platform right in front of the toy robot's face.

Mario lands on the conveyor belt in front of the robot. The robot is large enough to have its own gravity field, but instead, the forces of gravity always pull Mario straight down. He must use the green surfaces on the robot (they have the same texture as the pink surfaces on

a Power Star on the conveyor belt below. Mario drops to the conveyor belt, where he can bounce over to the Power Star as happy little robots look on approvingly.

A Magikoopa hovers near the robot's jaw, casting fireballs across the platform. Pick up the nearby Spring Mushroom to bounce to the top of the robot's head. Bounce over the Magikoopa and stop on the ledge right in front of the robot's eyes. There are two coins here.

TIP

If the Magikoopa hits Mario with a fireball, he loses the Spring Suit. There is another Spring Mushroom under the robot's right ear.

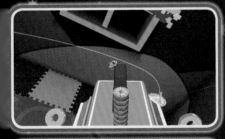

To stop the robot, bounce high into the air and ground pound the tall stack of stone circles atop the robot's head. When the stack is destroyed, the robot malfunctions and explodes, leaving

Psst!

Welcome to one of my favorite galaxies in the game: Toy Time Galaxy. There's just something about a game that enjoys looking "fun," and that's precisely what this galaxy does. The giant toy robot, the colors that are likely exploding off your television screen right now, and the fun jumps across cakes and popsicles are all deliriously fun to look at as well as play. And that's one of the coolest things about Super Mario Galaxy—the game relishes in its pure fantasy. Seriously, if you can play this entire galaxy without smiling, you need to be checked out.

MARIO MEETS MARIO

TOY TIME GALAXY
Mario Meets Mario

Start

A

B

C

The second mission in Toy Time Galaxy sends Mario to a flattened facsimile of the hero's younger days. Mario must recover five Silver Stars from this Marioesque landscape in order to discover this galaxy's hidden Power Star.

Gold Leaf Galaxy

Sea Slide Galaxy

Toy Time Galaxy

Bonefin Galaxy

Bowser Jr.'s Lava Reactor

Sand Spiral Galaxy

TOY TIME GALAXY

SUPER MARIO GALAXY

As always, Mario arrives in the Toy Time Galaxy at the train station. Let the Toads drive Mario to the Launch Star on the track's left side. The Launch Star blasts Mario across the galaxy, sending him through several rings of Star Bits. Wave the cursor over the Star Bits as Mario soars. The planet he lands on has no Launch Star—it must be constructed out of five Star Chips.

The fourth Star Chip is on a blue screw. After picking up the Star Chip, spin on the screw. This actually spins a much larger screw that makes up part of the planetoid.

The first Star Chip is on the large flat surface surrounded by electrical fields. It's right over a little robot's head, but be careful—that robot can shoot lasers.

Now, Mario can run up the giant screw's side to pick up the last Star Chip at the top. This creates the Launch Star that sends Mario to the 2-D planet that looks just like himself.

The next Star Chip is on the side of the green block with the spring. Bounce on the spring to grab the Star Chip.

NOTE

There is a hungry Luma on this planetoid, dancing on a nub surrounded by electrical fields. It wants 50 Star Chips to create a new planetoid. After collecting the Power Star for this mission, return here to seek out the hidden Power Star of Toy Time.

Walk from the spring to the right. The third Star Chip is inside a crystal. Spin to shatter the crystal and free the Star Chip.

Planet C

LEGEND

⭐ Silver Star

🍄 1-Up Mushroom

TIP

There is a lone 1-Up Mushroom on the planetoid. Pick it up but, again, try to leave as many green squares intact as possible.

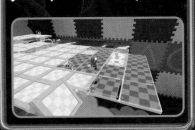

The flat planetoid is constructed of the green platforms that shrink underfoot and yellow squares that rotate when Mario touches them. Crossing this planet to collect the five Silver Stars is extremely tricky, since the ground seems to always be falling out from under Mario. The best way to get all five Silver Stars is to always keep moving. Staying still will dump Mario either into space or onto the lava that comprises the red part of the planet's overalls.

Make the rounds on the flat planetoid, ending with the Silver Star to the starting point's right. If Mario leaves enough green platforms untouched, he can long-jump back to the starting block and pick up the Power Star. If necessary, and if Mario has extra health, he can always bounce on the lava in hopes of reaching the Power Star.

The closest Silver Star is on the yellow platforms to the right. Instead of just running for it, though, jump across as many green squares as possible.

When all five Silver Stars are assembled, they create the Power Star—which is placed at the starting point on this planetoid. Leave green squares behind so Mario can backtrack to the beginning to pick up the Power Star.

SUPER MARIO GALAXY

PRIMA Official Game Guide

This planetoid is another one of Super Mario Galaxy's cooler moments—the giant 8-bit Mario planetoid is a neat idea. And when Mario returns to this galaxy after the purple comet arcs through the heavens, the giant 2-D Mario turns into an 8-bit Luigi.

BOUNCING DOWN CAKE LANE

TOY TIME GALAXY
Bouncing Down Cake Lane

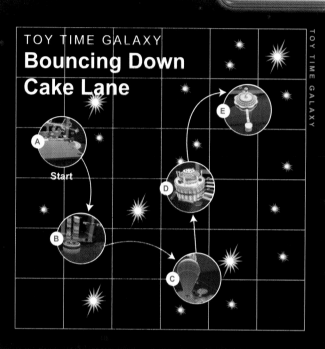

The Toy Time Galaxy isn't just about playthings— it's home to some of the most delicious goodies in the universe. Giant tarts, ice cream cones, and chocolate bars orbit the galaxy, beckoning Mario to see if he can indeed have his cake and eat it, too.

Mario lands on a planetoid made entirely of cake. The only way to get off this confection is straight up, so grab the nearby Spring Mushroom so Mario can vault high into the air. Jump between the two cakes. When he touches one cake, he bounces off to the other cake, much like a wall jump. Bound between the two cakes until Mario reaches their frosted rooftops.

Planets A, B, and C

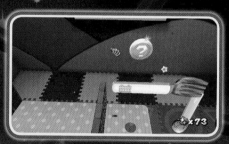

The train is right there to pick up Mario when he returns to the Toy Time Galaxy. Ride it around the track to the Launch Star on the ring world's side. While blasting through space, point the cursor at the cereal spoons hanging in the sky. There are Star Bits on each one.

Bounce over the giant chocolate bars on the conveyor belt. There is a Prize Block and a giant coin above the chocolate bars—each releases Star Bits.

Drop from the conveyor belt to a plate of orange cake. There is a Spring Mushroom on a spoon just in case Mario lost the Spring Suit. Vault to the slice of cake's top, then bounce across the fork bridge to the cake itself.

The cake is on a spinning platter. Mario must bounce around the cake as it revolves, avoiding forks and holes where slices have been removed. There

is a wall of white chocolate on the cake's far side. Bounce to the chocolate and jump to the Launch Star.

⭐ Planet D ⭐

The Launch Star rockets Mario to the bottom of an ice cream cone that has its own gravity field. March up the cone's side to the frozen scoop, then jump out to the popsicle sticks dangling from popsicles.

Mario can either cross the popsicle sticks or wall jump between the actual popsicle. There is no gravity on the popsicles, so Mario must watch his balance. Jump across the treats' tops to reach a Prize Block full of Star Bits. At the last popsicle's edge, jump down to a tray of rotating lollipops.

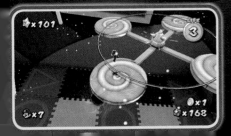

A mean robot sends shock waves across the lollipops. Hop over the shock waves as the treats spin.

The lollipops lead to a series of frozen bars occupied by crawling Electro-goombas. Jump across the bars, stunning the monsters with Star Bits so they don't hassle the hero. Ride the rotating lollipop on the bars' other side. More shock waves ripple across the lollipops, so jump over them until the candy suckers close in on a frozen ledge.

Run to the frozen platform's rear and wall jump up the alcove to grab a Life Mushroom. There is a cannon atop the block, so drop into it and aim at the next Launch Star in the skies.

SUPER MARIO GALAXY

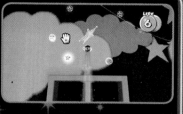

The Launch Star blasts Mario toward a colossal cake. Judging by all the forks and spoons sticking out of the cake, it looks like everybody's ready to dig in.

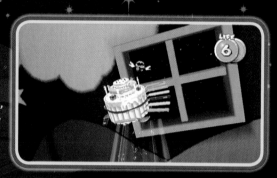

After Mario lands on the blue spoon at the cake's base, jump to the red spoon behind him. A green warp pipe is on the spoon's head and leads to a secret chamber full of prickly plants. The giant coin in the chamber emits a trail of musical notes. Collect all the notes before they vanish to earn a 1-Up Mushroom.

Planet E

After collecting the Mushroom, climb to the cake's top on the staircase made of forks. This must be a birthday cake—there are candles on it. Blow out the candles by standing next to them and spinning. After extinguishing the candles, will Mario's wish come true? Not unless he wished for a surprise attack by a nasty mole in a cannon.

LEGEND

- Life Mushroom
- Spring Mushroom

Boss Battle: Cannon

Watch out for the two fire cannons at the base of the gumball canister.

Sitting atop a canister of gumballs, a mean-spirited mole blasts the birthday cake with fireballs from his cannon. The fireballs streak through the sky, burning anything they touch. (The two Mecha-Bowsers crawling around the cake aren't helping much, either.) Mario must avoid the fireballs and jump on the cockpit three times to make this cake edible again.

TIP

Spring into the Life Mushroom hanging over the cake to replenish Mario's health. He can also squash the Mecha-Bowser toys to earn coins.

The first thing Mario must do is capture the Spring Mushroom so he can vault to the cannon's cockpit. The Spring Mushroom is on a small ledge lined with candies. Once Mario has the Spring Suit, he can bounce back up to the cake and fling himself high into the air.

After each hit, the mole increases the number of fireballs he shoots. After the second strike, the mole quickly spins the cannon around the cake, filling the air with fireballs. Duck under the fireballs and bounce up to the gumball canister's base. Just as the mole fires, bounce up to the cockpit and deliver the final blow.

Ground pound the glass cockpit to rattle the mole inside. Mario must now hit the cockpit two more times.

The Power Star appears on top of the gumball canister.

Gold Leaf Galaxy

Sea Slide Galaxy

Toy Time Galaxy

Bonefin Galaxy

Bowser Jr.'s Lava Reactor

Sand Spiral Galaxy

SUPER MARIO GALAXY

PRIMA Official Game Guide

THE FLIPSWITCH CHAIN

Feed the hungry Luma from the "Mario Meets Mario" mission to uncover the hidden Power Star on the Toy Time Galaxy. The Luma transforms into a collection of colorful blocks covered with floor switches. Turn all the switches yellow to earn the secret Power Star.

Hungry Luma

Return to the hungry Luma on the strange doorknob-shaped planetoid. Feed the Luma the required 50 Star Bits and enjoy the fireworks. The pleased Luma rockets into space and transforms into a planetoid covered with floor switches and rolling rocks. Use the resulting Launch Star to visit the new planetoid and start earning that hidden Power Star.

> **NOTE**
>
> To earn enough Star Bits, Mario must scoop up all the Star Bits in the air as he sails between planets.

To uncover the Power Star, step on every switch on the planetoid, turning them all yellow. Much like the Cyclone Stone, Mario must duck under the empty sides of the crushing cubes that rumble around the planetoid. Fortunately, most of these cubes are perfectly positioned so their empty spaces come down right on the floor switches.

The smooth edges mean Mario can step all the way around the planetoid without worrying about falling off. Run around the planetoid's ring, which is covered with glass panels, turning the floor switches yellow.

After completing the glassy ring, run to the little robot. Jump from the glass panel to the blue block. The two surfaces are close enough that the gravity of the blue block grabs Mario and pulls him to the new surface.

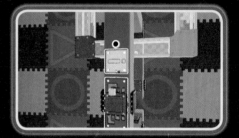

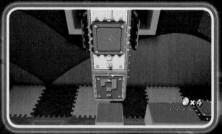

There are many more floor switches on the blue blocks, and they appear in threes. A few rolling stones are on the blue blocks. Mario must mainly worry about jumping over sliding platforms lined with razor-sharp spikes.

The gaps between the blocks are narrow enough that Mario can jump between and be captured by the next surface's gravity.

The rolling block on the blue surface doesn't place its empty side toward the switches. Mario must stand along the ledge and wait for the block to pass before touching the switches.

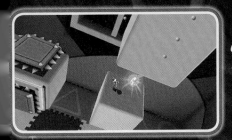

When all the switches are yellow, the Power Star appears on the orange block.

FAST FOES OF TOY TIME

The razor-edged platforms and rolling rocks on the Chain Planet must have gobbled some candy while Mario was at the Comet Observatory, because they're now running around twice as fast as before. Turn those switches yellow to pick up the fifth Power Star in this galaxy.

Speedy Switches

Mario returns to Toy Time Galaxy, landing directly on the floor switch planetoid. The sliding platforms and rolling stones are moving double time, so Mario must sprint across the surfaces to hit all the switches before getting poked or squished. Follow the same strategy as the first visit to this planetoid, but just watch out for those fast-moving enemies.

When standing on a switch with a Prize Block, jumping up to pop the block does not change the switch back to blue.

After stomping the switches on the glass-covered ring, jump to the blue blocks and start stepping on the switches while avoiding the sliding platforms and the spikes.

If Mario's ever injured, ride on the platforms to safely pick up a coin and replenish lost health.

The Power Star appears in the same place as before—on the orange block. All the platforms stop sliding, but the spikes still hurt, so be careful when jumping to the orange block.

BONEFIN GALAXY

Bonefin Galaxy is a dark and foreboding corner of the universe where few people dare to tread—and once Mario gets an eyeful of the teeth on the leviathan that rules this planet, he'll understand just why it's such a lonely place. To get the Power Star from Bonefin Galaxy, though, Mario must dive into this grim waterworld and do battle.

Gold Leaf Galaxy

Sea Slide Galaxy

Toy Time Galaxy

Bonefin Galaxy

Bowser Jr.'s Lava Reactor

Sand Spiral Galaxy

SUPER MARIO

Deep Sea Scares

Mario arrives at the Toad spaceship in orbit around the Bonefin Galaxy's only planet. After collecting the Star Bits on the spaceship, use the Sling Star to dive down to the watery planet and meet the local sea life.

When Mario splashes down on the planet, the Bonefin swims into view. This near-mythical juggernaut has teeth larger than a house and swims through the water like a torpedo. Mario must somehow defeat this behemoth with five attacks; as soon as the Bonefin starts circling the planet, immediately seek out a shell.

After Mario lands two hits on the Bonefin, the behemoth calls in reinforcements. Skeletal fish rise out of a hole in the seafloor and run interference, blocking shells and zeroing in on Mario like Bullet Bills. With each additional hit, more fish swim out of the hole to cloud the waters. The school of skeleton fish follows Mario doggedly through the water. To get rid of a fish, hit it with a shell.

Shells are all over the seafloor. Most of them are green shells that require precision aim. However, swim over to the unicorn-like horn sticking out of the seabed to pick up a red shell. These home in on a target, which keeps the Bonefin from swimming away by the time Mario lets fly with the shell.

CAUTION

It will take some time to land five hits on the Bonefin, so always keep an eye on Mario's air supply. Swim through bubbles to keep him in the fight.

TIP

There is a shimmering treasure chest on the seafloor. Throw a shell at it to reveal a 1-Up Mushroom.

Use the beacon on the shell's front to aim at the brute. Shake the Wii Remote to release the shell.

Bonefin soon starts smashing the rock formations on the seafloor. This shattered stone reveals a Life Mushroom.

After landing the fifth hit on Bonefin, the leviathan crumbles and all his skeletal minions disappear. The Power Star appears over the hole that the skeleton fish emerged from. Mario is still underwater, so make sure he has enough air to reach the Power Star.

What could be worse than outlasting Bonefin only to run out of air inches away from the Power Star?

BOWSER JR.'S LAVA REACTOR

BOWSER JR.'S LAVA REACTOR
King Kaliente's Spicy Return

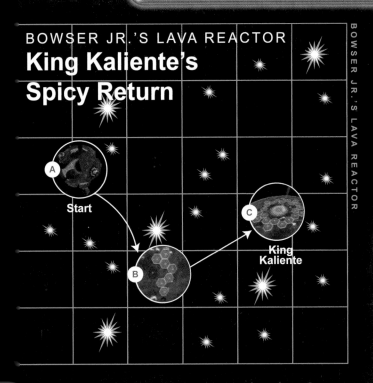

Start

King Kaliente

While Bowser licks his wounds elsewhere in the galaxy, Bowser Jr. steps up to stop Mario before he can thwart any more of his dad's plans. Bowser Jr. calls on the help of a familiar face: King Kaliente.

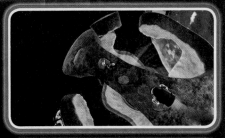

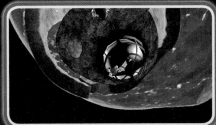

To break open the cages, Mario must get the attention of the Bullet Bills streaking around the planetoid. Once the Bullet Bills spot him, they give pursuit. Lead the projectiles around the planetoid, keeping far enough ahead to jump over gaps without the Bullet Bills catching up. Lead the Bullet Bills into the cages to fetch the 1-Up Mushroom and coins. After collecting the treasure, lead one last Bullet Bill to the Launch Star.

Planet A

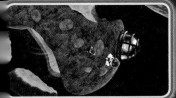

Mario lands on a small planetoid in distant orbit above the boiling Lava Reactor. The planetoid is being devoured at its core by the black hole—very little of the surface is left but a snaking walkway. A few cages on the surface contain treasures, such as a 1-Up Mushroom and coins, but the real prize is the Launch Star that rockets Mario down to the Lava Reactor.

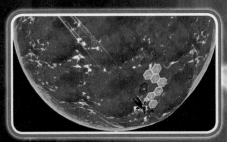

The Launch Star arcs Mario through the atmosphere surrounding the Lava Reactor, dropping him down on a series of metal platforms.

SUPER MARIO

★★ Planet B ★★

Two squid pop out of craters in the lava that spit coconuts and fireballs at Mario. Spin-attack the coconuts to knock them back at the squid. Mario must defeat both the monsters to get Bowser Jr. to bring his airship down to the Lava Reactor's surface.

Several enemies float across the lava to knock Mario into the scorching molten earth. Jump across the metal platforms, never standing still long enough for the platform to completely sink into the lava. There is a Life Mushroom on a stone ledge in the lava that doesn't sink, so jump out to fetch it before returning to cross the steel platforms.

Bowser Jr. is determined to finish off Mario and make big Bowser proud.

Boss Battle: King Kaliente

King Kaliente's first volley is a trio of fireballs. Avoid them, but don't stray too far because the next attack is a coconut, and Mario must hit King Kaliente as soon as possible. Spin-attack the coconut as it zips over the steel platforms. It wings back across the lava and strikes King Kaliente right on the noggin.

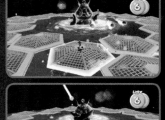

King Kaliente rises out of the lava once again, thrashing his tentacles about in a show of force. The second duel with this boss unfolds much the same, except now Mario cannot find stable ground from which to launch attacks. While batting the coconuts back and forth, keep moving so Mario doesn't sink into the burning lava.

King Kaliente doesn't wait long to call for help. After rising from the attack, the king issues forth burning blue monsters. Avoid the fireball attack again, then volley the next coconut back and forth twice before it catches King Kaliente off-guard and smacks the crown right off his brow.

Boss Battle: King Kaliente (cont.)

NOTE

If Mario loses health, zoom over to the lone coin on the steel platforms to stay in the fight.

After the second hit, King Kaliente calls down a meteor shower. Exploding stones bombard the steel platforms, forcing Mario to watch the skies as well as the ground. Dodge fireballs until King Kaliente spits out another coconut. Bat the coconut back and forth three times. The third hit knocks out King Kaliente. Mario can now claim the Grand Star powering the Lava Reactor.

Mario takes the Grand Star back to the Comet Observatory. It fuses with the beacon at the space station's heart, lighting the way to the final Dome: Garden. The Grand Star also opens up the Gate, where Mario learns the gift of flight.

SAND SPIRAL GALAXY

A hungry Luma lingers outside the Engine Room, waiting patiently for Mario to feed it a snack. After Mario feeds the Luma 1,000 Star Bits, it transforms into a new galaxy: Sand Spiral Galaxy.

Choosing a Favorite Snack

This short-'n'-sweet galaxy gives Mario a choice of suits: Boo or Bee. Each suit allows Mario to hover through a tunnel of rushing sand, but different obstacles present different problems depending on the suit chosen.

Through the Tunnel

Mario begins the mission on the bow of a ship, right in a Magikoopa's line of sight. Immediately dodge the Magikoopa's attacks, then charge forward to the

Sling Star on the ship's front. The Magikoopa vanishes as Mario closes in, appearing on the sliding platforms in front of the tunnel.

When Mario lands in front of the Magikoopa again, don't retreat from the fire spell. Instead, rush forward and jump on the Magikoopa's head to eliminate it. If Mario misses and the Magikoopa retreats, it will remain in the tunnel until Mario reaches the Sling Star at the very end.

251

At the tunnel's entrance, two Toads offer Mario a snack. The left Toad offers a Boo Mushroom; the right Toad is standing next to a Bee Mushroom. Each suit has its strengths and weaknesses in the tunnel. Boo Mario has to avoid the sweeping spotlights while Bee Mario has to find places to rest.

It's easier to avoid the lights, so choose the Boo Mushroom and float into the tunnel. Several spotlights sway from side to side, but the tunnel is wide enough for Mario to sail through without much worry.

The Power Star is atop the moon in the center of the spiraling rings. Jumping across the rings to reach the moon shouldn't be too hard, right? Wrong—the rings are covered with exploding mines. Fortunately, a Toad has a Rainbow Star for Mario!

Looks like Boo Mario has an admirer. When this pink Boo spots Boo Mario, it follows him to the tunnel's end. Don't stop moving or the pink Boo will catch up to Boo Mario and bump him right out of the suit.

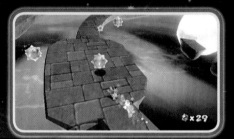

Float over the bubbles fired from the cannons. Hover through the gaps between the cannons to grab a 1-Up Mushroom.

The Sling Star is at the tunnel's end, on a small mesh bridge.

Use the Rainbow Star's invincibility to rush across the rings, smashing the mines as they fly at Mario. Hop across the gaps in the rings carefully so Mario isn't felled by gravity. When he reaches the innermost ring, long-jump out to the glowing moon.

If you chose the Bee Suit, Bee Mario doesn't have to worry about the spotlights—he

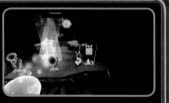

just needs to watch his fatigue. The signposts in the tunnel have spikes on them, so Mario must press on, finding respite on the rounded pipes poking out of the walls. Watch out for the bubbles, take a break on the bridge, then either use the Sling Star or buzz right out of the tunnel.

Climb across the lunar surface to pick up the Power Star and victoriously exit the Sand Spiral Galaxy.

GARDEN AND GATE GALAXIES

GATE GALAXY

Purple Coins

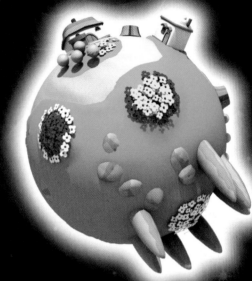

After Mario rescues the Grand Star from Bowser Jr. at the edge of the Engine Room galaxies, he opens up the final Dome on the Comet Observatory: Garden. However, there is a stop between the Engine Room and the Garden. On a small platform decorated by an inviting flowerbed is a link back to the Gateway Galaxy—the first planetoid Mario awoke upon after Bowser kidnapped Princess Peach.

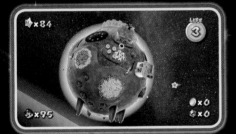

Before heading to the Garden, stop at the Gateway Galaxy. If Mario completes the mission there, he earns the power of flight. The red Luma on the Comet Observatory now offers Mario his Flying Suit, which lets him soar through the air free of gravity's constrictions.

Upon returning to the planetoid, Mario must visit Rosalina atop the small castle. She looks longingly at the heavens. She cares so deeply for the Luma, but there's a piece of her heart lost among the stars. She has always stopped near this planetoid—her favorite—every 100 years. This time, however, the malicious Bowser halted her journey. Rosalina pledges to keep helping Mario find Princess Peach before she returns to the Comet Observatory, leaving Mario in the company of a playful little red Luma.

Garden and Gate

Gate Galaxy

Deep Dark Galaxy

Dreadnought Galaxy

Melty Molten Galaxy

Matter Splatter Galaxy

Snow Cap Galaxy

The red Luma offers Mario the gift of flight. If he picks up the red star in front of him, he will don the Flying Suit. With just a jump and a quick flick of the Wii Remote, Mario blasts off the ground and sails through the sky. Collect all 100 purple coins on this planetoid, and the red Luma lets Mario use the Flying Suit on the Comet Observatory.

After Mario finds the last purple coin, the red Luma gifts him the Flying Suit and awards him a very special Power Star. Mario now has the two Power Stars of the Gateway Galaxy.

High and Low

As soon as Mario gets the Flying Suit, jump in the air and soar through the ring of purple coins that circles the planet. The coins jingle at the edge of the planet's atmosphere—Mario cannot fly much higher than the coins. Soar through the coins, filling his pockets. When the Flight Suit wears off, Mario drops back down to the surface, but picking up another red star sends him back to the sky to finish collecting the purple coins.

> **NOTE**
> Once Mario defeats Bowser for the first time, the purple comet appears in the sky and unlocks a new mission in 15 galaxies. Completing these 15 missions is the only way to gather all 120 stars.

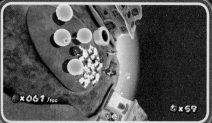

There are many purple coins right around the castle. Drop to the ground and circle the castle to collect even more coins. The small cottages at the castle's base are also sparkling with purple coins. Mario can backflip to the rooftops to reach the high coins, but it's easier to just zoom over the houses and grab them. There is another red star between the houses in case the Flight Suit wears off.

RACING THE SPOOKY SPEEDSTER

After Mario completes the purple-coin grab inside the Gateway Galaxy, a hungry Luma appears outside. Feed the Luma 1,200 Star Bits, and it transforms into a new galaxy: Boo's Boneyard Galaxy. Mario catches up with the Spooky Speedster again, and the Boo is ready for a rematch. He's even putting up another Power Star as the prize!

Purple coins are everywhere on this planetoid. Fly over the surface, looking down for the treasures. There is no time limit for collecting the coins, so enjoy zipping through the air and barnstorming the ground to find all 100 purple coins.

Boo Suit, Please?

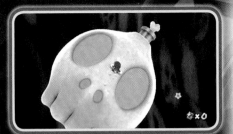

When Mario first arrives in Boo's Boneyard Galaxy, he touches down on a creepy skull-shaped planetoid. An orange warp pipe is atop the skull. Follow the pipe to the race course, where the Spooky Speedster waits patiently for his rival.

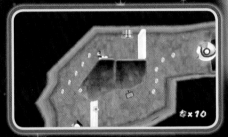

When Mario drops out of the warp pipe, he immediately spots a line of coins leading to a Boo Mushroom. Drop to the ground to transform into Boo Mario. Now he can disappear and pass through the walls the separate him from the Spooky Speedster.

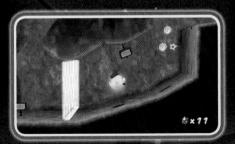

Float up to the Spooky Speedster, collecting even more coins.

The Race

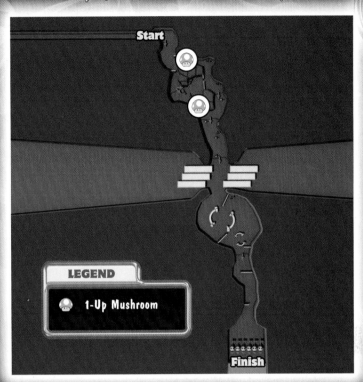

LEGEND

1-Up Mushroom

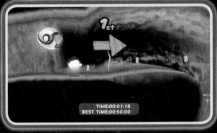

Boo Mario and the Spooky Speedster pull up to the starting line. The best race time for the course is 50 seconds—can Boo Mario best that? Even if he doesn't beat the record, as long as he crosses the finish line first, he earns the Power Star prize. When the race begins, follow the trail of coins, ready to drop into the course's vertical caverns.

Use Boo Mario's invisibility to slip through the walls and investigate side passages. Extra treasures are off the main path, such as 1-Up Mushrooms and Star Bits. Huge fans fill the caverns with howling winds that Mario can use to keep ahead of the Spooky Speedster. Some of the fans are inactive, but flying through the giant coin in front of them turns them on, creating powerful currents to carry Mario across the course.

Gate Galaxy
Deep Dark Galaxy
Dreadnought Galaxy
Melty Molten Galaxy
Matter Spatter Galaxy
Snow Cap Galaxy

PRIMA Official Game Guide

Just as Boo Mario reaches a wall, shake the Wii Remote so he turns invisible. Do this too early and Boo Mario might reappear and bounce right off the wall, costing precious time.

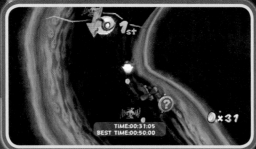

Watch out for springs in the middle of the course; they bounce Boo Mario backward, costing time. The Spooky Speedster is skilled at avoiding them.

The final stretch is littered with Star Bits. While Boo Mario descends, wave the cursor over the Star Bits along the cavern's walls and over the skull eyes to pick up oodles of Star Bits. The skulls mark the finish line, so drift toward them as quickly as possible.

Severe winds ahead! When Mario enters the chamber with the rib bones, fly to the right and grab the giant coin to activate a dormant fan. The fan blows Boo Mario straight down the chamber, giving him a huge lead over the Spooky Speedster. Just watch out for the walls.

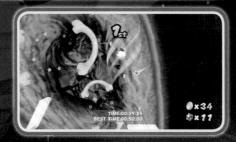

The Spooky Speedster is a good sport—he graciously awards Mario the Power Star for besting him on the racetrack.

GARDEN GALAXIES: DEEP DARK GALAXY

The Deep Dark Galaxy is a creepy landscape that's swallowed many ships, dragging them down to the murky depths where their secrets are kept forever. Mario must carefully explore this galaxy to uncover these secrets and locate the Power Stars.

DEEP DARK GALAXY
The Underground Ghost Ship

A
Kamella
Start

DEEP DARK GALAXY

Legend tells of a secret shipwreck in the Deep Dark Galaxy that contains a treasure worth more than gold in its haunted hull. Mario must discover the secret entrance to the ship's final resting place and then challenge any malevolent forces that try to wrest the treasure away from him.

Planets A, B, and C

LEGEND

1-Up Mushroom

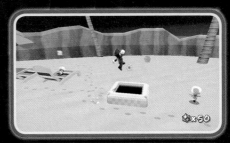

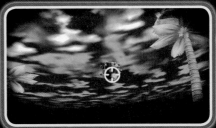

Gate Galaxy

Deep Dark Galaxy

Dreadnought Galaxy

Melty Molten Galaxy

Matter Spatter Galaxy

Snow Cap Galaxy

Grab the green shell in the water and bash open the treasure chest. There's a 1-Up Mushroom inside.

Life's a beach for the Toads lounging on the edge of the Deep Dark Galaxy's main planet. They've set up chairs on the sand and have built a cannon that will likely put off more sparks than any bonfire. The entrance to the lake that hides the ghost ship is blocked right now, so nose around the beach for goodies.

After collecting all the treasures on the beach, check out the Toads' cannon. Hop in the hole in the ground to squeeze into the barrel, then aim at the skies. There are two planetoids in orbit—the right one is partially obscured by a palm tree. Blast to the one on the left first—it's crawling with little creatures. Aim Mario right through the Rainbow Star.

Backflip to the roof of the Toads' spaceship to find a 1-Up Mushroom.

The blue crabs on the beach release 1-Up Mushrooms when defeated. Also, spin in the shell ring for Star Bits.

With the Rainbow Star's power, Mario can clean up the entire planetoid and collect a slew of Star Bits. After clearing the planetoid, use the Sling Star to return to the beach.

PRIMA Official Game Guide

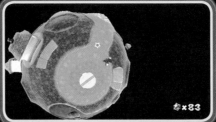

Be sure to smash the stones in this passage to discover hidden coins.

Now, aim for the planetoid behind the palm tree. Mario crashes onto the planet's surface. It looks peaceful enough—just a few Goombas meandering between the pleasant little cottages. Kick the Goombas off the planetoid and then locate the gold screw at the pole.

Deep Sea Diving

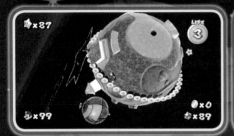

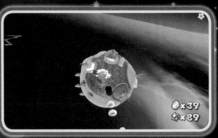

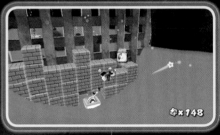

Spinning on the screw creates a ring of coins that circle the planetoid. However, the hole in the planet's crust is letting all the air out. The planetoid quickly shrinks to nothing, so run around the ring of coins and collect as many as possible before the planet goes "poof!" When the planet vanishes, Mario is snared by the other small planetoid's gravity. Good thing he already cleaned up the planet before being unceremoniously dumped to the surface. With the coast clear, grab the Fire Flower on the opposite pole from the Sling Star. Now, jump on that Sling Star and drop back to the beach.

Slip under the waves and swim straight down. A helpful arrow made of Star Bits points Mario in the right direction. The arrow leads to a brick wall. Smash the bricks to reach a lever, then spin to throw it. The gate beyond the bricks rises, clearing the path to the ghost ship.

Before Fire Mario's powers vanish, hurl fireballs at the two darkened torches flanking the huge door on the beach. (If Fire Mario loses his suit, just use the cannon to return to the planetoid and grab another Fire Flower.) When both torches are lit, the door opens.

Before going through the brick wall to find the ship, swim to the lake's bottom and use shells to dispose of the nasty Gringills there. This one leaves behind a 1-Up Mushroom.

A Magikoopa waits for Mario beyond the door. Bop its head to clear the way to the lake.

Watch for mines as Mario swims up to the surface beyond the gate.

Crackling jellyfish guard the lever that opens the gate at the watery passage's top.

There it is—the ghost ship! And what would Mario expect to find on a ghost ship? How about a bunch of Boos? The Boos contain coins, so lead the feisty spirits into the beams of light seeping through the cracked dome over the ship; the Boos disappear, leaving behind only the coins. Before heading for the ship, explore the narrow ledges to the right. There is a Life Mushroom atop the ledges, as well as Stars Bits and coins.

T.I.P. Dive under the ghost ship and pick up the spinning giant coin. This creates two rings of Star Bits, giving Mario more than enough to earn another extra life.

Boss Battle: Kamella

Kamella returns to finish what she started—defeating Mario before he gets another Power Star. The mammoth Magikoopa soars down from the night sky and challenges Mario to a battle on the ghost ship's bow. The winner gets the Power Star; the loser becomes another forgotten fixture of the old ghost ship.

The battle unfolds largely the same as last time. Kamella hangs back, casting fireball spells at Mario from beyond the railing. When her wand lights up red, she's casting a fireball. But when the magic mist around the wand turn green, the Magikoopa is about to unleash a shell. Spin to grab the shell as it crashes to the ship, then return fire. Make sure to jump high enough to clear the railing.

Need extra health? Shoot Star Bits at the lamps on the ship's mast to release coins.

(continued on next page)

Gate Galaxy

Deep Dark Galaxy

Dreadnought Galaxy

Melty Molten Galaxy

Matter Splatter Galaxy

Snow Cap Galaxy

PRIMA Official Game Guide

After hitting Kamella with two shells, she takes the fight to the crow's nest.

Spooked by Mario's skills, Kamella calls in some Magikoopas to help her defeat her rival. Two Magikoopas appear on the crow's nest, casting only fireballs at Mario. Dodge the fireballs and get close to the little Magikoopas so Mario can jump on their heads and get them off the ship. He must clear the way to Kamella. When she casts a shell down to the crow's nest, grab it and return fire to finish off the boss. (That is, until the Daredevil Comet arcs over the ghost ship and revives her for a tough rematch.)

BUBBLE BLASTOFF

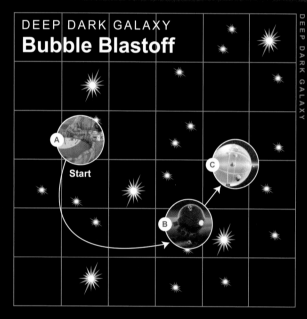

DEEP DARK GALAXY

DEEP DARK GALAXY
Bubble Blastoff

The skies above Deep Dark Galaxy are not well traveled—a lack of Launch Stars keeps visitors from taking any unwelcome trips. Mario must find another way to explore the galaxy. Perhaps he can use those bubble cannons?

When Mario returns to the beach, he sees that a mean mole has taken over the Toads' cannon. The mole has turned the cannon into a bubble blaster and is peppering the beach with multiple volleys. Before seeking out the beach's goodies (such as Star Bits in shell circles and the invisible creature full of Star Bits), Mario must get rid of that mole. Triple jump across the beach to reach the cockpit and ground pound the glass. It takes three hits to shoo the mole away from the beach.

Planets A and B

LEGEND

- 1-Up Mushroom
- Ice Flower

CAUTION

If a bubble hits Mario, he flies across the beach and slams into a wall. Use beach furniture, like chairs and umbrellas, to block bubbles, while getting close enough to launch an attack.

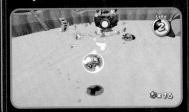

Light the two torches outside the entrance to the ghost ship's lake. There is a third torch just beyond the entrance. Light it to make an Ice Flower appear, but don't get it just yet. Take out the nearby Magikoopa first and smash the rocks for coins.

Ice Mario can run across the lake's surface to the opposite beach containing the pink Toad. However, watch out for the Magikoopa hovering over the lake. Dodge its attacks and keep moving—the Ice Suit wears off quickly. Mario must jump up the water fountains above the pink Toad, turning each spout into a frozen platform to reach the pole.

After Mario runs the mole off the beach, he can jump into the cannon and aim for the planetoid in orbit. Again, pass through the Rainbow Star in the sky before crashing down to the planetoid. When Mario lands, run around the planetoid blasting through the little monsters until the surface is clear (capture those flying Star Bits with the cursor). After finishing off the monsters, pluck the Fire Flower on the planet's opposite side from the Sling Star. Now, get in that Sling Star and bounce back down to the beach.

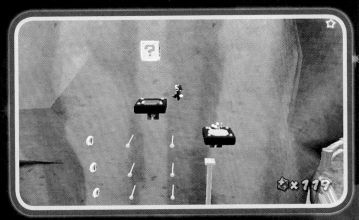

Climb the pole to reach the high ledge. Jump from the ledge to the Prize Block, and empty it to earn extra Star Bits.

Another Magikoopa appears! Weave around its fireballs on the way to a colorful circle platform hanging high over the lake. When Mario grabs the giant coin on the platform, it turns into small Sling Stars. Use the Sling Stars to vault up to the next set of ledges.

Gate Galaxy

Deep Dark Galaxy

Dreadnought Galaxy

Melty Molten Galaxy

Matter Spatter Galaxy

Snow Cap Galaxy

SUPER MARIO GALAXY

Mario rides the bubble to a small planetoid in the heavens over Deep Dark. Several Cheep Cheeps bounce around the shallow water, so watch out for their flying flippers. Three wooden pegs are on the planetoid. Ground pound all of them to activate the bubble cannon.

Mario must jump in front of the bubble cannon so he's launched even farther up the ledges. Pick up the Star Bits as he ascends the ledges. Jump over the fire cannons while running to the left. Jump to a tall orange pole to ascend to the top of Deep Dark's main planet.

Jump in front of the bubble cannon to blast off for the last planet in the system.

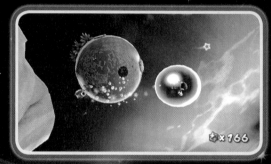

Watch out for the Magikoopa between the two poles.

There is a bubble cannon on the ledge at the second pole's top. Hop over the firetrap and hitch a ride in a bubble.

GUPPY AND THE UNDERGROUND LAKE

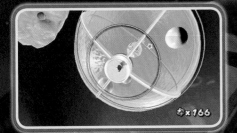

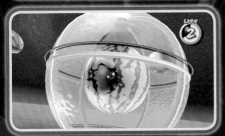

Mario lands on a giant glass sphere. The surface is rippled with shock waves; jump over them while investigating the sphere's contents. There are three tennis balls rolling around the sphere's interior. At the very center is a tiny watermelon. To solve this odd puzzle, Mario must ground pound over the tennis balls as they roll around the sphere's surface. The tennis ball then drops to the watermelon, which grows a little bit.

DEEP DARK GALAXY
Guppy and the Underground Lake

Start

Guppy is a long way from the friendly waters of the Sea Slide Galaxy. The toothy titan has found a Power Star but won't give it to Mario unless the plumber plays with him. Follow Guppy around the lake in a little race so the shark gladly gives up the Power Star.

To the Lake

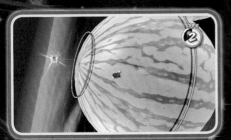

After hitting the third tennis ball into the watermelon, the fruit breaks through the glass sphere. The Power Star appears at the watermelon's top. Hop over the shock waves that still cross the surface to recover the Power Star.

This mission starts on the beach again. Mario can comb the beach for treasures at his own pace, getting rid of blue crabs for 1-Up Mushrooms and breaking open the treasure chest in the water for another extra life. After emptying the beach of goodies, head through the open gate flanked by torches, and run for the lake. Another Magikoopa waits, but just bounce off its head to send it packing.

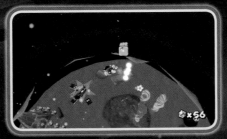

Swim to the lake's bottom. Guppy patiently waits for Mario, but before chatting up the shark, explore the lakebed for treasures.

Gate Galaxy

Deep Dark Galaxy

Dreadnought Galaxy

Melty Molten Galaxy

Matter Splatter Galaxy

Snow Cap Galaxy

SUPER MARIO GALAXY

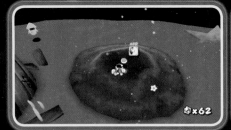

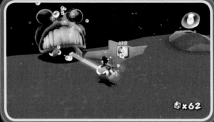

Use the green shells on the lakebed to get rid of monsters like Bloopers and gain coins and Star Bits. The Gringills at the lake's edge have returned, so smack them with shells for treasures, such as Star Bits and a 1-Up Mushroom.

When Mario's ready, swim over to Guppy. The shark is happy to see Mario again and issues a playful challenge to follow his lead around the lakebed, swimming through eight rings. If Mario passes through all eight rings before any of them vanish, Guppy will give Mario the Power Star he found.

Ring 6 is in the middle of the three Bloopers behind another shipwreck. Carefully pass between the Bloopers. If Mario hits one, he loses his shell.

Guppy leaves Ring 5 between four jellyfish. Just like Ring 6, Mario must carefully avoid the jellyfish or he loses the shell.

In Guppy's Wake

Guppy swims a little faster in this mission than in the Sea Slide Galaxy. The rings he leaves behind don't last as long either. They blink before they vanish, so if one is flashing, he better pick up the pace.

Ring 8 is over the bed of mines around the sunken ship. Swim through the ring, but watch out for the mines. If Mario's hit, he's slowed down enough that it's hard to pursue Guppy.

Guppy cuts across the lakebed, leaving Ring 4 in the kelp next to the urchins.

Guppy swims over the urchins on the lakebed, leaving behind Ring 7. After passing through the ring, pick up a shell so Mario can keep up with Guppy.

Guppy drops Ring 3 just next to the urchins.

Error

Cut to the right to follow Guppy along the lakebed's edge and swim through Ring 2.

Tricky Guppy drops Ring 1 right in the middle of three fast-moving currents. Thread the narrow space between the currents to reach the ring and satisfy Guppy's challenge.

Swim to Guppy in the lakebed's center to pick up the Power Star!

Gate Galaxy

Deep Dark Galaxy

Dreadnought Galaxy

Melty Molten Galaxy

Matter Spatter Galaxy

Snow Cap Galaxy

BOO IN A BOX

There is a strange cube in orbit around Deep Dark Galaxy's main planet. What could possibly be inside of it? The more pressing question, though, is how will Mario even reach the cube to investigate?

Spooky Star

Begin the "Underground Ghost Ship" mission and enjoy all the great stuff on the beach, including Star Bits and 1-Up Mushrooms. Follow all the steps to open the gate to the lake where the ghost ship resides. Instead of breaking off and following the Star Bits arrow, keep swimming to the chamber's bottom.

Pick up a green shell and swim toward the minefield next to the shipwreck. From a safe distance, stop and aim for the mines around the wreck's base. All the mines explode in a spectacular chain reaction, revealing a different kind of sunken treasure—a Launch Star.

Mario pops into the cube, landing next to a Boo. This Boo has swallowed a Power Star, and Mario must somehow get that prize out of the Boo's belly. Use the pegs on the wall to flip up to a green switch on the wall. This switch orients the gravity inside the cube. Spin to flick the switch so it points to the blue wall.

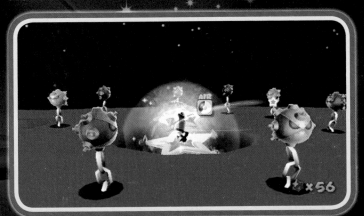

Use the Launch Star to blast out of the lake and to the mysterious cube in the sky above.

265

Collect the coin on the blue wall, then use the spring to bounce up to the switch again. The switch flips so Mario "falls" to the chamber's ceiling.

The waterlogged ceiling has another coin and a bubble cannon. Jump on the spring in front of the cannon and let Mario get swallowed by a bubble. Ride the bubble to the switch; spin to flick it so it points to the blue wall to the right.

Smash the crystal in the hole in the wall's middle. This lets a sunbeam into the cube's interior.

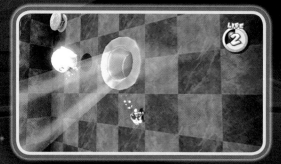

Mario returns to the ghost ship in a bid to ruin Kamella once and for all. Kamella drops from the moon to gladly confront Mario again, especially since the hero can only withstand one hit during the course of the entire battle. On the ship's deck, Kamella begins by lobbing alternating spells. Her first volley is a fireball, but she follows it with a shell. Swipe the shell and jump above the railing to make sure the shot clears it.

Use the nearby spring to bounce up to the switch again. Spin next to the switch so it points back to the floor. Now, lead the Boo into the pool of light on the ground. The Boo vanishes, leaving behind the Power Star. Pick it up to end the mission.

Kamella whizzes close to Mario for her second attack, dancing around him on the ghost ship's deck. Watch her spectral trail to make sure she doesn't surprise Mario.

DAREDEVIL RUN TO THE GHOST SHIP

Kamella is back, and she's discovered a second Power Star at the ghost ship in the Deep Dark Galaxy. Mario must return to challenge Kamella, but the Daredevil Comet overhead saps him of almost all his strength. Can he best Kamella with the odds stacked against him?

Gate Galaxy

Deep Dark
Galaxy

Dreadnought
Galaxy

Melty Molten
Galaxy

Matter Spatter
Galaxy

Snow Cap
Galaxy

Watch out for those shell spells. Even though these are beneficial for Mario, if one hits him before he grabs it, he must restart the battle.

After bopping Kamella on the crow's nest once with a shell, she calls for additional help. If Mario dispatched either of the Magikoopas, it returns to help Kamella. Avoid the fireballs that Kamella unleashes on the crow's nest in threes while waiting for the next shell spell. Grab that shell and put Kamella out of business.

After finishing off Kamella, grab the Power Star to rocket back to the Comet Observatory so Mario can explore another galaxy.

...fter two successful hits, Kamella ...s to the crow's nest, calling for ...stance from two Magikoopas. The ...e worms do her bidding, blasting ...balls across the crow's nest at Mario ...e he tries to survive long enough to ...ture another shell.

DREADNOUGHT GALAXY

The Dreadnought Galaxy is a massive system of floating platforms and orbital weapons that Mario must infiltrate and disable in order to rescue the galaxy's six captured Power Stars. Watch out for giant lasers, blasting cannons, and wicked robots when exploring this galaxy's intricacies.

Infiltrating the Dreadnought

It may be easier for Mario to get rid of the Magikoopas before concentrating on Kamella—especially since he must hit her twice on the crow's nest to finish the battle. Either jump on the Magikoopas, or use shells to attack from a safer distance.

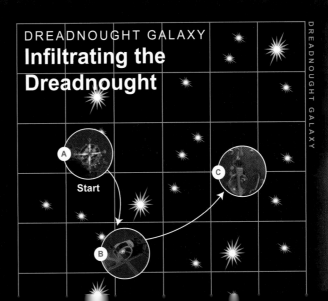

DREADNOUGHT GALAXY
Infiltrating the Dreadnought

A Start

C

B

Blast through the interior of the Dreadnought's largest battle platform to discover the Power Star on its far side. The heart of the battle platform is full of traps and tricks, so Mario must watch his balance and execute precision jumps to survive.

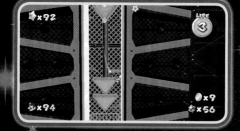

Planets A and B

Mario lands on a satellite outside the battle platform and is immediately under siege by four lasers. The satellite is large enough to have its own gravity field, so run across its base and avoid the lasers.

After landing inside the platform, run to the right and jump between the two walls as they close in on each other.

Long-jump over the gap between the two walls to gather a Life Mushroom and increase Mario's health.

When Mario walks off the base's edge, he flips to the hourglass-shaped center of the satellite's hull. More lasers rotate around the satellite. Weave between the lasers to avoid damage and jump up to be captured by the gravity of the satellite's top half. Pick up the Star Bits and avoid the lasers while trekking to the satellite's roof. Bounce off the purple robot's head (avoid those shock waves) to reach the Launch Star that sends Mario crashing down to the Dreadnought battle platform.

Three robots wander around a warp pipe. Spin to knock the robots on their backs, then stomp their vulnerable undercarriages. When all three are gone, the force field around the warp pipe vanishes, granting Mario entry to the battle platform's interior.

Jump over three rising platforms to reach a gravity switch in the corner. Bump the switch with a spin attack to reorient gravity. The right wall becomes the new floor.

The interior has normal gravity—for now. Mario must navigate through the maze to reach the exit, but getting there is no cakewalk. The interior is closely protected by cannons and moving walls that will squish Mario if he gets trapped between them.

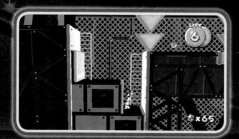

Now carefully backflip up the three rising platforms so Mario isn't smashed.

Jump between the cannonball volleys coming from the guns in the floor. There is another gravity switch against the right wall.

That gravity switch turns the right wall into the floor again. Now Mario must use the spring to bounce between two platforms as they spread apart.

Two purple robots guard the warp pipe that leads back outside. Bounce on their springy heads to reach the warp pipe.

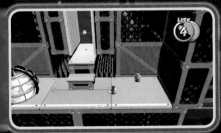

Back outside the battle platform, Mario must bounce on the heads of little green Topmen to vault up the side of a collapsing structure. Once he leaves

one tier of the structure, it falls away. Keep bouncing on Topmen until Mario reaches the rounded structure's top and lands on stable ground. There is a 1-Up Mushroom in a cage here, but Mario cannot open it just yet. Wall jump between the two moving surfaces over the spikes to reach the area's top.

Pick up the Bob-omb at the top, then drop back down to the cage. Throw the Bob-omb at the cage before it explodes, then reap the rewards. Now, wall jump back up to the Launch Star (stopping on the little ledge with the three coins) and use it to leave the battle platform.

★ Planet C ★

LEGEND

🍄 1-Up Mushroom

⭐ Power Star

Gate Galaxy

1
Deep Dark Galaxy

Dreadnought Galaxy

Melty Molten Galaxy

Matter Splatter Galaxy

Snow Cap Galaxy

SUPER MARIO GALAXY

The Sling Star rockets Mario to another satellite loaded with lasers. Walk around the satellite, avoiding the beams, to find a small Sling Star that bounces Mario over to the last planetoid in this mission. The Power Star is there, but reaching it requires the dangerous mixture of water and electricity.

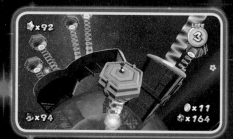

The planetoid's floor is dry. Mario must fix that. Drop to the planetoid's metal core and walk around until a Bullet Bill sees him. Guide the Bullet Bill around the steel girders to a cage, inside of which is the water valve. Breaking the cage turns on the water and floods the planetoid's core.

Jump from the steps to the top of the laser beams that were searing the planetoid's core. Ride the lasers over the water to reach a long grassy ledge that is also guarded by lasers. Jump off the laser to the platform, grab the nearby 1-Up Mushroom, and then weave around the laser beams that crisscross the walkway leading straight to the Power Star.

Swim through the water and hop onto the platform that looks like three steps.

If Mario waits for a second, a robot turtle swims by. Hop on the back of this harmless 'bot and collect all the Star Bits in its path.

DREADNOUGHT'S COLOSSAL CANNONS

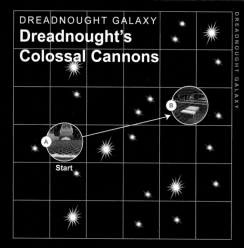

DREADNOUGHT GALAXY
Dreadnought's Colossal Cannons

Start

The Dreadnought platform is armed with the same cannons that graced the Battlerock Galaxy's exterior. Mario must run the gauntlet, avoiding the onslaught of cannonballs while riding a series of moving platforms.

Beware of Chomp

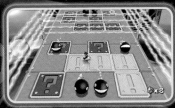

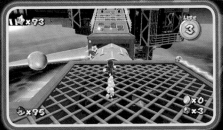

When Mario arrives at the Dreadnought again, he faces a huge field of floor switches below what looks like a collection of...doghouses? Mario must cross the bolts between the starting point and the switches to infiltrate the Dreadnought, but before heading over, make a little pit stop.

When Mario reaches the ramp with the switches, dozens of Chomps stream out of the little houses. The Chomps roll down the ramp, trying to run Mario off the field. To turn off the electrical barrier in the field's middle, step on all the switches in the first batch, turning them from blue to yellow. Now, continue up the ramp and step on the remaining switches. When the last one turns yellow, every Chomp on the field turns into Star Bits. Collect the treasure and move on to the bolts just beyond the field.

 NOTE *The Chomps roll in a straight line, so watch the houses and plot a course up the ramp that avoids the patterns of rolling Chomps.*

 Gate Galaxy

 Deep Dark Galaxy

 Dreadnought Galaxy

 Melty Molten Galaxy

Matter Spatter Galaxy

Snow Cap Galaxy

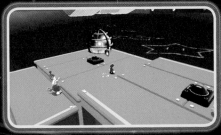

Drop off the starting platform's left side. A ledge down has a caged 1-Up Mushroom. Take a Bob-omb from one of the dispensers and destroy the cage to grab the power-up. Use the nearby Launch Star to bounce back up to the platform facing the switches.

There are two sets of bolts Mario must spin to reach the Launch Star in the distant cage. When he jumps to the second set of bolts, two squid pop out of barrels. While trying to negotiate the bolts, Mario must now deflect both of the squid's coconut attacks with spins. After bopping a coconut at each squid, the cage falls, opening the way to the Launch Star.

 CAUTION *Those bolts don't spin only one way. If Mario stands on the bolts' left side, they actually retreat, putting the hero farther away from his goal.*

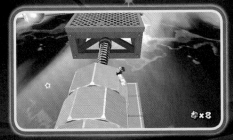

Run on the bolts' edges so he moves across the threads. Don't stand still or the bolts will keep turning, dumping Mario right off.

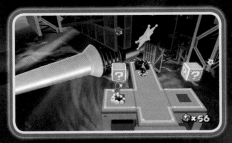

Open each Prize Block to discover Star Bits before jumping over the Bob-omb to reach the Launch Star.

PRIMA Official Game Guide

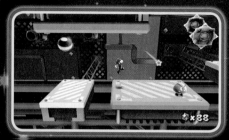

While soaring to the cannon gauntlet, scoop up flying Star Bits with the cursor.

dangerous distractions. Even though the Star Bits inside would be great to pocket, Mario cannot let the orange platform get too far ahead or he'll be stuck and will have to wait for another platform to come by.

Cannon Alley

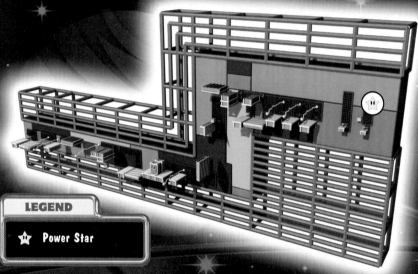

LEGEND

⭐ Power Star

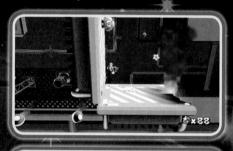

Jump back down to an orange platform that rolls along the screen's bottom. Mines are in the area now, so Mario has a new threat to watch for. Goombas also invade the area, but quickly dispel them with Star Bits and a swift kick.

When Mario drops down in front of the cannon, he lands on an orange platform. Orange platforms move while yellow ones remain stationary. The platform rattles and starts crawling to the right. The cannons in the Dreadnought's hull explode into action, filling the air with shells. Unlike the ride across the Battlerock's side, Mario must run and jump on the orange platform's top to avoid the shells. When the orange platform slides under a yellow platform, jump over the obstacle quickly so Mario's ride doesn't get away from him.

Soon, Mario's platform stops. He must jump up and be captured by the gravity of the platform above him. The gauntlet begins again as Mario rolls to the right, dodging incoming shells and jumping over stationary yellow platforms and ledges. ? Blocks start decorating the scene, but these are

The gauntlet gets weird when Mario's platform crashes into some mines and is disabled. The cannons don't stop attacking, so the only way to go is up. Jump to the next orange platform, allowing gravity to pull Mario's feet to the new "down." Ride the platform straight up, avoiding obstacles and cannon fire.

At the column's top, Mario's platform crashes into more mines. Quickly jump to a yellow platform to the right and ride along the ceiling. The yellow platforms are higher up here, so plan early with a backflip or spin at the top of a normal jump to grab the yellow ledge's edge and pull Mario up.

Electric barriers force Mario to ride the next orange platform that rolls along the gauntlet's bottom. The cannon fire intensifies, filling the skies with exploding shells. Avoid the cannonballs in the "valleys" between the yellow platforms. Between shots, scale the yellow ledges and get back down quickly as the orange platform rolls beneath.

Mario finally rolls beyond the wall of cannons, but there's no time to celebrate. Two purple robots on ledges blast shock waves across space. Jump over the waves as the orange platform

slides toward the Dreadnought's outside wall. When the platform finally docks, jump on the purple robot to the right to stun it. Its neck springs up, bouncing Mario straight into the Power Star.

REVENGE OF THE TOPMAN TRIBE

DREADNOUGHT GALAXY
Topman Tribe Speed Run

A — Start
B
C
D
E — Topman Maniac

DREADNOUGHT GALAXY

Topmaniac has found a new galaxy to rule: Dreadnought. The Topman tribe has followed their leader to this distant corner of the universe to offer their support in stopping Mario from taking any more of their coveted Power Stars.

Planets A, B, and C

At the Dreadnought Galaxy's edge, the Topmen have installed a satellite that looks remarkably like their leader, Topmaniac. They've stationed only one Topman to guard the galaxy's outer perimeter. Bounce off the Topman's head, into the small Sling Star in the sky. This Sling Star bounces Mario up to a small planetoid.

Gate Galaxy

Deep Dark Galaxy

Dreadnought Galaxy

Melty Molten Galaxy

Matter Splatter Galaxy

Snow Cap Galaxy

A Luma is trapped behind a force field at the planetoid's northern pole. Slam two Topmen into the field to dismantle it. None of the Topmen guarding the Luma are close to the fields, so Mario must shuttle them across the surface with repeated spin attacks. Once the Luma is free, it becomes a Sling Star that rockets Mario up to another satellite.

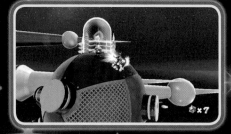

The Pull Stars lead to a large Launch Star that zooms Mario down to the Dreadnought battle platform's surface.

TIP

Before using the Sling Star, backflip to the top of the highest tower on the planetoid to fetch a 1-Up Mushroom.

Planet D

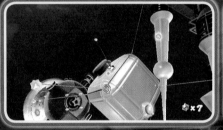

Mario lands on another small satellite. Several Star Bits are at the ends of the antennae sticking out of each corner of the satellite, so scoop them up with the cursor. There's no way off the satellite just yet, so ground pound the red button to make five blue Star Chips appear. Assemble all five to have a string of Pull Stars lead him away from the satellite.

Mario lands in front of a field of mines and Pull Stars. He must pull himself through the minefield via the Pull Stars, but the Topmen aren't about to make things that simple. They have installed cannons alongside the minefield to fill the air with exploding shells. So, before braving the minefield, run to the bottom of the cylinder Mario landed on and pick up a Life Mushroom. He'll need the extra health if things start going wrong.

Four of the Star Chips are within easy reach, but the last one hovers too high over the satellite to reach with a normal jump or even a backflip. Therefore, spin-attack the green Topman to push it under the Star Chip. Now, bounce off the Topman's noggin to reach the Star Chip and create the Pull Stars.

TIP

Don't use the Pull Stars just yet! There is a 1-Up Mushroom over the satellite. Push the Topman underneath it (look for the shadow on the satellite's surface), then bounce off the little green robot to reach the power-up.

Watch the cannon's fire patterns and drag Mario across space just as the shell passes between the two Pull Stars.

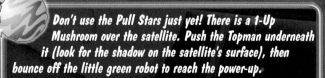

There are Koopas on the tarmac as well. Bop them and steal their shells so Mario can break open the treasure chests on the tarmac. The first two chests are full of Star Bits, but the third one (the chest closest to the Launch Star) contains a 1-Up Mushroom.

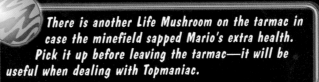

TIP

There is another Life Mushroom on the tarmac in case the minefield sapped Mario's extra health. Pick it up before leaving the tarmac—it will be useful when dealing with Topmaniac.

Getting the 1-Up Mushroom near the minefield's end isn't easy, especially with the cannons going off in Mario's face. To grab the Mushroom, pull Mario toward one of the two Pull Stars just beyond it. Then, halfway to the Pull Star, quickly grab the other Pull Star to divert Mario to the Mushroom.

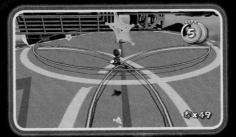

The Launch Star is at the convergence of three shock waves. Time Mario's jumps over the waves, then leap into the Launch Star to rocket out of harm's way—for now.

Planet E

After Mario reaches the Launch Star at the minefield's end, he drops to a long tarmac. The tarmac is covered with robots that send shock waves rippling across the ground. Jump over the shock waves as Mario crosses the tarmac, zeroing in on the Launch Star on the far end.

Boss Battle: Topmaniac

Top

(continued on next page)

Gate Galaxy

Deep Dark Galaxy

Dreadnought Galaxy

Melty Molten Galaxy

Matter Splatter Galaxy

Snow Cap Galaxy

SUPER MARIO GALAXY

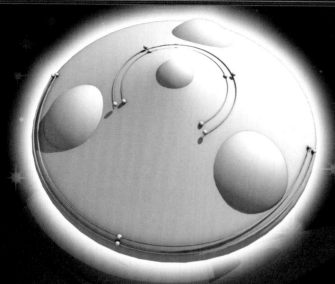

Bottom

Are those little Topmen giving Mario trouble? Bash them into the electrical barriers, too. They pop and sizzle before disappearing off the planetoid.

Mario lands on the bottom of Topmaniac's throne. Several red Topmen with spikes on their heads ricochet around the ship's bottom, trying to soften Mario up before Topmaniac gets his turn. Spin to back them into the electrical fields, then run topside.

Each time Topmaniac gets off the ropes, he spits out Star Bits. Collect these while planning the next attack.

There is another blue Luma on the planetoid's top selling power-ups. If Mario already has six health, purchase the 1-Up Mushroom. The cost is only 30 Star Bits; if Mario is a little short, just circle the world and pick up the extra Star Bits.

It takes three hits to defeat Topmaniac, but this isn't the last time Mario will see the Topman king. When the Speedster Comet bathes the Dreadnought Galaxy in red, Topmaniac will be back for his revenge.

When Mario is ready, jump to the arena on the planetoid's top. Topmaniac drops from the skies to challenge Mario, and he brings reinforcements before the fight even begins. Two red Topmen with spikes also bound around the arena, running interference for their boss. To score the first blow, jump on Topmaniac's head; while he's stunned, spin-attack to nudge him into an electrical barrier. The boss is shocked, literally, by Mario's expert moves.

DREADNOUGHT'S AMMO DEPOT

A massive battle platform like the Dreadnought certainly needs its fair share of ammunition, but some misplaced trash is gumming up the depot. If Mario can help the robot running the depot clean out the trash, maybe it will share something cool it found while working at the depot. This hidden Power Star is found on the "Revenge of the Topman Tribe" mission.

⭐ Trash Day ⭐

As soon as the clock starts counting down, grab Bob-ombs and throw them as close to the lights on the ground as possible. Perfect aim isn't necessary because the splash damage is pretty extensive, but getting the Bob-omb as close to the light as possible will guarantee this mission ends in success.

When Mario returns to the "Revenge of the Topman Tribe" mission, he must ignore the action on the satellite's top and check the undercarriage. There's a green warp pipe! The pipe leads to the Dreadnought's ammunition depot, and the on-duty robot is angry that a Topman dumped garbage among the shells. The robot tells Mario if he helps clean out the depot within 30 seconds, he'll give him a reward.

This garbage-cleaning mission is a little tougher than the one Mario encountered in the Battlerock Galaxy—there's a lot more trash. Fortunately, visual clues on the ground indicate where Mario should throw the Bob-ombs to make the trash disappear.

TIP

Drop a Bob-omb in the middle of the two lamps in the garbage dump's center. The resulting explosion takes out five garbage piles rather than just three if Mario dropped the Bob-omb directly on the lights.

As the seconds tick down, Mario must hurry. Precision is paramount within the last 10 seconds of the mission.

Now, who would throw out a perfectly good Power Star?

DREADNOUGHT GALAXY

DREADNOUGHT GALAXY
Topman Tribe Speed Run

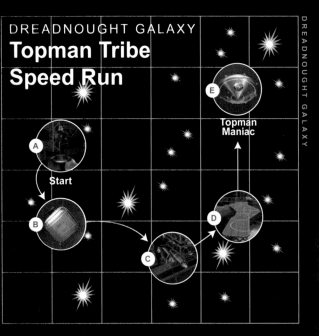

The Speedster Comet soars over the Dreadnought Galaxy's battle platform, beckoning Mario's return. The hero must scramble across the battle platform and defeat Topmaniac one last time to earn the fifth Power Star of the Dreadnought Galaxy.

Grab the Life Mushroom on the satellite's bottom before heading out into the minefield.

Blasting Through

To earn the Dreadnought Galaxy's fifth Power Star, Mario must blaze through the "Revenge of the Topman tribe" mission within six minutes. To succeed, keep moving and don't spend any extra time angling for Star Bits or coins that would take Mario too far off the main path.

Time Mario's movements through the minefield so he doesn't have to completely stop at the Pull Stars. Drag him to the Sling Star and exit the minefield within one minute.

When the mission begins, immediately try getting off the first satellite by bouncing through the Sling Star and rocketing up to the planetoid with the trapped Luma. Ignore the 1-Up Mushroom for now and concentrate on slamming two Topmen into the electrical barriers around the Luma.

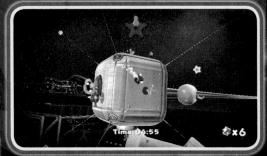

The Luma turns into a Sling Star and zips Mario up to the small satellite containing the five blue Star Chips.

Don't worry about breaking open the treasure chests on the tarmac. Just run to the Launch Star as fast as possible, jumping over the shock waves to avoid damage. The Life Mushroom is still behind the second chest, so pick that up. Mario needs as much health as possible when closing in on Topmaniac.

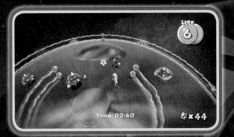

Time: 02:40 &x44

*Don't spend any time with the Topmen
on the bottom of Topmaniac's arena.
Just get topside and bring the boss
down for the final duel.*

Concentrate solely on Topmaniac. If any of the Topmen get
close enough that Mario bops them into the electrical fields while
defeating Topmaniac, great. Otherwise, just keep jumping on
the boss's head so his spikes disappear, then budge him into the
electrical fields to quickly end the fight. Mario should have about
one minute left on the clock. Grab the Power Star and finish the
mission, blasting off from Dreadnought to the Comet Observatory.

MELTY MOLTEN GALAXY

The Melty Molten Galaxy is a planetary system comprised entirely of fire and brimstone. The highly hazardous
galaxy is a volatile place, full of lava geysers and crashing meteors. The Power Stars here are difficult
catches, but if Mario can keep his cool in the hottest corner of the universe, the rewards will be worth the
effort.

Sinking Lava Spire

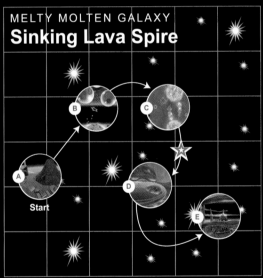

MELTY MOLTEN GALAXY
Sinking Lava Spire

Start

Planet A

The first Power Star in Melty Molten Galaxy is
atop a rocky spire. Normally, climbing a mountain
wouldn't be a problem for Mario, but with burning
lava melting the spire's base, reaching the summit
suddenly got a lot harder.

Gate Galaxy

Deep Dark
Galaxy

Dreadnought
Galaxy

Melty Molten
Galaxy

Matter Spatter
Galaxy

Snow Cap
Galaxy

MELTY MOLTEN GALAXY

PRIMA Official Game Guide

There is no rest in the Melty Molten Galaxy. After touching down, Mario must immediately start crossing the main planet. The ground erupts with fiery geysers and Lava Bubbles pop out of pools of molten earth. There are several crystals that somehow don't melt. Shatter them to gather up Star Bits. Use a spin attack to easily blow out Lava Bubbles that float after Mario and a kick to destroy them.

Follow the trail across the planet, gathering more Star Bits. Wait for the geysers of molten lava to cool before trying to jump across the wide lava field. When Mario reaches the other side, look left and wave the cursor over the sea of lava to grab more Star Bits.

Carefully cross the network of metal bridges that span the sea of lava. They sink under Mario's weight, so move quickly, picking up the coins between the bridges. The long green bridge leading to the cliffs is already dipping into the lava, so swiftly cross it. Watch out for lava bursts arcing over the bridge.

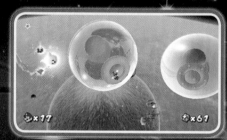

Wait for the field of geysers to pause, then slip through to the alcove carved in the cliffs. Backflip up to the stone circle under two coins. Ground pound the circle to lower the granite plug to the right. When the plug drops into the lava, wall jump up the new alcove to reach the cliffs' top. Grab the coins there, then run to the right.

Vault to the active volcano via the small Sling Star on the cliffs. Mario drops into another Sling Star on the volcano's side. Use it to bounce up to the Launch Star in the volcano's mouth.

If Mario doesn't spin in the Sling Star on the volcano's side, he slides down a ledge. He can then cross back to the cliffs and try again.

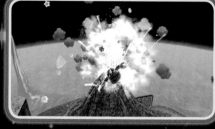

Boom! The volcano roars to life, blasting Mario across the galaxy.

Planets B and C

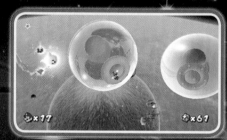

Mario lands on a small trio of spheres. Gravity pulls him to safety. A hungry Luma is on the left sphere, but it needs to wait—Mario must get the Power Star from the lava spire now. The spheres lead to a field of Pull Stars. Drag Mario across space into the Pull Star field, but don't go too fast; the field soon fills with deadly explosions.

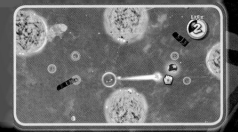

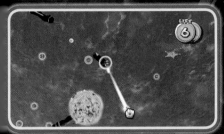

There are five Star Chips on the newly forming planetoid. Gathering them is complicated by a horde of Lava Bubbles and fire geysers. Carefully step over the geysers as they die down to pick up the Star Chips. Spin to disable the Lava Bubbles and kick them to destroy them.

After collecting the fifth Star Chip, a large Launch Star rises out of the lava near the planetoid's edge. This Launch Star rockets Mario over the sea of furious energy and to the lava spire.

Arcs of solar energy burst from the lava balls in the Pull Star field. Wait for the bursts to die down before pulling Mario across the field. A Life Mushroom in the field restores any lost health and acks Mario up to six. The extra health is nice to have, because he'll probably burn his feet more than once while finishing the mission. Follow the Pull Star path to large Launch Star and use it to blast ack down to the Melty Molten Galaxy's urface.

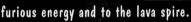

Mario soars under titanic arcs of cosmic energy as he closes in on a small planetoid half-swallowed in the boiling lava soup.

Use a small Sling Star on a crashed saucer to reach the cooling surface of

★★ **Planet D** ★★

Front

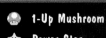

LEGEND	
🍄	1-Up Mushroom
⭐	Power Star

Gate Galaxy

Deep Dark Galaxy

Dreadnought Galaxy

Melty Molten Galaxy

Matter Spatter Galaxy

Snow Cap Galaxy

Back

Watch out for boulders near the caves. If caught unexpectedly, Mario is pushed into the lava. He loses only one wedge of health at the first touch, but he also briefly loses control. If he doesn't get back to safe ground quickly, he'll burn through his remaining health.

When Mario touches down on the path leading to the spire, he discovers that this area is sinking. With every step, the sea of lava swallows a little more of the spire, so get moving, and keep moving, to survive the primal forces of nature and reach the Power Star before fire consumes the entire spire.

Circle the spire, picking up Star Bits that crash down to the surface, but ignore the crystals loaded with Star Bits. Stopping too long to collect the goodies can be disastrous. Keep moving at all times. When confronted by Lava Bubbles, spin to snuff their flames, but then keep moving.

Ground pound the stone button at the dead end. The cliff breaks away from the spire and sinks into the lava, creating an alcove Mario can scale with wall jumps. As he hops up the alcove, the lava consumes more and more of the spire.

The hanging lava rock drops as Mario closes in, creating a temporary platform for him to cross the wide gap in the path around the spire.

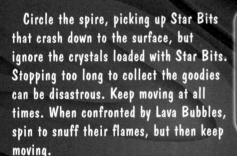

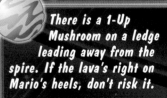

T·IP

There is a 1-Up Mushroom on a ledge leading away from the spire. If the lava's right on Mario's heels, don't risk it.

There are tons of Star Bits on this spire, all designed to tempt Mario into slowing down and filling his pockets. Resist the urge and keep going for the summit. The greatest prize, the Power Star, is just ahead!

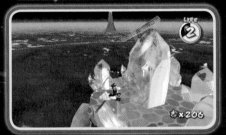

When Mario spots a ledge with a railing, he's almost there. Ignore that Prize Block—there's no time to pop it for Star Bits. Jump to the step right below the summit and spin to dispose of the Lava Bubble blocking the path. As Mario reaches the summit with the Power Star (encased in a crystal), the lava relents. Smash the crystal to free the star and get out of this primordial mess.

THROUGH THE METEOR STORM

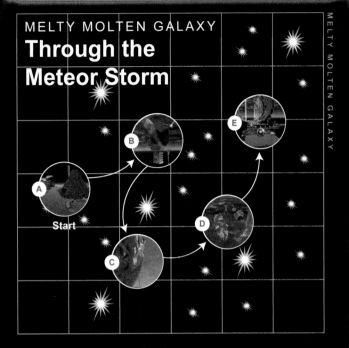

MELTY MOLTEN GALAXY
Through the Meteor Storm

It's not just the burning ground that Mario must watch in this mission—he must also watch the sky, lest a fiery meteor clobbers him. Surviving the meteor shower is only part of finding the Power Star in this mission, so get ready for some intense action across fields of bubbling lava.

★ Planets A and B ★

When Mario arrives back in the Melty Molten Galaxy, the main planet is strangely devoid of life—because the sky is falling! Meteors crash to the ground, exploding on impact. Watch for shadows to see where the meteors are about to hit. When a shadow appears on the ground, get out of the way as soon as possible.

Gate Galaxy

Deep Dark Galaxy

Dreadnought Galaxy

Melty Molten Galaxy

Matter Spatter Galaxy

Snow Cap Galaxy

SUPER MARIO GALAXY

PRIMA Official Game Guide

Avoid the meteors and zoom in on the pair of unlit torches next to the sea of lava. Mario must light these to make a Launch Star appear. Fortunately, a couple Lava Bubbles rise from the soup just in time. Lead them to the torches, where they ignite them with just a touch. Now, use that Launch Star to get out of here before Mario gets beaned by a meteor.

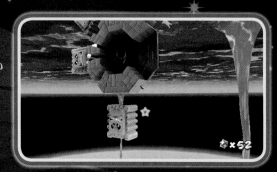

The Launch Star vaults Mario to a stone octagon in the sky, which is dominated by Thwomps.

A cooled stone platform rises from the sea of lava. There are five Star Chips on the platform that must be assembled to create a Launch Star. The first Star Chip is inside the wooden crate on the left. Watch out for nasties while scouring the surface for the remaining four Star Chips. Shoot star bits at them to kill them.

Run under the Thwomps as they rise into the air. Jump over the pits just as meteors streak into them.

TIP

Take refuge in this nook below the third Thwomp. There's a 1-Up Mushroom in the shallow gap. Duck down so the Thwomp doesn't squish Mario.

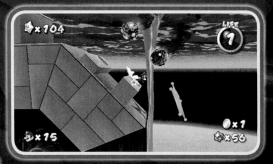

Watch out for meteors as Mario jumps to the Sling Star at the end of the octagon's track.

There is a Life Mushroom on the surface's right side. Collect it before moving across the planetoid to gather the remaining Star Chips, such as the one on the sloping platform just off the main landmass. When all the Star Chips are joined, the Launch Star appears on the landmass's far end.

The Bullet Bill shatters the cage, allowing Mario to use the Launch Star within to blast across the galaxy to a huge lava tunnel.

Mario lands on a U-shaped planetoid high above the lava sea. The Launch Star to escape this planetoid is under a cage, to find a Bullet Bill. Walk across the planetoid, looking out for Lava Bubbles between the ramparts. Spin and kick these monsters out of the way. The stonework finally gives way to pure rock. Jump over the lava gap at the base of the U.

 **Planet E**

The Power Star waits for Mario right in front of the massive lava tunnel. Unfortunately, it is trapped inside a ball. Mario must roll the sphere across the 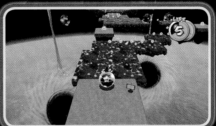 lava squares and through the tunnel to reach the machine that can crack it open.

Watch out for Lava Bubbles at the crook in this U-shaped planetoid.

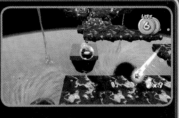

TIP It's a risky move, but Mario can hop to a 1-Up Mushroom on a barren square. Prepare to slow down by tilting the Wii Remote back just as Mario lands so he doesn't roll right off.

At the planetoid's far end is a Bullet Bill cannon. Jump in front of a Bullet Bill and let it follow Mario back across the planetoid. Weave between the walls that were once guarded by Lava Bubbles

Hop across the sliding lava squares, rolling through the lines of coins. There is another 1-Up Mushroom on a waypoint—a calm stationary tract of land. Jump from the waypoint to another sliding square, then roll the Power Star right up to the tunnel's mouth.

Gate Galaxy

Deep Dark Galaxy

Dreadnought Galaxy

Melty Molten Galaxy

Matter Spatter Galaxy

Snow Cap Galaxy

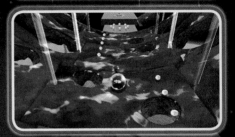

The tunnel is moving. Rings of giant lava squares rotate, pushing the sphere around and making it hard to steer straight through the tunnel. Fortunately, there is another waypoint in the tunnel's center where Mario can rest and get his bearings before pushing through the rest of the hazardous landscape. The last few rings of squares are full of holes. Carefully steer around them, jumping only when necessary to avoid certain doom.

Jump across the last few lava circles to reach the machine that breaks open the sphere and releases the Power Star.

MELTY MOLTEN GALAXY
Fiery Dino Piranha

A
Start

F

Dino Piranha

B

E

C

D

MELTY MOLTEN GALAXY

The Dino Piranha of the Good Egg Galaxy may be long gone, but apparently the branches of its family tree extend all the way to the Melty Molten Galaxy. Mario must somehow fight his way across the chaotic lava field to reach this burning boss's nest.

Planets A and B

LEGEND
1-Up Mushroom

TIP

Don't smash the brick on the large rock in the steel platform's middle. Backflip to climb atop the brick, then jump straight up to claim a 1-Up Mushroom.

Mario again lands on the large landmass on the Melty Molten Galaxy's lava sea. His mission is imperiled by aggressive Lava Bubbles and a splashing geyser that erupts with intense frequency. Mario must cross this hostile world and leap over a major gap in the ground to reach a series of small metal platforms.

Jump from the small platforms to an alcove carved in the cliffs opposite the large volcano Mario had to dive into before. Wall jump up the alcove's sides to reach a warp pipe at the ceiling, but look out for geysers that spurt blistering air out of the walls.

Jump across this network of tiny metal platforms as they sink into the lava. Don't stand still, lest the floor vanishes into the molten earth. Jumping across these small platforms is tricky. If Mario falls in the lava, he bounces right out (sans one health wedge) but is hard to control for a moment, which can lead to him falling right back in.

The warp pipe leads to an overturned saucer in the lava. A small Sling Star on the saucer's edge vaults Mario up to a pair of planetoids forming from the lava sea.

These new planets are still extremely hostile. As they churn and spin in the lava, Mario must cautiously cross the cooled platforms before they sink back into the lava. Watch out for geysers along the edges that will knock Mario into the lava. No Launch Star appears on the first planetoid until Mario eliminates all the Lava Bubbles. Spin to snuff one out, then kick it to finish it off.

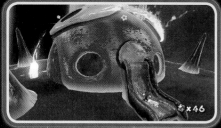

Walk up the ramp leading to the next planetoid. This cooled crust is also being recycled into the lava, so run across it to reach a Launch Star on the mass's far end. Lava balls arc through the air over the planetoid, so watch out. If one hits Mario, he's likely to tumble into the lava.

Dash across the steel platforms to reach a series of small Sling Stars to bounce Mario over the lava.

Jump to the Launch Star to get off this unstable planetoid.

CAUTION

Keep shaking the Wii Remote whenever Mario lands in the next Sling Star or he falls right into the lava.

Planets C and D

Mario lands on a disc of rotating platforms. Gravity always pulls him to the disc's center, so he can ride the platforms as they spin around the core. The platforms often brush against each other, so jump to the next one so Mario isn't pushed into the lava. There are five Star Chips and a Life Mushroom on this disc. Collect all five Star Chips to craft the Launch Star that leads to the mission's end.

On the last ledge before the Launch Star that vaults Mario to this galaxy's boss, purchase either a Mushroom or a 1-Up Mushroom from a blue Luma. The price is the same for both: 30 Star Bits.

The Star Chips are on each ring of the disc. Ride the platforms around, ducking down to keep from being pushed, and jump to grab the necessary pieces. After collecting all five pieces, the Launch Star appears on a ledge on the outside disc's ring.

Boss Battle: Fiery Dino Pirahna

Like the Dino Piranha in the Good Egg Galaxy, Mario must strike the ball at the end of the monster's tail three times to win. However, this tail is often on fire! Mario must dodge the boss until the ball cools down enough that he can attack without burning himself.

After the first successful attack, the Fiery Dino Piranha picks up the pace while walking around the planetoid, and it's burning tail leaves a fire trail behind it. Avoid the flames while waiting for the tail to cool down for the next strike.

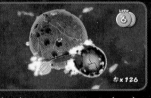

When Mario lands on the Fiery Dino Piranha's nest, he cracks the shell, waking the brute. The monster starts blindly stomping around the planetoid, since it cannot see outside the shell. While the monster is aimlessly tromping about, shatter the crystals to earn Star Bits. Leave the coins and the coin flowers alone for now. Mario may need those goodies during the battle. Wait for the Fiery Dino Piranha's tail to cool down, then spin-attack it. The shell is broken and the monster roars with fury.

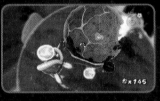

After the second attack, things get even worse. The Fiery Dino Piranha leaves a trail of untouchable fire, and it spits fireballs that bounce across the small planetoid. Mario must avoid these while closing in on the tail ball.

When the fire trail dies down, zoom in and deliver the third attack that ends the monster's reign over Melty Molten Galaxy.

To blast off from this galaxy, grab the Power Star at the planet's southern pole.

Gate Galaxy

Deep Dark Galaxy

Dreadnought Galaxy

Melty Molten Galaxy

Matter Spatter Galaxy

Snow Cap Galaxy

289

PRIMA Official Game Guide

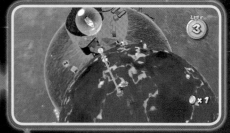

MELTY MOLTEN GALAXY
Burning Tide

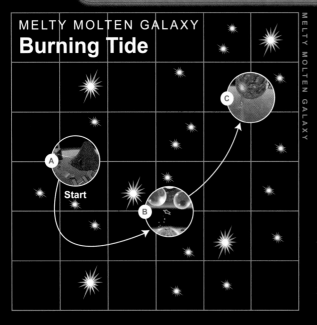

Start

While crossing to the spire in this galaxy's first mission, Mario spied a hungry Luma—apparently hoping for a hot lunch. Feed the Luma 80 Star Bits so it blasts off and transforms into a new planetoid.

Silver Star 2: Climb the pole as the lava rises to capture the next Silver Star and avoid getting burned.

Silver Star 3: The third Silver Star is on safe ground, but three Lava Bubbles surround it.

Silver Stars

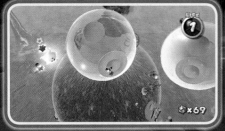
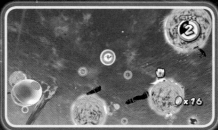

After escaping the main landmass from the first part of the "Sinking Lava Spire" mission, head for the trio of spheres hanging over the Melty Molten Galaxy. The hungry Luma up here requires 80 Star Bits to create a new planetoid. If Mario is short on Star Bits, enter the Pull Star field and run the cursor over the lava balls to pick up a few extra.

Silver Star 4: Jump on the block in this fire trap's center to grab the next Silver Star. Wait on the block until the lava subsides, then run for the next Silver Star.

The Luma transforms into a pulsing lava sphere. The tide of molten earth rises and falls, revealing a network of walkways. Rush between the few safe places to stand during a high lava tide while collecting five Silver Stars. After bringing the five Silver Stars together, the hidden Power Star appears.

TIP

Scramble atop the Prize Block as the lava rises to escape danger and pick up a Life Mushroom.

Silver Star 1: To get this star, cross the first pathway that appears as the lava drops.

Silver Star 5: Two rings of geysers surround the last Silver Star. The rings alternate, so wait for the outer ring to blow, then inch close and hold back until the inner ring falls silent.

Find a safe spot to stand once the Power Star is revealed. When the lava ebbs, make a break for the Power Star to end the mission.

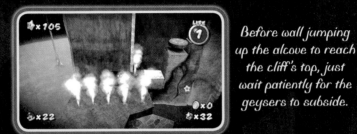

LAVA SPIRE DAREDEVIL RUN

Ascending the sinking spire was tough enough with full health—does Mario have the chops to reach the summit again with only one sliver of health?

⭐ Hot-Stepper ⭐

This mission unfolds exactly like Mario's first visit to Melty Molten Galaxy, but having only one wedge of health and no means of getting more adds a tough wrinkle. Use the strategy from that mission to reach the Power Star, but watch out for these difficult areas when trying to avoid that one horrible hit.

Before wall jumping up the alcove to reach the cliff's top, just wait patiently for the geysers to subside.

Hold Mario's position on each Pull Star and don't make a move until the lava bombs that arc between the spheres have passed.

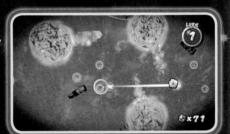

Avoid the gushing geysers and Lava Bubbles on the main landmass. Don't even try snuffing out the Lava Bubble; just run from it and don't look back.

Waste no time on the sinking steel bridges. Mario must jump as far as possible onto the green platform since its edge is already touching the lava.

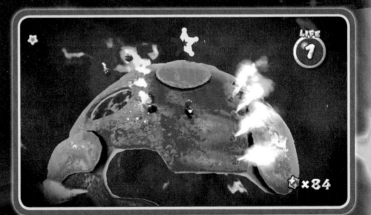

Be careful gathering the Star Chips on the planetoid in the lava. Watch out for the wall of geysers that guard the fourth Star Chip.

Gate Galaxy

Deep Dark Galaxy

Dreadnought Galaxy

Melty Molten Galaxy

Matter Spatter Galaxy

Snow Cap Galaxy

SUPER MARIO GALAXY

PRIMA Official Game Guide

Back

LEGEND

🍄 1-Up Mushroom

⭐ Power Star

Forget about Star Bits. Just keep running up the spire.

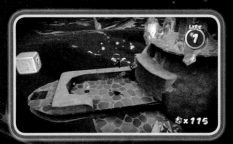

Front

When Mario reaches the lava spire, time is of the essence. The spires start sinking the moment Mario sets foot on the base, so don't slow down or stand still. He must keep as far ahead of the lava as possible.

Quickly hop over the platform created by the falling rocks on the spire's side. The lava can easily catch up to Mario if he hesitates.

The Lava Bubble in front of the Power Star is troublesome. As soon as Mario approaches, jump and spin to snuff it out before it can bump him back to the spire's base. After hitting the Lava Bubble, just jump to the Power Star and break it out of the crystal.

MATTER SPLATTER GALAXY

The farthest galaxy from the Garden Dome is an odd place indeed. Matter Splatter Galaxy is in constant flux, disappearing and reappearing as balls of mass are tossed back and forth. As it does this, Mario must nimbly jump from one surface to the next without hesitating—because in Matter Splatter, one second the floor is there and the next it's vanished into the cosmic ether.

Here Today

Mario arrives in Matter Splatter just in time to watch a bit of the show before making his first move. Drops of matter bounce around, temporarily exposing pieces of a landscape. As matter bounces away, the ground seems to melt, only to reappear when another droplet of matter bounces along again.

The galaxy's next area is pitch-black until matter droplets start fleshing out the level. Walls and walkways suddenly appear in blinding contrast to the darkness, but within seconds, they collapse back into the void. Run to the Right and wall jump up the shaft as matter droplets reveal the level.

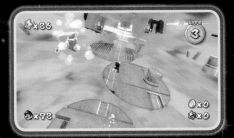

Mario's goal is a warp pipe on the fluxing landscape's far end. As he jumps across the pieces of the galaxy that appear, Magikoopas cast fireballs in an attempt to make Mario dodge—right into the void. Avoid the fireballs and keep pushing ahead. Don't try to defeat the Magikoopas—just keep moving.

Coins and Star Bits offer hints as to where solid ground might appear.

Keep bounding across ledges as they appear out of the void. More Magikoopas fly in to fling magical fireballs at Mario; just keep running and drop down the warp pipe at the room's top.

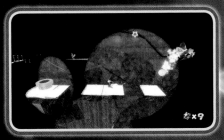

The warp pipe never disappears. It is one of the rare constants in Matter Splatter.

Gate Galaxy

Deep Dark Galaxy

Dreadnought Galaxy

Melty Molten Galaxy

Matter Spatter Galaxy

Snow Cap Galaxy

PRIMA Official Game Guide

Hope Springs Eternal

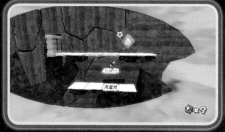

Spring into the Sling Star at the chamber's top. It's tough to see since it is flat—it looks like a sliver of gold against the green cosmos.

Matter Splatter's next area is painted against a swirling field of green ether. A moving window, crawling upward, reveals the stage piece by piece. Keep pace with the window of visible land. Pink grates appear that Mario can jump through. But as these grates get farther and farther apart, he must use the Spring Mushroom to close the gaps.

Vanishing Point

Use high bounces to vault through the small grates. Aim those bounces well, because if Mario springs into solid ground, he will bounce right into the void.

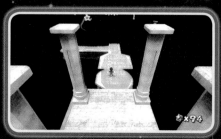

The final section of Matter Splatter is a road, but only a few feet of it appear at a time. And as new ground is revealed, previously seen walkways melt away. Mario must keep pace with the moving window as he closes in on the Power Star at the galaxy's end. Use the following pictures to chart a course through the area and arrive safely at the Power Star.

CAUTION

Just use small bounces to climb ledges like this. There's no need for dramatic jumps when little hops will do.

Spring over to the swinging platform with the 1-Up Mushroom, then bounce straight up to pass through a grate as it appears.

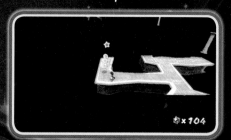

Grab these three coins, then run back to the other fork in the road. Take the route on the right.

At the stage's top, a giant coin hangs in the air. Bounce into the coin to create a twinkling field of Star Bits. Bounce into the field and pick up as many of them as possible with the cursor.

This route ends abruptly, so jump to the left when the new area appears.

294

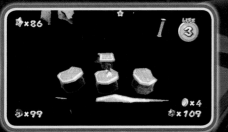

Take the center route; the other two are dead ends.

More Magikoopas! The road is wide enough for Mario to jump off their noggins and get rid of them without worrying about spilling into the void.

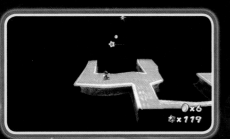

Once Mario reaches the pink road, stick to the left.

Grab the coin in the middle of this split route, but then keep to the left.

Ignore the last Magikoopa and run straight for the Power Star before the road beneath it vanishes.

SNOW CAP GALAXY

The hungry Luma outside the Garden Dome transforms into a new galaxy if Mario feeds it 1,600 Star Bits. The Luma blasts into the cosmos and becomes the Snow Cap Galaxy, a playful paradise for a trio of star bunnies. If Mario would just play a little game of hide-and-seek with them, surely they could find some way to show their gratitude?

⭐ Snow Day ⭐

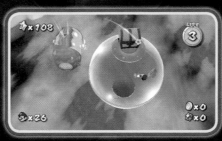

Mario drops into Snow Cap Galaxy, landing on a small sphere that overlooks the galaxy's main planetoid, which is a long cylinder covered with a light dusting of snow. To reach the planetoid and talk to the star bunnies, break open the chest with a shell. The shell is on the sphere's opposite side, so make a lap around the sphere to pick it up. Break open the chest and follow the Sling Star to visit the bunnies.

The three bunnies ask Mario to play a game with them. They will run and hide in different places on the snowy planetoid. If Mario can find them

within 150 seconds, the bunnies will share something special.

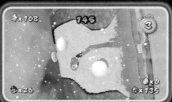

First, step on all the floor switches. Most of them are buried under the snow, which can be brushed away with the cursor. He runs slower in the snow, so always sweep a path for the hero.

Gate Galaxy

Deep Dark Galaxy

Dreadnought Galaxy

Melty Molten Galaxy

Matter Spatter Galaxy

Snow Cap Galaxy

The last switch is on the planetoid's bottom. When Mario steps on it, the lid slides backs, revealing a small collection of Star Bits and a Fire Flower. Without the Fire Flower, Mario cannot melt away the snow and find all the bunnies.

The third bunny is hiding in one of the little holes obscured by the snow. Brush away the snow over this hole to make the bunny hop out.

The first bunny is hiding inside this snowman. Melt the snowman with a fireball to reveal it. The bunny hops away, but a beacon over its head always lets Mario know where it is.

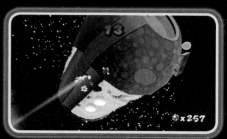

Melt the snowdrifts and snowmen with fireballs to reveal piles of Star Bits.

Finding the bunnies is one thing; catching them is another thing entirely. The bunnies hop around, begging Mario to give chase. Some of them will hop through the snow. Remember to sweep a path ahead of Mario as he runs so he can catch up with those bunnies and win the game. The best way to catch the bunnies is to chase them into one of the rings on either end of the capsule.

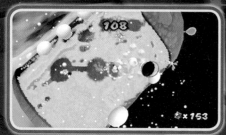

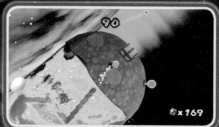

The second bunny is inside the treasure chest on the grassy knoll on the opposite end of the planetoid from the Fire Flower. There's no shell out in the open, but if Mario melts this snowman, he uncovers a green one. Pick up the green shell and quickly break open the chest to reveal the second bunny.

Hooray! Mario won the game. The bunnies are happy to present him with the promised prize, a Power Star.

BOWSER'S GALAXY REACTOR

LAST BATTLE

After Mario recovers the fifth Grand Star from Bowser's Dark Matter Reactor and has collected 60 Power Stars, the Comet Observatory gains enough power to finally give pursuit to Bowser. There are still dozens of Powers Stars to seek out at this point, but Mario's eagerness to rescue Princess Peach as soon as possible is understandable. When Mario confirms to Rosalina that it's time to fly to the heart of the cosmos and launch the attack, Rosalina flies the Comet Observatory into deep space.

Using her magic, Rosalina steers the Comet Observatory next to the Mushroom Kingdom's floating castle. Mario runs across a sky bridge that extends between the Comet Observatory and the castle. While Mario goes to save Peach, Rosalina transforms the Comet Observatory into a powerful starship. She will keep Bowser's airship armada busy while Mario engages the villainous Bowser at the Galaxy Reactor, an incredible machine that Bowser has constructed to create a new universe for him to rule with Peach at his side.

Psst!

You don't have to visit Bowser's Galaxy Reactor the moment it becomes available. When you choose to chase down Bowser is entirely up to you. You earn a star for completing this mission, though, which goes toward the 120 stars hidden across the galaxies.

Gravity Bounce

The sheer power of Bowser's Galaxy Reactor is tearing the palace apart. As the pieces drift away, Mario must avoid drifting into the void himself. The reactor shoots forth giant beams of artificial gravity, creating moving spotlights that Mario can walk through. The catch is that he must keep up with the gravity spotlights if he wants to walk up the vertical surfaces.

SUPER MARIO GALAXY

At the stage's beginning, Mario must use the artificial gravity to scale the palace walls. If he steps outside the spotlight, he will float away. There are a few Dry Bones patrolling the palace walls, but you can easily avoid them. Should one get too close, use a spin to reduce them to a pile of old bones.

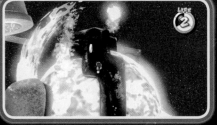

Keep moving along the walls, keeping Mario bathed in the gravity spotlight. There are a few Star Bits near the point where two spotlights intersect. Don't try jumping from one spotlight to another—only cross when the spotlights actually touch. Right before Mario must scale a wall guarded with fire traps, pick up a 1-Up Mushroom.

> **TIP**
>
> *Jumping outside the safety of the spotlight is dangerous, but as long as Mario is firmly within the boundaries of the artificial gravity, he can bounce over small gaps in the ground or leap over the fire traps.*

Mario lands on a safe platform on the orb—this is the only spot on the bubbling surface that's safe to idle. As soon as Mario jumps to the steel cages and the other rock platforms, they start sinking into the lava. The cages sink downward while the stone platforms topple sideways. Pillars of fire belch from the orb's core, and flashes of cosmic energy arc through the orb's low orbit.

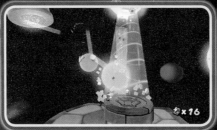

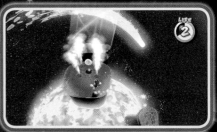

Two Dry Bones are chattering around the palace tower's top. Hit the skeletal Koopas with a spin, and then walk to the pad, emblazoned with Bowser's symbol, atop the tower. Before setting foot on the symbol, use the cursor to sweep up the Star Bits in the space between the tower and the orb. When Mario steps on the symbol, he's pulled off the tower and through space to a small orb of burning energy and bubbling lava.

> **TIP**
>
> *This mission isn't timed, so slow down and collect every Star Bit possible. Bowser pulls out all the stops for his last stand, so you must bank as many extra lives as possible.*

A black platform cycles through the lava, pushing up momentarily only to disappear within seconds. Mario must run along the platform as it rolls out of the lava, collecting the lone coin to replenish any lost health. There is a 1-Up Mushroom on a small steel platform. Reaching it requires some risky jumps. Mario can either long jump off from the black platform or leap from the rock platform just to the right of the 1-Up Mushroom before it's pulled below the bubbling surface. There is another coin just before the gravity beam that will pull Mario off this burning orb, but it's sitting in the middle of four fire geysers. Wait for the geysers to stop spewing, swipe the coin, and then leap into the gravity spotlight.

The beam drops Mario on a small ice sphere. A series of blocks are pulled to the frozen surface as Mario walks ahead, but they do not last very long. The ice blinks and then vanishes after just a few seconds, so Mario must keep moving. If he falls off the blocks and drops down on the icy sphere, he takes damage, just as if he fell into lava.

There are two 1-Up Mushrooms on the ice sphere. The first is on a tall block that snaps into place as Mario closes in on it. Use a backflip to scale the block and grab the 1-Up Mushroom, and don't linger. The ice vanishes quickly. Keep following the blocks to the stone platform rising from the sphere—there

is a gravity beam here that pulls Mario to the next orb. The second 1-Up Mushroom is to the stone's right. Jump out to it and immediately backflip up to the stone before the ice block blinks out of existence.

Unlike the fire or ice orbs, Mario cannot step on the sand sphere. Like the quicksand in the Dusty Dune Galaxy, one misstep results in a sad fate. Mario must cross the rotating stone spindles in the sand to reach the next gravity beam.

Jump over the fire traps on the two sets of rotating platforms and then make a big jump to the tall ledge beneath the gravity beam. As soon as Mario touches the beam, he's yanked off the sphere and pulled to a tricky set of moving blocks.

NOTE

While Mario is flying through the gravity beams, sweep the cursor around the screen to scoop up Star Bits.

Mario is dropped on a small platform of cosmic blocks. As he runs right, more glowing bricks slam into place. However, as new blocks appear, old ones vanish and never return. Keep moving forward so the ground doesn't disappear out from under Mario's feet. When the bricks start creating a vertical wall, use wall jumps to scale the area. Don't worry about jumping out into space—blocks snap into place just in time. There is a 1-Up Mushroom at the shaft's top, but watch out—if Mario misses the 1-Up Mushroom on his first attempt, he must keep moving to the left before the blocks vanish.

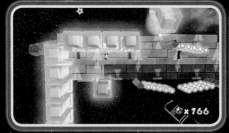
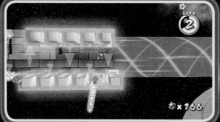

There are two gravity fields at the blocks' top. The pink field pulls Mario up while the blue field pushes him down. Blocks keep appearing along the "bottom" of each field, but spinning fire traps make it tough to remain in one field or the other. The blocks keep disappearing after just a few seconds, so always move to the right and bounce between the fields until reaching the final gravity beam.

Claiming the 1-Up Mushroom beneath the Thwomp in the cylinder is tough. Jump out to the platform just as the Thwomp rises. While Mario grabs the 1-Up, the steel platform rises out of the lava, giving him a safe place to jump to after claiming the prize.

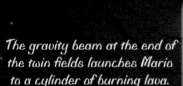

The gravity beam at the end of the twin fields launches Mario to a cylinder of burning lava.

T·I·P

It's tough to shake the multiple Bullet Bills following Mario. Try making a sharp turn right in front of the Bullet Bills so they crash into each other and explode.

Run the Gauntlet

As soon as Mario drops into the cylinder, he must start running a gauntlet of moving platforms and Bullet Bills. The Bullet Bills, fired from large cannons in the cylinder, are determined—and the number of these foes unleashed on the plumber grows. With only small platforms to travel on, dodging incoming Bullet Bills is tricky. Lure the Bullet Bills into the Bowser statues. Some of the statues release a coin when popped with a Bullet Bill.

As Mario moves up the rotating cylinder, Thwomps enter the equation. These heavies come crashing down on the platforms with such force that Mario is squished, no matter how much health he has left. Direct Mario under the shadow of the Thwomps, picking up goodies like coins and a 1-Up Mushroom. Look for the telltale shake of the Thwomp before it pounds the ground.

Toward the cylinder's end, two massive cannons fire Banzai Bills at Mario. These behemoths do not give pursuit like the smaller Bullet Bills—they just block passage for a few seconds. When a Banzai Bill screams down the cylinder, Mario must step aside and take cover. While you hide, Bullet Bills will not be far behind. As soon as the first Banzai Bill passes, hop across the floating platforms and run around the Banzai Bill cannon.

The second Banzai Bill cannon is flanked by at least six Bullet Bill cannons. Mario must avoid the Banzai Bill and cross the last of the lava so he can step in the Launch Star at the cylinder's end and confront Bowser. Jump across the rotating platforms, sidestepping the Banzai Bill. When the Bullet Bills close in, zigzag so they crash into each other and explode.

Shake the Wii Remote as soon as Mario reaches the Launch Star—Bowser must be stopped!

BOWSER'S LAST STAND

Mario escapes the lava-filled cylinder and touches down on a long staircase that extends into the heavens. Bowser taunts Mario from the top of the stairs, revealing that Bowser Jr. has Princess Peach aboard his airship. Bowser Jr. keeps Princess Peach just out of reach, teasing Mario up the stairs into a confrontation with his father, the great Bowser.

Mario must climb the stairs to reach Bowser. Halfway up the stairs, Bowser Jr. volleys several fireballs at Mario, splintering the steps beneath his feet. There is a 1-Up Mushroom and a Life Mushroom on the steps. Mario must grab them before reaching Bowser.

At the top of the stairs, Bowser reveals his plans to Mario. His Galaxy Reactor will cause this universe to collapse upon itself, giving birth to a new cosmos that Bowser will control. His reign will last 10,000 years with Princess Peach at his side. Mario cannot allow Bowser to wreak such destruction on the universe, so he challenges the brute to a final showdown. Bowser is more than happy to oblige. Twisting gravity for his own use, he pulls Mario to a series of small planetoids that orbit the Galaxy Reactor. Mario must reach the Galaxy Reactor, but he has to get through Bowser first.

TIP

If Bowser strikes Mario, he loses one health wedge. There are coins frozen in ice that replenish health. Once you deplete those, though, Mario must trick Bowser into smashing the prickly flowers (wait for Bowser to start rolling at Mario, then lead him through the plants). Each squished flower releases a coin.

When Bowser crashes down on the first planetoid, he immediately causes trouble for Mario. The tyrant stomps the surface repeatedly, sending shock waves around the planetoid. Mario must jump over each shock wave while avoiding the prickly flowers on the surface.

After knocking Bowser out of the boulder, the giant Koopa spins wildly around the planetoid. He's vulnerable to another spin attack, so watch his trajectory and strike him as he rattles by. Mario must smack Bowser twice to knock him off this first planetoid, inching closer to the reactor.

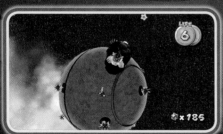

After the third shock wave, Bowser attracts cosmic matter, turning himself into a giant boulder and rolling after Mario. Mario must get close enough to strike Bowser with a spin attack, but the Koopa King is fast. Mario must intercept the boulder and spin into Bowser's exposed face just as he rolls up to him. The attack shatters the boulder, sending Bowser flying across the planetoid.

Second Planetoid

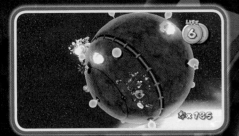

Mario chases Bowser to the second planetoid. As soon as Bowser pulls himself to his feet, he starts breathing fireballs that encircle the sphere. These fireballs take a while to burn out—some go around the planetoid more than once, so keep a close watch on where the fireballs are traveling when they disappear over the horizon.

Bowser is breathing fire, so Mario keeps his distance. The rubbery plants on this planetoid's surface are Bowser's undoing. If Mario can get close enough to bop one of the plants into Bowser, the brute loses his balance and skitters across the surface, completely open to attack.

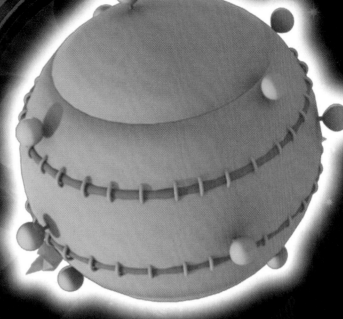

To defeat Bowser on this planetoid, Mario must hit him with the rubbery plants. Stand on the opposite side of the bulb and spin to smack the plant into Bowser, either when he's breathing fire or rolling around inside his shell. It takes just one hit to flip Bowser on his back. Just as before, this is when Bowser is vulnerable, so chase him down and spin attack him twice to knock him off this sphere and onto the reactor.

After searing the surface with fire, Bowser curls into his spiky shell and rolls around the planetoid. Mario cannot touch Bowser in his shell; he must keep his distance, lest Bowser knock him down. After rolling around the planetoid's circumference a few times, Bowser explodes from his shell and starts breathing fire again.

TIP

Low on health? There are coins inside the ice crystals, the prickly plants, and the lamp posts (while Bowser is fleeing, shoot the lamp to find a coin and restore some health).

SUPER MARIO GALAXY

★★ Reactor ★★

NOTE
There are only a handful of coins on the reactor, encased in ice. Bowser tends to shatter the ice while in his shell; when he does this, Mario has only a few seconds to claim the coin before it vanishes.

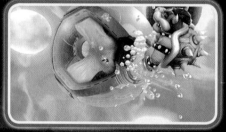

After striking Bowser twice on the second planetoid, the pair takes their fight to the Galaxy Reactor. This battle goes down much like previous showdowns on other reactors—Mario must trick Bowser into slamming down on the glass that contains the quantum reactor inside

the sphere. However, Bowser isn't going to fall for it so easily this time. The Koopa King uses different attacks between his jumps, such as shock waves and shell assaults.

Bowser unleashes a series of shock waves by stomping on the reactor's exterior. Mario must jump over the shock waves as they ripple around the reactor. After the third shock wave, Bowser rolls into a ball, using his impenetrable shell as a weapon. Mario must avoid the spikes—there are no rubbery bulbs to use against Bowser on the reactor.

When Bowser finally jumps around the reactor, Mario must lead the beast to one of the bluish glass sheets using Bowser's shadow as a guide. Stand on the glass as Bowser vaults into the air. When the shadow darkens the glass, immediately move. Bowser slams down on the reactor, shattering the glass and burning himself on the pure energy gurgling inside the reactor.

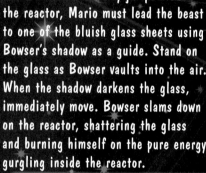

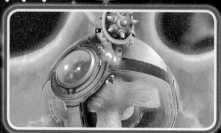

Just as before, Bowser runs around the reactor with his tail on fire. He knows he's in trouble, so he purposefully flees

prima games.com

om Mario. If Bowser spots Mario in his
...th, he turns and runs in the opposite
...rection. Run after Bowser and hit him
...hile he is changing directions.

Finally, Bowser stops to take a breath.
...hile Bowser is stopped, Mario has
...ly two seconds to hit Bowser's tail
...th a spin attack. If he doesn't make
...in time, Bowser recovers and starts
...leashing shock waves again. When
...ario strikes Bowser's singed tail, the
...llain spins around the reactor on his
...ck. Mario must strike Bowser in this
...eakened state to inflict damage.

After Mario hits Bowser, the Koopa
...ing scrambles to his feet and preps
...nother series of attacks. He starts
...ith shock waves, but instead of only
...tomping out three waves, Bowser sends
...ve across the reactor. Just as he rips
...ut the fifth wave, Bowser collapses into
...is shell and starts rolling around the
...eactor in hopes of perforating Mario
...ith his spikes.

**Use the reactor's
transparent shell to
keep an eye on Bowser
when he's either rolling around
inside his shell or bouncing
across the surface after Mario
strikes his tail.**

Mario must follow
the same pattern as
before to finish off
Bowser. After tricking
him into smashing a
glass plug and burning
his tail, Mario must
catch up with the giant as he stops to nurse his wound. When
Mario hits Bowser's tail for a second time, Bowser flips on his
back and skates around the reactor. Bowser is now vulnerable to
a spin attack, but Mario must hit him twice. After the first hit,
Bowser ricochets away. Mario must intercept the shell one more
time and hit him with a devastating spin attack to finally stop
Bowser's universe-rending scheme.

*Mario's final hit sends
Bowser into the sky.
Mario leaps after the
scoundrel and delivers
a galaxy-rattling shot
to the bully's jaw. The
blow is so strong that
Bowser is jettisoned
into the cosmos, leaving behind a Grand Star.*

*When Mario captures
the Grand Star, the
reactor starts to go
critical. Mario must
escape the reactor
before it explodes.*

*Using the Grand Star's power, Mario rockets to Princess
Peach. He takes her hand and flies through the heavens,
pulling her away from the reactor.*

SUPER

Bowser is left behind as Mario and Peach escape. He casts a pathetic shadow against the pulsing materials of his failed reactor. He slowly sinks into the lava, cursing Mario as the reactor finally explodes.

Mario and Peach manage to escape Bowser's immediate fate, but the reactor's force is too strong. Fortunately, Rosalina has the power to shield them from the blast that threatens the very fabric of the universe. In Rosalina's calming presence, Mario learns that the universe holds many mysteries about the great cycle of life: birth, death, and rebirth. Change is the only constant in the cosmos. Bowser tried to bend this force to his will, and in the end, he paid the price.

Rosalina sends Mario into a bright light, and the universe displays its awesome power. When Mario awakens, he is lying in a grassy field in the Mushroom Kingdom. A butterfly flits around his face. He opens his eyes to see Princess Peach and all the Toads in the kingdom. The castle is back in its original place. Even Bowser is there, shaken by his narrow escape from a horrible fate. Mario smiles at his friends and casts his eyes to the heavens, welcoming new life into existence. Somewhere, far from the Mushroom Kingdom, a young galaxy with its own stories yet to be told is shining brightly.

And maybe, one day, Mario will get to see it.

Congratulations! You have defeated Bowser and saved Princess Peach. Or have you? You have not yet earned all 120 stars, so the next time you start the game, Mario is back on the Comet Observatory in Rosalina's presence. The floor beneath the star map now shows how many Power Stars are left in the galaxies. Mario can now resume his planet-hopping in search of the remaining Power Stars. However, defeating Bowser's Galaxy Reactor unleashes a new force in the universe—the purple comet. How does this new comet affect the different galaxies? Is it the key to discovering the hidden Power Stars still out among the skies? Turn the page to find out...

HIDDEN GALAXIES

TRIAL GALAXIES

After Mario locates the three special green Power Stars, the green Launch Star on the Comet Observatory is ready for use. This special Launch Star is pointed at a planetoid just outside the Comet Observatory's orbit.

Three green Luma on the planetoid wait for Mario's arrival. Each one directs him to one of the three Trial galaxies, a collection of courses designed to test Mario's hero skills. He earns a Power Star for completing each Trial Galaxy. Mario needs these three Power Stars to finish his collection of Power and Grand Stars. A very special reward awaits for collecting all 120 stars and restoring peace and order to the universe.

BUBBLE BLAST GALAXY

The two-part obstacle course in the Bubble Blast Galaxy tests Mario's piloting skills. He must jump inside a series of six bubbles and float through a maze of buzzing walls, Bullet Bills, and sliding mines.

THE ELECTRIC LABYRINTH

The Electric Labyrinth is divided into two parts. The first half of the course requires Mario to seek out five yellow Star Chips that assemble into a Launch Star, which bounces him to a high-speed pursuit through a perilous maze. With Bullet Bills on Mario's tail, he must reach the Power Star as quickly as possible to escape the galaxy.

First Half

Star Chip 1

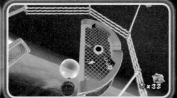

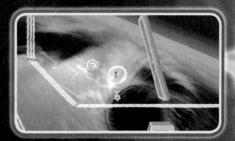

Mario starts on a star-shaped platform containing five warp pipes. Each warp pipe leads to a small maze that ends with Mario finding one of five Star Chips. Start by walking through the top warp pipe to appear on a metal platform. The nearby bubble machine has transportation for Mario. Just step into the bubble.

Carefully blow Mario across the course to the right, staying away from the electric walls. Fly through the giant coin to create a trail of coins that leads right to the Star Chip.

SUPER MARIO GALAXY

PRIMA Official Game Guide

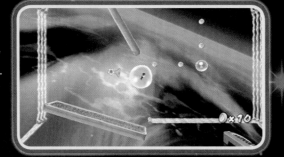

Follow the coins while floating around the rotating platforms. The Star Chip is floating in a small bubble too.

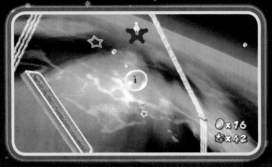

After picking up the Star Chip, float farther north to the Sling Star, which leads Mario back to the star-shaped platform.

Star Chip 3

Slip through the third warp pipe to zoom to the maze's next phase.

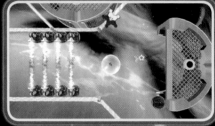

After jumping into the bubble, inch Mario toward the fire cannons that create an intense wall of flame.

Star Chip 2

Drop into this warp pipe to start the search for the next Star Chip.

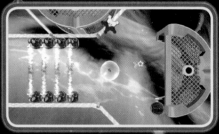

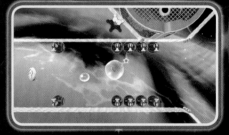

Jump into the bubble and float north. Avoid the sliding electrical fence and aim for the 1-Up Mushroom.

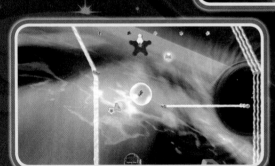

When the cannons fall silent for a few seconds, blow Mario to the Star Chip. Push through the second set of fire cannons to pick up a giant coin.

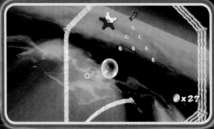

The Star Chip is in the center of two sets of rotating fences. Carefully inch toward the Star Chip, waiting for the path to clear before grabbing it. Float around to the giant coin to create a field of coins near the Sling Star.

The giant coin creates a trail of coins that runs back through the gauntlet of fire cannons and ends at the Sling Star.

Star Chip 4

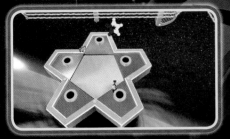

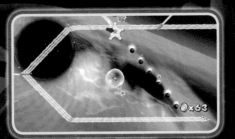

Float around the bouncing projectiles en route to the Sling Star.

Almost done! Jump into this warp pipe to head to the next Star Chip's location.

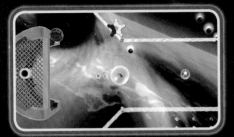

Star Chip 5

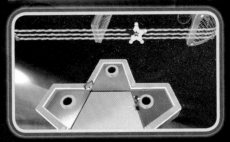

The fifth Star Chip is just beyond this warp pipe.

Hey, the Star Chip is right at the start of this leg of the labyrinth. Getting to the Sling Star is the hard part—there's a field of fast-moving projectiles bouncing around the maze.

TIP

Look for Star Bits all along the electric fences' exterior. Park Mario in a safe spot, then run the cursor over the Star Bits.

Jump right into the bubble and breeze over to the giant coin to create the trail of coins that leads to the Star Chip.

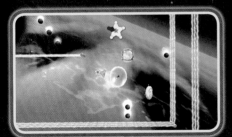

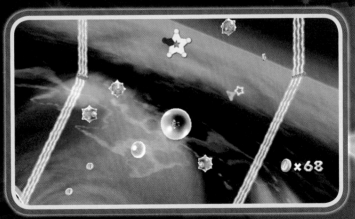

Want more cons? Float through the projectiles to pick up this giant coin. Then, follow the trail of coins to the Sling Star.

Watch for floating mines while blowing Mario's bubble into the Star Chip.

SUPER MARIO GALAXY

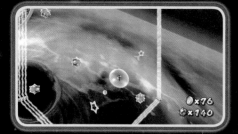

The Sling Star that leads back to the star-shaped platform is farther to the south, beyond another collection of mines.

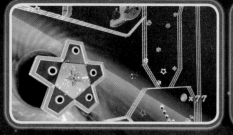

A series of rotating green platforms try to push Mario into the electrified walls. Push through the walls as quickly as possible, as more Bullet Bills are on Mario's tail.

After collecting all five Star Chips, a large Launch Star appears in the star-shaped platform's center. This launches Mario to the maze's back half. If he falls in the maze's second half, he starts at the beginning of the second half.

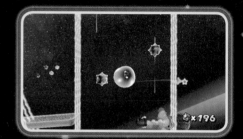

Second Half

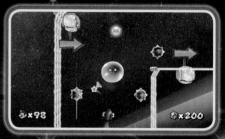

When Mario lands on the Electric Labyrinth's back half, he must hop into the waiting bubble and float south. At the southern stretch's bottom, Mario encounters the first of many Bullet Bill cannons. Bullet Bills pursue him through the majority of the maze, giving the chase a sense of urgency. Flee from the first Bullet Bill and lead it into a caged 1-Up Mushroom.

Mines appear more frequently as the path through the maze curves back to the north. Most of the mines slide along predestined paths marked with thin purple lines. Bullet Bills still give chase, so blast through the maze quickly.

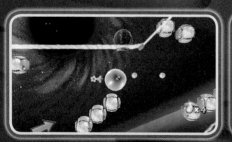

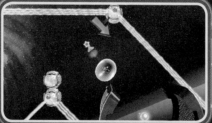

There are several inflatable bulbs in the maze that will bounce Mario into fences and other hazards. Carefully steer around them, especially when Bullet Bills are present. Mario soon arrives at a rotating red cage. Slip into the cage, grab the 1-Up Mushroom, and then keep moving.

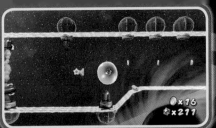

As Mario zooms toward the homestretch, the maze narrows. He floats between a gauntlet of Bullet Bill cannons. There is no slowing down after this point. Quickly push to the right, keeping away from the fences as they close in. Watch out for a bumper in front of the Power Star. Breeze around it, escaping the last of the Bullet Bills as Mario picks up the Power Star.

LOOPDESWOOP GALAXY

The penguins love their ray-surfing fun and have constructed an even more elaborate course for testing their skills. Remembering how Mario wowed them on his run through the Loopdeloop Galaxy, the penguins invite him to shred the new Loopdeswoop course.

The Galaxy's Greatest Wave

Finish

Start

LEGEND
🍄 1-Up Mushroom

SUPER

The course begins similarly to the Loopdeloop Galaxy, with Mario surfing his manta ray up a wide swath of water. As before, watch for the green caps of 1-Up Mushrooms on the course, as well as arrow signs signaling an especially sharp turn ahead.

What goes up must eventually come down. The course keeps pressing farther skyward, but just as Mario flies through a series of yellow loops, the course suddenly drops right out from beneath his manta ray. As Mario sails down, steer his ray so it doesn't veer off course and fall out of the galaxy. There are coins and a 1-Up Mushroom in the air, so steer into them as the manta ray glides back to the track.

Another big drop follows the loop. There is a 1-Up Mushroom on the way down, but the turn at the bottom is so sharp Mario should prep for that rather than aim for the power-up. The ray bounces big-time after hitting the bottom. Twist the Wii Remote to the right just before the ray touches down to bounce into the turn rather than right off the track.

The finish line is just one more sharp turn away. When Mario surfs through the finish line, the penguins award him a Power Star for his brilliant performance. Before grabbing the Power Star and ending the mission, jump over to the adoring penguins to the right of the winner's box. The Sling Star near there sends Mario soaring around the track, allowing him to pick up all Star Bits he passed while concentrating on the race.

The track soon narrows after the first big drop. Stay close to the center, as the turns don't allow much room for error.

CAUTION

When Mario reaches the blue ring, the course turns devilish. No longer do arrows indicate sharp turns and the track gets even narrower.

A giant loop sends Mario soaring through the sky. The track is narrowest at the loop's top, so keep that manta ray in the track's middle.

ROLLING GIZMO GALAXY

As soon as Mario reaches the Rolling Gizmo Galaxy, he's gifted with the Power Star—but too bad it's trapped inside a sphere. Mario must roll the sphere through a toy-filled obstacle course, at the end of which is a machine waiting to free the prize.

Gizmos, Gears, and Gadgets

When Mario first arrives at the course, little Goombas threaten to make things difficult. Roll the sphere away from the safety of the blue starting platform and gingerly splatter the Goombas without accidentally bouncing off the narrow bridge. The bridge leads to a red platform containing several stone blocks. Jump into the blocks—the sphere's toughness shatters them.

Roll out to a revolving bridge. It locks in place for just a couple seconds, giving Mario a chance to steer onto a few cogs and grab a 1-Up Mushroom.

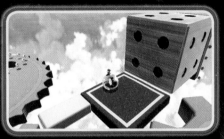

A huge silver dice slides along the bridge after the last cog. Wait for it to slide back into place, then roll ahead of it so it doesn't push Mario off.

There's a wall on the blocks' other side. Pull back and then push forward, jumping into the wall. The wall falls down, creating a bridge and a checked blue platform with more stones. Shatter the stones and drop into the tiny hole to bounce up to the green circle. Roll the sphere around the circle's edge, collecting coins before dropping through the empty space in the center.

Mario rolls along a section of track before reaching a large orange platform. Several Goombas crawl about the platform—smash them to earn coins. Coins decorate the red-lined hole in the orange platform. Carefully inch across the line that stretches across the hole to pick up the treasure.

Mario rolls out onto a large orange coin-covered cog. The treasure would be easy pickings if not for the four Bob-ombs milling about. Avoid the bumbling Bob-ombs. The force of an explosion will bounce him right off the course. The biggest threat isn't a Bob-omb hitting the sphere, but two or more Bob-ombs running into each other and causing a chain reaction. When Mario leaves the cog, he rolls to some machinery that flings the sphere through the skies over the course.

There are two giant coins on the next orange cog. Each creates a ring of coins on the cog. Pick them up—hopefully Mario now has enough coins to earn an extra life.

After collecting the 100 purple coins from the galaxy's special course, Mario earns the final Power Star for that galaxy, and the tiny crown appears next to its name.

While the requirement of finding 100 purple coins is always the same, the conditions for doing so change depending on the galaxy. Some missions are as straightforward as touring the galaxy and looking behind every rock and under every tree for the 100 coins. Some missions require collecting the 100 purple coins under a specific time limit. Some missions let Mario run through the course only once. If he misses a purple coin, he must restart and try again.

After Mario finds all 15 of the Power Stars associated with the purple coins and his total count reaches 120, he can return to the universe's center to challenge Bowser one last time for a very, very special surprise.

Just one more narrow bridge separates Mario from the course's end. Two silver dice slide around the bridge. Inch forward and jump to grab the 1-Up Mushroom over the bridge, then roll past the dice and up to the final blue platform. Roll the sphere into the ring to crack it open and retrieve the Power Star within.

PURPLE COINS

Even after completing the Trial Galaxies and rescuing every Power Star from the Dome missions, Mario still has only 105 stars. Where are those last 15 Power Stars? They appear under the shadow of the purple comet, a phenomenon that colors the sky only after Mario defeats Bowser at the center of the universe.

Check the star map on the Comet Observatory to see where the purple comet was last seen. When a purple comet appears over a galaxy, travel to that Dome and look over the map to see it. Visit that galaxy and collect 100 purple coins while the comet flies

GOOD EGG GALAXY
Purple Coin Omelet

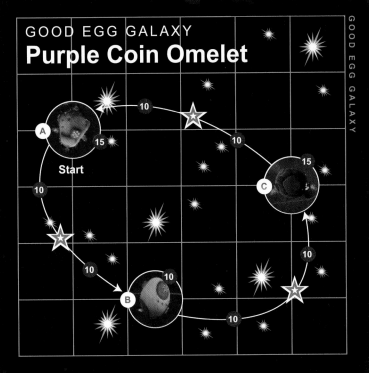

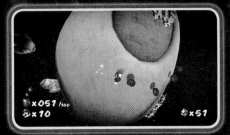

The 100 purple coins in the Good Egg Galaxy are spread across the galaxy's many planetoids, and they run the length of the Launch Star highways between them. To collect all 100 coins, Mario must travel all roads.

The egg-shaped planetoid is the third stop on Mario's final tour of the Good Egg Galaxy. After he uses the Launch Star there, he has 70 purple coins. Find the remaining 30 purple coins along the extra routes in the skies. To find these extra routes, use the Launch Stars that intersect the previously taken routes.

When Mario lands in the Good Egg Galaxy, he must scour each planetoid for its bounty of purple coins. There are no hidden coins here—just diligently run around the galaxy to earn the Power Star. After cleaning out each planetoid, hit the skies and pick up the dozens of purple coins hanging in deep space.

On the way back to the red planetoid, use the Launch Star to rocket to a new path.

From the red planetoid, bounce across the galaxy to the egg-shaped planetoid to collect additional purple coins. Mario automatically picks up all the purple coins along the Launch Star paths—the coins are placed right along the flight path.

x070 /100

The new route sends Mario soaring through 20 purple coins.

There are 100 purple coins hidden on Honeyhive Galaxy's main planet. Mario never has to leave the planet to complete the collection. Most of the purple coins are out in the open, but a few are slightly out of the way.

x000 /100   x275

After vaulting off the Good Egg Galaxy, use the Launch Star at the midpoint to find the remaining 10 purple coins.

x096 /100

x005 /100   x275

★★ Honeyhive ★★ Galaxy ★★

x2

x4

x14

x8

When Mario lands on the Honeyhive kingdom, he immediately sees a huge number of purple coins. Some are in the river next to him; others are on the slope headed down to the riverbank. However, before exploring too far away from the starting point, turn around and look at the ledge where Mario normally picks up a 1-Up Mushroom. There is a purple coin back there.

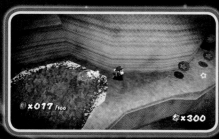

x017 /100   x300

Check the alcove behind the ledge where the Piranha Plants guarded the warp pipe to the secret chamber. Wall jump up the alcove to pad Mario's pockets.

LEGEND

🪙 **Purple Coin**

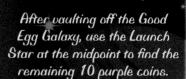

Look behind the waterfall, just under the main cavern that originally led to the Queen Bee.

Check the planet's top. Wall jump to fetch the coins on the twin walls.

Check the planet's back side to find purple coins on the final leg of his race with Cosmic Mario.

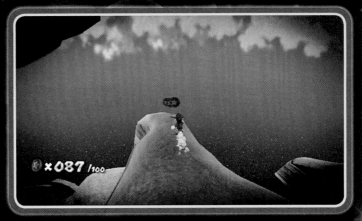

These three coins are easy to miss—they're on the edge of the rounded wall that overlooks the giant tree. Be careful not to slip!

Backflip onto the lone block hovering above the ledge overlooking the mission's starting point. A purple coin hangs just above it.

When Mario backflips on top of the rounded wall behind the twin walls, the camera pulls back to reveal purple coins on a series of ledges leading down the planet's back side.

Carefully walk the wooden fence that runs the length of the planet's left side.

Finally, check the upper ledge behind the waterfall. Grab the purple coins here and drop down at the end to finish off the 100.

SPACE JUNK GALAXY
Purple Coin Spacewalk

Some of the purple coins are at dead ends, so Mario must backtrack and try a different route to reach the rest of the coins.

Make sure to jump straight across the gaps in the paths. If Mario missteps, he falls straight into the void and must restart the mission.

Mario returns to the Space Junk Galaxy to collect 100 purple coins from the debris field where he previously rescued the five Silver Stars. He has only two minutes to walk across the rapidly constructed-deconstructed paths to collect all 100 purple coins.

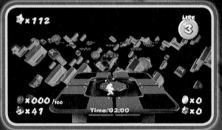

Look over the debris field to spot 10 groups of 10 purple coins. It's not difficult to collect all 100 purple coins within the time limit, but watch Mario's step. The debris field's general layout is different than before.

Mario must pick up the Power Star before time is up. If time runs out, he must restart the mission—even if he's just three feet from the Power Star.

To start things off, run straight ahead to the first circle of 10 purple coins. The path snaps into place as Mario runs. When he reaches the coins, a platform pops up underneath them. The platform remains as long as Mario stands on it but disappears when he jumps away.

Follow the paths between the circles of purple coins.

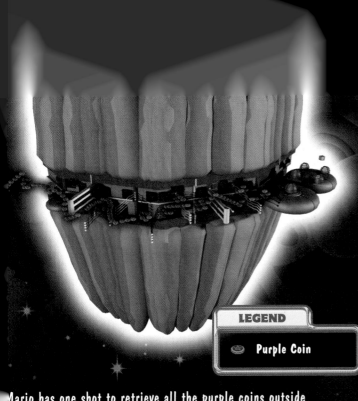

What a treat! There's a 1-Up Mushroom sitting in the middle of these six purple coins.

Mario has one shot to retrieve all the purple coins outside the Battlerock Galaxy. He must ride a disc across the battle platform's exterior, dodging cannonballs while grabbing every last purple coin. This is a one-way trip, after all.

As the disc floats close to the battle platform, Mario can see the general layout of the field of purple coins. He must jump through the air to grab coins placed higher than the disc's flight path as well as dip to the disc's underside to collect those floating underneath laser fences.

The trail of coins arcs over two electrical fences. Either use a backflip or a side-jump to collect these coins.

When passing under the first wall, stand on the disc's side to pick up an errant purple coin.

If Mario collects all 100 purple coins, the robot at the planet's end awards him the Power Star. If he misses even one, he must restart from the beginning.

The purple coins are not all positioned in a straight line. Mario must veer on and off the path to collect the bounty.

Beach Bowl Galaxy

Walk up the palm trees' bowed trunks to collect purple coins hidden among the lush fronds.

Purple coins are hidden around the waterfall's top. Don't forget to look in the actual water.

There's a Spring Mushroom on the waterfall's edge. Use this power-up to vault to the island's top and collect more purple coins.

LEGEND

Purple Coin

It's a fine day in the Beach Bowl Galaxy to do a little beachcombing for 100 purple coins. Mario has no time limit for collecting the purple coins on this ocean paradise—and that's a good thing, because some of the coins are cleverly hidden!

From the starting point, Mario can see about half the purple coins in the Beach Bowl Galaxy. The find the others, search the fronds of the palm trees, slip under the waves, and bounce to the island's top.

Pick up the easy ones first. Traipse across the little islands and, while picking up purple coins, talk to the penguins. They offer clues about where to find the not-so-obvious coins. For example, one penguin lets slip that there are only five purple coins in the sea.

Swing around the vine hanging near the starting point to collect two rings of purple coins.

Boing! The Spring Suit lets Mario easily check the trees.

There are several purple coins on the upper ledge behind the waterfall on the island's back side.

...ed the penguin's advice—there are ...five purple coins in the sea. Grab a ...and tour the seabed to pick them ...nce they're in Mario's pocket, he ...y off for good.

Ghostly Galaxy

Purple Coins in the Bone Pen

...are over 100 purple coins in the Ghostly Galaxy—picking ...0 of them to earn the Power Star will be easy, right? ...g. Mario has only 60 seconds to bounce around the field of ...Stars to gather 100 purple coins and to swing over to the ...Star.

...e minute to grab ...purple coins? ...s Mario going to ...ge that, even in ...rowded field of ...lies? Inertia is ...ey—as is thinking ...oves ahead. Mario cannot stay still in this galaxy for even a ...d; he must always be dragging himself through a line of purple ...to secure the needed 100 before time runs out.

Fortunately, many of the coins are positioned in straight lines between the Pull Stars, so immediately drag Mario through a few of these lines to start his collection.

Some of the purple coin lines curve around the hunks of space meat. To gather them, grab the Pull Star on the other side of the beefy bone and let Mario bounce away from the rib to pick up the arc of coins.

Watch out for mines. If Mario hits one, he loses precious time, making it very difficult to finish the mission.

Only seconds remain—get to that Power Star!

The Power Star appears in the center of the Pull Star field. As Mario closes in on 100 purple coins, set him up for a straight shot to the area's middle.

Gusty Garden Galaxy

LEGEND

🪙 **Purple Coin**

The purple coins of the Gusty Garden Galaxy are sprinkled across the cube where Mario had to chase down the bunny in return for the Power Star. There's no bunny in sight this time—just a hoard of purple coins. There are over 100 purple coins on the cube, but a time limit of 2:30 means Mario has some speedy collecting to do.

Over a dozen purple coins jingle atop the tricky trellises.

Each of the cube's six sides is covered with purple coins. Only a few Goombas wander the landscape. The topiaries and bushes that segment the purple coins serve as obstacles between Mario and the treasure. Mario must scale tall shrubs, balance across narrow trellises, and rustle through thick grass to complete his 100-coin collection.

When Mario finally pockets 100 purple coins, the Power Star appears back at υ on the side of the cube where he started.

Jump atop the garden maze to collect the purple coins from this side of the cube.

Freezeflame Galaxy

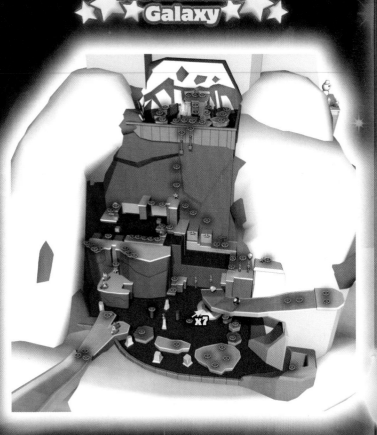

Several purple coins are hidden in the tall grasses. Always check on top of the thick shrubbery at each corner of the cube.

LEGEND

🪙 Purple Coin

Scale the bushes on this side of the cube to pick up another 10 purple coins.

→ x3

x026 /100   ⚡x10

Skate to the Ice Flower's left and wall jump up the alcove to find a side area with a couple purple coins.

x034 /100   ⚡x16

Use the Ice Flower to scale the water fountains and reach the upper frozen lake.

x062 /100

x075 /100

Freezy Peak, home of the infamous Baron Brr, hosts precisely 100 purple coins. To pocket all of them and earn the galaxy's final Power Star, Mario must check every-where, from the mountain's base to the highest points on its sharp crags.

Mario begins his trek up Freezy Peak at the edge of the freezing lake. Before starting across the frozen platforms, turn around and grab three coins from the base of the ramp that Mario uses to slide onto the planet. There are several purple coins on the lake, so fetch that Ice Flower.

x004 /100   ⚡x1

Ice Mario can skate around the lake and really start the hunt. Before starting the mountain ascent, check the four spikes surrounding the giant coin for a handful of purple coins.

x013 /100   ⚡x4

Baron Brr's throne area hosts many purple coins. Use the Ice Flowers to skate around the water and pick up the coins on the platforms; then wall jump up the alcove to fetch the purple coins on the plateau where Mario brawled with the coldhearted baron. Check the little caves underneath the plateau for purple coins behind the crystals.

x020 /100   ⚡x4

Use the Sling Star to the Ice Flower's right to bounce up to the ramp containing the Life Mushroom and 1-Up Mushroom. There are several purple coins up here.

There's even a purple coin on the very top of Freezy Peak!

Triple jump up the water fountains to use the small Sling Star and access Freezy Peak's top half. Melt the snowmen with fireballs to clear the paths.

Psst!

I mentioned that the hidden purple coin in the Beach Bowl Galaxy caused me some consternation. That was nothing compared to the two hidden purple coins on Freezy Peak. To spot the coins, stand on the summit and face the same direction the Toad is looking. Now, turn to the left and look down. It took me forever to find those—and even longer to reach them. The secret? Line up with the coins, then long-jump off the summit's edge. Mario will land right on top of the first purple coin. The next one is just a quick jump down. A Sling Star takes you back to the mountain's base to claim the Power Star.

Keep pushing up the peak, negotiating the narrow ledges. Without the ice bats dive-bombing Mario, this is a bit easier.

Dusty Dune Galaxy

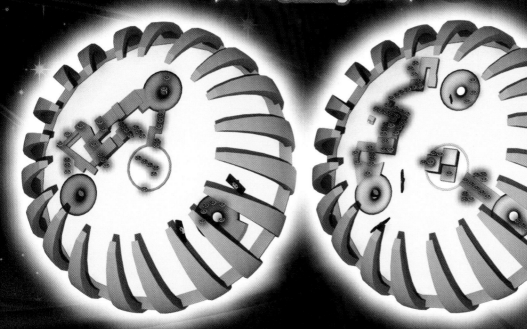

The purple coins of the Dusty Dune Galaxy are sprinkled across the giant sand disc with zigzagging stone pathways. There are still Dry Bones and plenty of tornados whirling around the quicksand-covered disc.

LEGEND

⬤ Purple Coin

SUPER MARIO GALAXY

When Mario lands on the sand disc, he can collect only a few purple coins right away—but he can clearly see the last few he must gather to release the Power Star. On the disc's bottom, use the switch on the tower's top to raise a platform on the disc's top. But between here and there are a dozen tornados and a lot of perilous quicksand.

The two tornados on the path to the tower are unlike the others. Bones and debris swirl around these tornados, so Mario must hitch a ride by jumping into the tornado's center. If he tries to walk into these tornados, the debris will knock him into the quicksand. There are two arcs of three purple coins on each side of these tornados, so Mario must take the risk to grab the treasure.

Pass through the first hole in the disc to access the other side. There are lots of purple coins over here. Use the tornados to snag the purple coins over the quicksand between the walkways.

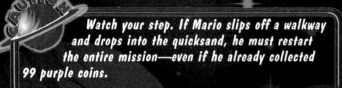

There are three purple coins on top of the Thwomp. Use a tornado to fly into the air just as the Thwomp smashes to the ground, then flutter over to grab the edge of its head.

Grab purple coins whenever Mario sees them. Even though he must return here after hitting the switches that move the tower from the disc's other side to this side, it's easier just to collect the coins when spotted.

Look for shadows on the quicksand to spot purple coins in the air. Then, use the nearest tornado to catch a lift.

Climb the tower and jump into the purple coins over the blue switch. After collecting the purple coins, ground pound the switch to drop the tower to the disc's other side. Now, run for the closest hole, because the tower only remains on the disc's other side for about 15 seconds. When the ticking speeds up, the tower is about to pop back to the disc's tan side.

GOLD LEAF GALAXY
Purple Coins in Gold Leaf

GOLD LEAF GALAXY

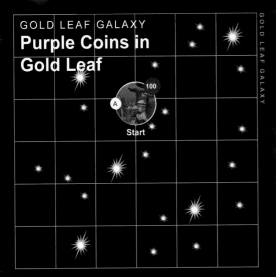

100
A
Start

This bee tells Mario he should have 70 purple coins before heading farther up the tower.

colors are settling over the galaxy—golds, oranges, ...ws...and purple? The Gold Leaf Galaxy is splashed with an ...ely new hue for the sixth and final mission. Mario receives a ... help from the bees in this galaxy. They tell him how many ... coins he should have before moving on to the next area.

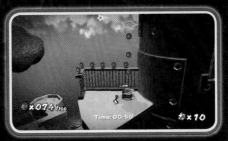

Carefully inch along the railing to pick up these purple coins. If Mario slips, he has quite a walk back up to the tower.

...en Mario lands on the Gold Leaf Galaxy, he spies a trail of ... coins leading up a series of blocks. This trail stretches to the ... of the giant tree that supports the crow's nest where the nasty ... with the bubble cannon harassed the bees earlier in Mario's ...ture. The purple coins in this galaxy are all pretty much out in ...pen—just check in with the bees before moving on to the area's ... section to make sure he has the proper number of purple coins.

Ground pound this stone circle to release the Sproutle that extends to the tower's top.

...er Mario collects ...e purple coins on ...e walkways (don't ...get the spring!), ... should already ... have 50.

There are 10 purple coins atop the tower. If Mario arrives with any less than 90 purple coins, he'd better head back down and find those he missed.

Spring up to the trapeze to start ascending the tower— collect the two purple coins at the height of the trapeze's arc before dismounting.

LEGEND

🪙 Purple Coin

The penguins of Sea Slide Galaxy are eager to share a tip with Mario when he arrives: There are no purple coins in the water. Stick primarily to the skies; the multitude of Bee Mushrooms on the planet will certainly help him take flight and stay aloft.

There is a Bee Mushroom close to the beach where Mario touches down. In his Bee Suit, he can flutter between the puffy clouds (no rain here) and seek out the purple coins that decorate the entire ring. If Mario ever slips into the drink and loses the Bee Suit, just find another Bee Mushroom and continue the search where he left off.

After clearing off the mangrove, buzz across the network of puffy clouds over the filtering station.

Buzz to the mangrove and search every branch. There is at least one purple coin on each branch, and several are on the puffy clouds that surround the giant tree.

Drop to the station to grab a small collection of purple coins before buzzing to the green Toad spaceship in orbit over the ring.

Once the Power Star appears, take no risks buzzing between the clouds. If Mario runs out of flight energy over the void, he must re-collect all 100 purple coins.

Explore the hillside over the twin tunnels that hide the nasty Gringills. Watch for those Piranha Plants. If they snap Mario, he loses his Bee Suit.

Toy Time Galaxy

Float to the water's surface and collect the purple coins at the castle tower's base.

TOY TIME GALAXY
Luigi's Purple Coins

100+

A

Start

Use the puffy clouds to reach the purple coins atop the tower. After collecting all 100 purple coins, the Power Star appears atop the tower's flagpole.

The 8-bit Mario planetoid in the Toy Time Galaxy is replaced with an 8-bit Luigi. His visage is covered with well over 100 purple coins, but this mission is anything but a cakewalk. Mario must collect 100 coins within three minutes, but the lava that Mario simply bounced off of with just a little damage has been replaced with dark matter. One touch and Mario must start all over.

Check for three purple coins atop the red Toad spaceship.

An incredible sea of purple is splashed across the Luigi-shaped planetoid. Collecting the coins requires calculated jumping, hair-trigger reflexes,

and a pinch of luck. To get a good start on the mission, jump as far away from the starting position as possible. The Power Star appears right where Mario is standing when he pockets the hundredth purple coin, so he needs a way back.

Take a counterclockwise route around the planetoid. Start by heading for the lines of purple coins over the dark matter to the right. Run across the yellow platforms to get the coins, but before they spin too far, duck down and long-jump over the dark matter. Mario picks up an entire line of purple coins and starts the mission off with a bang.

Got the 100 purple coins? Head for the starting position. The green platforms Mario jumped over at the mission's beginning are now ready to hold his weight as he comes back to claim the prize.

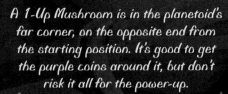

Small collections of five purple coins hang just outside the planet's edge. Jump out and spin to grab the coins while maintaining enough air to fall back to safety.

A 1-Up Mushroom is in the planetoid's far corner, on the opposite end from the starting position. It's good to get the purple coins around it, but don't risk it all for the power-up.

By the time Mario reaches this corner of the planet, he should have over 60 purple coins. It's now time to start heading back around to the starting position.

Long-jump over the dark-matter voids to pick up purple coins. It's always easier to grab purple coins on the green shrinking platforms than the rotating yellow ones, so as Mario gets closer to 100, stick to the green platforms as much as possible.

DEEP DARK GALAXY
Plunder the Purple Coins

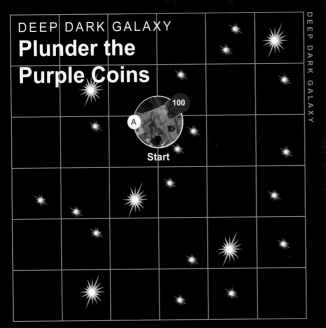

The ghost ship of the Deep Dark Galaxy contains a precious bounty: purple coins. Exactly 100 purple coins are either around, on, or under the ghost ship. There are no enemies causing trouble during this mission, so take it slow and be methodical about collecting every hint of purple Mario can see.

When Mario drops into the drink just outside the ghost ship, he must swim around the wading pool and collect the purple coins within. After clearing the pool (check under the box that Mario hops on to exit the water), move on to the large chamber that houses the ghost ship. Several purple coins are right on the beach, so use the wooden crates to jump high enough to pluck them out of the air, then smash open the wooden crates to pick up some regular coins.

Jump on the ledges opposite the ghost ship. There are several purple coins on each tier of the ledges. Look for shadows on the ground to indicate a purple coin spinning overhead.

After grabbing all the purple coins off the land, jump into the water. Swim around the lake's edge to pick up purple coins, then paddle over to the ship. Swim around the ship, jumping to grab purple coins on each side of the vessel. Be sure to pluck the purple coins out from between the ghost ship's idle cannons.

Dive deep to spot a line of purple coins under the ship. Check the underwater ledges and don't ignore the chains running between the anchors and the ship's hull.

PRIMA Official Game Guide

x064 /100

x080 /100

After emptying the lake and collecting all the coins on the ship's sides, board the vessel. Several purple coins are right on the deck, and more hang over and under the crow's nest. Use the orange pole to reach the crow's nest. A purple coin hangs under a stalactite. To grab the coin, long-jump from the railing of the crow's nest. Mario will swipe the purple coin while he flies through the air.

Dreadnought Galaxy

LEGEND

🟣 Purple Coin

The cannons of the Dreadnought battle platform guard the 100 purple coins. Just like the run through the purple coin mission of Battlerock Galaxy, Mario must follow the moving platforms as they pass in front of the cannons only once. If he misses a coin, he must start all over. And if the platform gets too far ahead of Mario while he collects tough-to-reach purple coins, he must wait for another to come along.

x97
LIFE 3
x003 /100
x70
x0
x6

LIFE 6
x009 /100
x11

When the platform starts rumbling to the right, pick up a Life Mushroom and the first batch of purple coins. The Life Mushroom's extra health is beneficial for surviving cannon attacks, but getting blasted by an exploding shell often makes Mario miss a purple coin while he recovers.

The platforms follow the same track as the "Dreadnought's Colossal Cannons" mission, so Mario should be familiar with the general lay of the land.

Gravity fields play tug-of-war with Mario when he jumps between the "ceiling" and the "floor." Don't miss any purple coins while bouncing between the gravity fields.

When Mario jumps to the first upper platform, he should have 17 purple coins.

The moving platforms slip under stationary blocks and ledges, giving Mario stable ground to leap off of and grab airborne purple coins.

Not all the purple coins are in a straight line. Sometimes, Mario must run in a little circle to grab all the purple coins on a platform.

After safely ducking under the Thwomp, backflip to grab the purple coins over its head.

Mario's platforms smash into mines, stopping them cold. Quickly jump to another moving platform, such as this vertical one, before they pull away.

When the platform pulls away from the cannons, Mario should have 95 purple coins. Four more coins are over the purple robot's head on the dock's right. Bounce off the robot's springy head to grab the four purple coins. Then jump over to the purple robot under the Launch Star.

Jump into the Launch Star to rocket high above the Dreadnought battle platform. The final purple coin is along the arcing path Mario takes through space before landing right next to the Power Star.

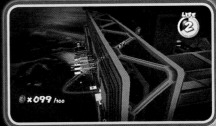

PRIMA Official Game Guide

Melty Molten Galaxy

x5

LEGEND

⬤ Purple Coin

Mario must hotfoot it around the main landmass in the Melty Molten Galaxy to collect the 100 purple coins required to bank the Power Star. Many of the purple coins are positioned dangerously close to the surface of the lava sea, so be ready to jump as soon as he corners his quarry. Hesitation leads to burnt toes.

The main landmass on the Melty Molten Galaxy is still pulsing with primordial energy. Heat geysers explode out of the ground. Lava pillars blast into the air. Avoid these hazards while sweeping purple coins off the mission's first part. After collecting all the purple coins on the landmass, head for the steel bridges that lead to the cliffs.

⬤ x008 /100

⬤ x17

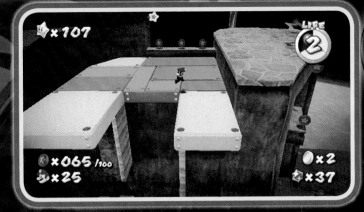

When Mario reaches the cliffs' top, he spots some purple coins over the side that faces the volcano.

There are purple coins both over and under the bridges. To collect those under the bridges, stand on them until they sink into the lava. Just as the purple coin pokes through the grating, run over it, then jump before the lava burns Mario's feet.

Step off the edge to collect the purple coins down the cliffs' right side.

Hop across the tiny platforms in the lava to collect more purple coins at the cliffs' bottom.

Follow the green bridge to the cliffs, but linger long enough to collect the three purple coins just above the lava lake's surface.

There are five purple coins atop the heat geysers in front of the cliff. Wait for the blasts to die down, then scoop up the coins.

When Mario has the 95 purple coins from the landmass, step into the Sling Star pointed straight at the volcano. The Sling Star rockets Mario toward the active cone, but the arc falls just short. Quickly shake the Wii Remote as Mario touches the Sling Star on the volcano's side to bounce right inside. The final five purple coins are at the volcano's bottom. After collecting all 100, use the Sling Star to escape and grab the Power Star.

★★★ 335 ★★★

After completing all the purple-coin missions, you should have 120 stars and a crown next to the name of every galaxy on the star map. You've beaten the game and saved the universe, right? Don't touch the power switch just yet. There's a little surprise that you're going to love.

Return to Rosalina on the Comet Observatory and tell her you want to go fight Bowser at the center of the universe again. Bowser is more than happy to brawl again. Complete the mission just as before, surviving the strange gravity fields and the huge lava tube. After defeating Bowser, the giant falls back into the lava and the credits roll. Watch the credits. (Pay attention, too. Those people worked really hard on this game.) When the credits end, listen closely.

"Did the game just say what I think it said?" I asked aloud when this first happened to me.

Yes, I heard correctly: Super Luigi Galaxy.

That's right. If you beat Bowser again after collecting all 120 stars, you get to play the game as Luigi. And let me tell you, the game is a little tougher as Luigi because the bro with the green duds jumps and runs differently than Mario. Luigi jumps higher and further, and also runs faster,

but has trouble stopping. They each have the same moves, such as the long-jump or backflip, but the difference in their basic jump, running speed, and stopping ability makes completing the game harder.

And what happens when Luigi gets all 120 stars and defeats Bowser?

That's when you turn the power off.

And go outside to look up at the stars.

STAR LIST

GALACTIC CHECKLIST

Mario must collect 120 stars in order to rid the galaxies of Bowser's evil influence and restore peace to Rosalina's travels. Gathering all the Power Stars and Grand Stars takes Mario from one end of the known universe to the other, visiting crazy places like the haunted Ghostly Galaxy or the sun-soaked Dusty Dune Galaxy.

We've shown you exactly how to locate and retrieve all 120 stars—but for quick reference, here's a complete checklist of every star in the cosmos, organized by galaxy. Missing a star in the Dreadnought Galaxy? Check the page number and then flip straight there to read our star-searching strategy. You'll have entire collection in no time!

Gateway Galaxy

🪐 Gateway Galaxy

Location: Grand Star Rescue

Location: Gateway's Purple Coins

Terrace

🪐 Boo's Boneyard Galaxy

Location: Racing the Spooky Speedster

🪐 Good Egg Galaxy

Location: Dino Piranha

PRIMA Official Game Guide

Location: A Snack of Cosmic Proportions

Location: King Kalienfe's Battle Fleet

Location: Purple Coin Omelet

Location: Dino Piranha Speed Run

Location: Luigi on the Roof

Honeyhive Galaxy

Location: Bee Mario Takes Flight

Location: Trouble on the Tower

Location: Big Bad Bugaboom

Location: Honeyhive Cosmic Mario Race

Location: Luigi in the Honeyhive Kingdom

Location: The Honeyhive's Purple Coins

Loopdeloop Galaxy

Location: Surfing 101

Flipswitch Galaxy

Location: Painting the Planet Yellow

Sweet Sweet Galaxy

Location: Rocky Road

Bowser's Jr.'s Robot Reactor

Location: Megaleg's Moon

Fountain

Space Junk Galaxy

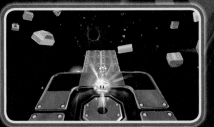

Location: Pull Star Path

Location: Kamella's Airship Attack

Location: Tarantox's Tangled Web

Location: Pull Star Path Speed Run

Location: Yoshi's Unexpected Appearance

Location: Purple Coin Spacewalk

Battlerock Galaxy

Location: Battlerock Barrage

Location: Breaking into the Battlerock

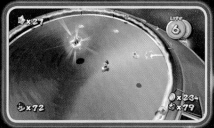

Location: Topmaniac and the Topman Tribe

Hurry-Scurry Galaxy

Location: Shrinking Satellite

Sling Pod Galaxy

Location: A Very Sticky Situation

Bowser's Star Reactor

Location: The Fiery Stronghold

Kitchen

Beach Bowl Galaxy

Location: Sunken Treasure

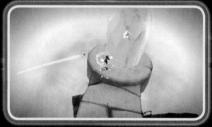

Location: Passing the Swim Test

Location: The Secret Undersea Cavern

Location: Wall Jumping up Waterfalls

Location: Fast Foes on the Cyclone Stone

Location: Beachcombing for Purple Coins

Ghostly Galaxy

Location: Luigi and the Haunted Mansion

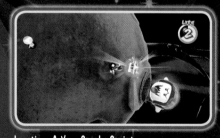

Location: A Very Spooky Sprint

Location: Beware of Bouldergeist

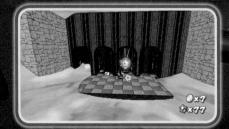

Location: Matter Splatter Mansion

Location: Bouldergeist's Daredevil Run

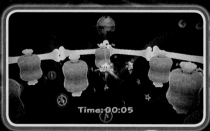

Location: Purple Coins in the Bone Pen

★★★ 340 ★★★

Drip Drop Galaxy

Location: Giant Eel Outbreak

Buoy Base Galaxy

Location: The Floating Fortress

Location: The Secret of Buoy Base

Bubble Breeze Galaxy

Location: Through the Poison Swamp

Bowser Jr.'s Airship Armada

Location: Sinking the Airships

Gusty Garden Galaxy

Location: Bunnies in the Wind

Location: The Dirty Tricks of Major Burrows

Location: Gusty Garden's Gravity Scramble

Location: Major Burrow's Daredevil Run

Freezeflame Galaxy

Location: The Freezy Peak of Baron Brr

Location: The Golden Chomp

Location: Purple Coins on the Puzzle Cube

Location: The Freezy Peak of Baron Brr

Location: Conquering the Summit

Location: Freezeflame's Blistering Core

SUPER MARIO GALAXY

PRIMA Official Game Guide

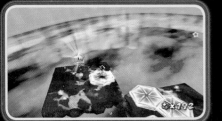
Location: Hot and Cold Collide

Location: Frosty Cosmic Mario Race

Location: Purple Coins on the Summit

Dusty Dune Galaxy

Location: Soaring on the Desert Winds

Location: Blasting through the Sand

Location: Treasure of the Pyramid

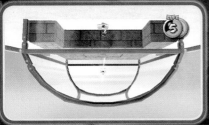
Location: Sunbaked Sand Castle

Location: Bullet Bill on Your Back

Location: Sand Blast Speed Run

Honeyclimb Galaxy

Bigmouth Galaxy

Location: Purple Coins in the Desert

Location: Scaling the Sticky Wall

Location: Bigmouth's Gold Bait

Engine Room

Bowser's Dark Matter Reactor

Gold Leaf Galaxy

Location: Darkness on the Horizon

Location: Star Bunnies on the Hunt

Location: Cataquack to the Skies

Location: When It Rains, It Pours

Location: The Bell on the Big Tree

Location: Cosmic Mario Forest Race

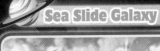
Sea Slide Galaxy

Location: Purple Coins in the Woods

Location: Going After Guppy

Location: Faster Than a Speeding Penguin

Location: The Silver Stars of Sea Slide

Location: Hurry, He's Hungry

Location: Underwater Cosmic Mario Race

Toy Time Galaxy

Location: Purple Coins by the Seaside

Location: Heavy-Metal Mecha Bowser

Location: Mario Meets Mario

Location: Bouncing down Cake Lake

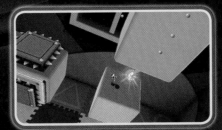
Location: The Flipswitch Chain

Location: Fast Foes of Toy Time

Location: Luigi's Purple Coins

Location: Kingfin's Fearsome Waters

Garden

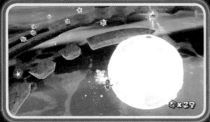

Location: Choosing a Favorite Snack

Location: King Kaliente's Spicy Return

Location: The Underground Ghost Ship

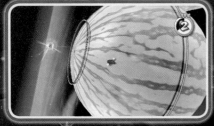

Location: Bubble Blastoff

Location: Guppy and the Underground Lake

Location: Boo in a Box

Location: Ghost Ship Daredevil Run

Location: Plunder the Purple Coins

Location: Infiltrating the Dreadnought

Location: Dreadnought's Colossal Cannons

Location: Revenge of the Topman Tribe

Location: Dreadnought's Garbage Dump

Location: Topman Tribe Speed Run

Location: Battlestation's Purple Coins

Location: The Sinking Lava Spire

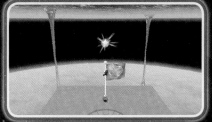

Location: Through the Meteor Storm

Location: Fiery Dino Piranha

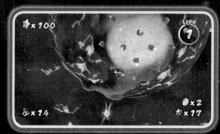

Location: Burning Tide

Location: Lava Spire Daredevil Run

Location: Red-Hot Purple Coins

Matter Splatter Galaxy

Location: Watch Your Step

Trial Galaxies

Snow Cap Galaxy

Loopdeswoop Galaxy

Bubble Blast Galaxy

Location: Star Bunnies in the Snow

Location: The Galaxy's Greatest Wave

Location: The Electric Labyrinth

Last Battle

Rolling Gizmo Galaxy

Location: Gizmos, Gears, and Gadgets

Bowser's Galaxy Reactor

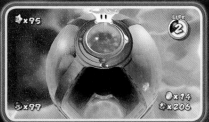

Location: The Fate of the Universe

PRIMA Official Game Guide

SUPER MARIO GALAXY CONCEPT ART

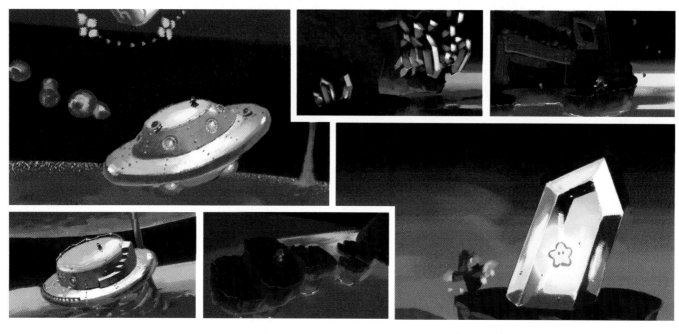

Rosalina

◄ In the early stages, we contemplated the idea that Rosalina was related to Princess Peach, so that is why their features are very similar. Her long bangs represent her outward strength and inner sorrow and loneliness.

Bowser's Ship

➤ I was a huge fan of Super Mario Bros. 3, especially Bowser's Ship. It was re-created in this game mainly due to my strong desire to see Bowser's Ship again!

Toad Brigade and Starshroom

▲ The whole idea of Toads exploring the galaxies in a mushroom-shaped spaceship was born from a random conversation and a simple scribble. Of course, Toads were already well known, but the idea of them being space travelers quickly gained popularity among the staff and ultimately was used in the game.

347

Buoy Base

Underwater Volcano

▲ This was an early-stage drawing of the Buoy Base. We simply drew a disc-shaped ocean floating in the sky. There is a fort in the center, displaying its dangerous element.

▲ We first envisioned it to be very dark and gloomy and located at the bottom of the deep sea, but we eventually changed the water to be shallow and expansive.

pdimagames.com

◀ *Originally, we were going to borrow the image of the friendly dolphin character from Super Mario World to maintain the Mario theme, but when Guppy's character image changed from "nice" to "wild," we decided to give him a scary face.*

SUPER MARIO GALAXY

Fortress

◄ The Fortress was designed at the very beginning of development. This is a memorable piece for all of us, because it really solidified the idea that the next Mario game was going to be *Super Mario Galaxy*. This fortress was rebuilt repeatedly. On the other side of the planet, you can spot some excavation sites for natural resources.

side
↓

Coach

◄ The single most important characteristic of this penguin is his large stature, which makes him easy to spot from far, far away. He teaches little penguins how to swim, so he is muscular and wears sporty colors, resembling a typical coach.

◀ Our intention was to emphasize Boos, so it was made dark and eerie. However, we didn't want to hinder game play, so we eventually made it brighter.

Concept Art and Captions by:
SMG Development Team

351

To All the MARIO Fans.
Explore the GALAXY!
これからも MARIO をよろしく！

REACH FOR THE STARS!

Find all 120 stars that unlock the super-secret ending.

We shine the light on every hidden star in the cosmos.

GIANT Glow-in-the-Dark **POSTER!**

Extra Content Exclusive to the Collector's Edition!

CLOTHES make the Mario— all of the hero's newest suits detailed.

Locate tons of hidden 1-up mushrooms to keep Mario in action.

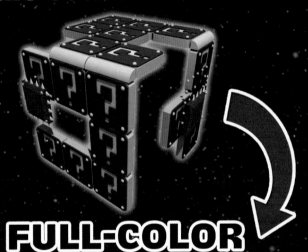

FULL-COLOR MAPS give you the layout of the galaxy before you even blast off.

ISBN 0-7615-5713-X

U.S. $29.99   Can. $35.95

Prima GAMES

Fletcher Black

™ & © 2007 Nintendo. All Rights Reserved.

The Prima Games logo is a registered trademark of Random House, Inc., registered in the United States and other countries. Primagames.com is a registered trademark of Random House, Inc., registered in the United States.

Visit us online at primagames.com®